Michael
Palin

Also by Jonathan Margolis
Cleese Encounters
The Big Yin
Lenny Henry
Bernard Manning

Michael Palin

A BIOGRAPHY

Jonathan Margolis

ORION
MEDIA

The right of Jonathan Margolis to be identified as the author
of this work has been asserted by him in accordance
with the Copyright, Designs and Patents Act 1988.

First published in Great Britain in 1997 by
Orion Media
An imprint of Orion Books Ltd
Orion House, 5 Upper St Martin's Lane, London wc2h 9ea

A CIP catalogue record for this book is available
from the British Library

ISBN 0 75280 504 5

Printed and bound in Great Britain by
Butler & Tanner Ltd, Frome and London

Every effort has been made to trace copyright holders,
but if any have been inadvertently overlooked,
the publishers will be pleased to make the
necessary arrangement at the
first opportunity.

CONTENTS

ACKNOWLEDGEMENTS

My profoundest thanks for assistance with this book go principally to Michael Palin who generously stood to one side to allow me to rummage through his life so far.

Many, many thanks also to: Graham Stuart-Harris, Robert Hewison, Terry Jones, Caroline Law, Gabrielle Morris, Bryony Coleman, Peter Todd, Edward Whitley, Richard Heath, Lynn Barber, John Peel, Francis Ravenscroft, Peter Goodman and Martin Dawes of the *Sheffield Star*, Tim O'Sullivan, Stephen Pile, Andrew Martin, Jemima Harrison, Sally Creighton, Judy Speed, and Gordon Knights of the *Canterbury Press*, Norwich, staff of the Motion Picture Academy Library, Los Angeles, and Graham McOwan of The Lighter Side Bookshop, Upper Richmond Road West, London SW 14.

PREFACE

Dr Michael Palin, honorary Doctor of Letters at the University of Sheffield, has been described over and over again as the fresh-faced, nice-looking one, the only member of the Monty Python team you can imagine appealing to a middle-class mum. The wardrobe lady who worked with the Pythons for years, and saw the six-man team daily at their most stressed, was smitten by this man's niceness. Ian Hislop, the editor of *Private Eye*, has admitted he would be hard pressed even to know how to start satirising Palin.

By a matter of weeks Michael Palin is the youngest of the Pythons. The closest of his colleagues in age is Eric Idle, who entered the world two months earlier than Palin, in March 1943. Palin is a Yorkshireman, from Sheffield – which may explain why he feels that people should not live in Surrey – and a hard-working Taurean, who enjoys his food and drink. With his untidy hair and impish, schoolboy smile, Michael Palin looks a little like the advertising executive his parents once wanted him to become. 'They wanted me to go into something sound. I remember the name Courtauld's being mentioned, and there was the usual careers master who twitched and told you you had to go into glass because he had twenty free Pilkington brochures stuffed into his desk. But we agreed on advertising. Advertising was the only thing they could think of which was both creative and sound.'

In the event, of course, he became a comic – the perfect occupation for someone who has been making people laugh since the time he accidentally fell off the stage during a school production of *A Christmas Carol*. 'It made me wonder why people walked around with gloomy, long faces when there was so much to laugh about,' he says of this incident now. Palin also became an Oscar-winning film star, a serious actor, a screenwriter, a television traveller, dramatist, do-gooder, novelist and millionaire. He is funny, clever, co-operative and talks ceaselessly. His close pal, John Cleese, once famously remarked that you can always tell where Michael has been because of all the donkeys' hind legs cluttering the place up.

He prefers, he confessed once to his Oxford friend Janet Watts, in a *Radio Times* interview, not to climb on political platforms. But he will stick his neck out on matters of public interest when he gets thoroughly fed up about public transport policy or people who have their car stereo playing too loud. Church of England as a boy, he now pointedly subscribes to no religion and avoids supporting causes because he thinks, he told Watts, 'then people think they know what you are, and listen to you far less'. Yet he insists that 'just because I can't take things seriously for very long, it doesn't mean that I don't want to be taken seriously at times'.

He is passionate about many subjects (travel, railways, art), is a Labour voter and his distaste for certain policies can intensify into moments of 'numbing pessimism'. But he admits he is lucky: 'I can use humour as a defence against the monstrous things in the world, just as I did to avoid getting bashed up at school.'

Michael Palin has absolutely no façade. He is one of the few people in showbusiness who not only appears to be, but actually is, unspoiled by success. On set, he is famous for paying special attention to even the lowliest member of the crew. He remains courteous, considerate and self-deprecating, in a typically English middle-class way, which paradoxically is fast becoming untypical of the English middle classes.

He has no discernible sense of himself as a bigshot. In a Boston restaurant once, while being interviewed about a film, the waitress interrupted Palin and the reporter from the *Boston Globe* with a note written on a napkin from a group of fans who had spotted him. They offered to send another bottle of wine to the table.

'That's awfully nice of them,' said Palin, as he wrote a thank-you note in return. 'I'm still not used to this kind of attention,' he explained in a genuine version of that diffident, Hugh Grant manner Americans love. 'I never know exactly what to do.'

'I could never see myself as a celebrity,' he told the reporter. 'That's one reason we conceived of Monty Python. It gave the troupe an identity beyond the individuals involved.'

Yet Palin winces when accused of 'niceness'. The best thing, the only good thing, about his Boy Scout reputation, he often says, is that no jury will convict him if he decides to take up serial killing.

'Oh that terrible stigma,' he told another old Oxford friend-turned-journalist, Lynn Barber. 'But of course it's true – I am extra-ordinarily nice. What I can't stand is when people say I'm the sanest of the Pythons. In fact, I'll sue you if you say that – it's a terrible slur. We are all completely mad.'

John Cleese says of Palin: 'Being liked, being popular, is enor-mously important to him. Like a lot of English people, he is not absolutely comfortable with direct communication if there is any hint of confrontation in it. He's not a man who will ever die on the barricades, but he will die with thousands of friends.'

This constant accusation of niceness has become, over the years, 'something of a joke'. 'I haven't got any skeletons in my closet, so people go on about my normalcy and my niceness,' Palin told the writer, Mark Lawson in the *Independent*.

'What really surprises me is that this quality, if I have it, is thought so remarkable. I mean, there must be nice people in showbusiness apart from me and Cliff Richard. Most of the people I know in the business are terribly nice. But it's true I tend to avoid confrontation.'

He says he simply finds it easier to get through life being nice to people and getting on with them. His one regret is that he does occasionally lose his temper. 'About twice a year it flares up and it always gives other people immense pleasure, but I hate it.'

A favourite time for celebrities to misbehave is when being photo-graphed by the press. They frequently want to appear cool by being dismissive or bored with the process, but at the same time are frantic to look their best. So when photographer Tim O'Sullivan took Palin and his eldest son, Tom, up to Hampstead Heath in spring 1997 to take a joint portrait for a *Sunday Times Magazine* 'Relative Values' piece, he wondered what to expect of Palin.

'When you meet people, you immediately think they are a bit tense or they are sort of negative,' O'Sullivan says. 'But he was neither of those. He is very relaxed, friendly, approachable. He was just a good bloke, and very humorous. He was saying lots of Monty Python lines under his breath as we were shooting, muttering away and burbling on with funny bits. He was absolutely brilliant. I loved him. The son was quite quiet, but bright. He seemed to be a chip off the same sort of block, a very, very easy-going person.

'I am not usually in awe of people,' O'Sullivan concludes, 'But I just wished he was my dad.'

Watching Palin at a July 1997 press lunch the BBC put on for his latest travel series, *Full Circle*, was fascinating. It was a hot, sweaty day in London, and we members of Her Majesty's press were the usual mixed and scruffy bag of misfits in ill-fitting clothes, people asking stupid questions in loud voices, people taking portable phone calls as Palin was talking, people taking copious notes that would probably never see the light of day. We must have been a highly unprepossessing sight and sound.

Yet Palin still couldn't help being funny. Indeed, he was like a force of nature unleashed, a little diffident and restrained at first, then rapidly getting into gear and performing as if this little gathering of hacks were the glossiest and most prestigious chat show in the world. A very tolerant, courteous and professional man.

He is – a vital test of a celebrity, this – not one to abandon old friends he has left behind him. Palin remains close and intimate friends with the boy who lived next door to him from the age of four, and is now a chartered accountant in Sheffield. Even when Palin was becoming highly successful as a TV performer in the sixties, he was as happy having a riotous time with an old university friend who hadn't quite made it in showbusiness, as he was to be with the other Pythons.

Robert Hewison, now a distinguished academic and writer, was an early comedy collaborator who was struggling a little professionally three or four years out of Oxford. 'Michael and I decided one day that we would go and see this dreadful sex film that I had written the script for,' Hewison recounts. 'I actually appeared in it too, but with my clothes on. So we both went to some trouble to find dirty macs, and brought them along. We went for a good lunch first, to the Jardin des Gourmets, then put on our dirty macs, walked down to Charing Cross Road, and sat in this afternoon cinema, glowing from lunch. All around us were these strange types who made scratching sounds. We waited until the titles came up and, when my name appeared, we went huuurrrraahhh! and all the scratching round us stopped.'

While such stories show how Palin loves to be slightly mad, what seems to trouble him even more than being known as nice, is the corollary; that nice equals boring. Some people wonder if his often very dangerous trips abroad are part of an attempt to demonstrate that he can be interesting too. If that is the case, at some albeit subliminal level, the attempt inevitably did not quite come off for everyone. The success of *Around the World in Eighty Days* and *Pole to Pole* brought – at long last – sneers from *Private Eye*, where the phrase 'to Palin' was coined, meaning to bore people stiff with your holiday videos. But the campaign typically did not not bother Palin. 'When *Private Eye* had a go,' he says, 'I thought, "At last, I've made it." My children are hoping I'll be on *Spitting Image* next – then I'll really have arrived.'

With such a sunny disposition, it is no surprise that on *Desert Island Discs* in 1979, Palin chose as his book Thackeray's *Vanity Fair*, and from it selected this passage: 'The world is a looking glass and gives back to every man the reflection of his own face. Frown at it, and it will in turn look sourly upon you; laugh at it, and it is a jolly, kind companion.'

What impresses as much as Michael Palin's character, his wit, his generosity, is his sheer output of words. He must have written millions of words since childhood, and far from all of them have been published or performed. He does not save up his funniest words or his finest writing for the big audiences. He can be as funny in a local radio interview, or in one destined to be published only in some far, obscure corner of the Internet, or on a one-to-one basis with someone he likes, as on a prime-time chat show in the United States.

In football terms – and Palin is a devout Sheffield Wednesday supporter – if Cleese is the flashy striker who saves his legs for big games only, Palin is the hard-working midfield playmaker, who puts as much heart into a reserve game with a hundred people watching as he does into the Cup Final.

Alongside the comedy, there is a far more serious and solitary part of him, which enjoys the projects he can completely control, such as novels or travel books. 'The two sides are still wrestling within me,' he says. 'But then, because I'm Oxford, and a bit woolly, I think, perhaps I should stick with comedy, and having a nice time.'

A funny man with a massive enthusiasm for life, Palin is also a man of great humanity. He seemed dumbstruck during his *Pole to Pole* series as he walked around a deserted village near Chernobyl, and his concern for victims of poverty in Africa is manifest. It seems only amazing that neither Palin, nor Cleese nor any of the Python gang have yet to receive so much as an OBE.

Perhaps Palin lacks the overweening ego which most successful people possess. Celebrities tend to need to become famous because of an enormous ego, and then grow an even bigger head as a result of their fame. Michael Palin seems to exist completely outside that cycle. 'I don't actually like bright, sharp, clever, pushy people, so I tend to go for the sort of characters that would infuriate them; those are the sort of characters I like to play,' he says.

'I've been very lucky,' the proud new holder of a doctorate from his home city's university admitted immediately after the ceremony. 'From the age of forty-nine onwards, my career has been fun. I am now doing what I only dreamed of at the age of nineteen.'

A man of forty-nine – now fifty-four – doing what he dreamed of at nineteen? If there is a single attribute which explains Palin in one, it is a childlikeness. Youth, it is said, is a quality which, once you attain, you never lose, and Palin is a prime example of this.

A few years ago, he was being interviewed in an airport cafeteria in Los Angeles about *A Private Function*, the Alan Bennett film he had just starred in as a chiropodist, along with a pig and Dame Maggie Smith. Palin was jetlagged, the *Los Angeles Times* writer Nancy Mills wrote, as he had flown in from Glasgow, where he had been required a few hours earlier to do a photocall with the Lord Mayor in a pen full of pigs, and was now directly on his way to Chicago. He was also hungry, and was tucking in to a none too appetising plate of tinned fruit salad.

'Despite all the privations, hardships, and smells, working with the pig was worth it,' he told Mills between mouthfuls. 'Next time I'd like to work with kippers. I could eat them afterwards.'

He chatted away, Mills records, about the film and life in general, pausing to mention a man he had noticed earlier in the day, sunbathing by an LA swimming pool. 'I thought he was wearing a jumper, but it turned out he was just incredibly hairy,' he told her. It was at about this point when Mills caught him staring perplexed at a mirror behind her. 'He looks puzzled,' she wrote. "Maybe I've disappeared," he mutters. Then he realises that he's looking at a room divider.'

Anyone with a five-year-old will recognise such lucid yet at the same time gloriously stupid observations. Michael Palin is one of the rare men lucky enough still to be able to make them in adulthood.

I

Whitworth Road

The accent was pure early BBC, stiff necked and emotionless, with the short 'A's pronounced as 'E's. in that curious upper-class English manner of the times, and the real 'E's stretched into an emphatic, yet clipped little vowel which does not really exist any longer:

It's six o'clock. Here is the news, end this is Joseph Macleod reading it. The Emericans are making steady progress beyond Mateur and their patrols are reported ten miles from Bizerta. Other Emerican patrols have reconnoitred Exis positions twelve miles from Tunis. British and French troops beat off enemy counter ettecks in the central sector yesterday.

Bomber Command's raid on Dortmund last night was one of the heaviest yet made on Germany,' the news bulletin continued. 'We hed more four-engined bombers out than ever before. Thirty of our aircraft are missing.

The war news on Wednesday, 5 May 1943, was relatively encouraging, despite those thirty missing bombers. But as he caught up with the latest from the BBC in the front sitting room at no. 26, Whitworth Road, Ranmoor, a smart suburb in the prosperous, and sometimes snobbish far west of Sheffield, Ted Palin's mind was not fully on the war effort. Upstairs, in the first floor front bedroom of the large, three storey rented house, while he was at work as a manager in a toilet paper factory, Palin's first son had been born, a brother to Angela, by then eight years old.

Michael Edward Palin had been conceived, a war baby, as the result of a unilateral decision by his mother, Mary. Ted Palin had never been as well-off as his upbringing and education might have predicted, and much of his efforts in life were devoted to trying to keep up appearances. He worked as a civil engineer, and was never well paid. For predominantly financial reasons, therefore, he had been hesitant over the question of whether the couple should have a second child. Mary Palin, on the other hand, was already in her late thirties and was quite certain of what she wanted, and made the decision for her husband. 'Whatever method of birth control my mother was using, she didn't use it on that particularly balmy night in 1942,' Michael Palin was later to say, 'and I was the result: the ultimate mother's story.'

Large-scale bettles are now being fought in the Kuban, where the Russians are using their air superiority to good effect. The Minister of Egriculture hes said he's working out a four-year plen for egriculture. The Lords heve discussed evecuees – their improved health and behaviour in their war-time homes. The death is announced of Lord Hewart, former Lord Chief Justice of England.

Sheffield, as the centre of the steel industry, had been savagely hit by the Blitz, although up in middle-class Ranmoor, bomb damage was a rarity. The Anderson shelter Ted had installed in the back garden of no. 26 had barely been necessary, anyway; the Luftwaffe's raids on the British equivalent of the industrial Ruhr had died out almost the moment the Palins moved in to Whitworth Road.

Ranmoor, both then and now, would hardly be recognisable to any southerner who imagined it to be Yorkshire of the clogs and 'trouble-at-mill' stereotype. Close to the city's university, the area is elevated both topographically and socially. Whitworth Road, furthermore, is one of the finest in Ranmoor, an avenue of beech trees which today are fifty foot tall and spaced a precise eleven yards apart. The substantial, honey-coloured, Yorkshire stone-built Victorian houses, mostly detached or so tenuously semi-detached as to make no odds, are set well back from the quiet road, down long, sloping front drives.

Ted and Mary Palin were not Sheffield people by birth or inclination. They came from Norfolk and Berkshire respectively, and Palin doubts they were ever really reconciled to living in the north. Ted Palin was a doctor's son, pretty much from the East Anglian upper class. There was a history of rather up-market clergymen in the family. A great-great-uncle appears in the *Dictionary of National Biography* as 'William Palin, divine', and Michael's great-grandfather was a Gloucestershire vicar. His side-whiskery portrait still hangs on the Palins' landing in London.

Young Ted – Edward was a traditional Palin family name – had gone to Shrewsbury school, then on to Cambridge, to India, and to a society wedding to the daughter of the High Sheriff of Oxfordshire. Yet the county balls petered out, his work took him to stints in Leeds, Hull and Sheffield, and 1943 found him a middle-aged man working for a lavatory paper manufacturer and doing his best for his family in a rented house in a suburb of war-ravaged Sheffield. Life, consequently, was a struggle of slightly faded gentility and penny pinching – and Michael Palin's father was a disappointed man who saw himself as a failure. The job in the toilet paper factory soon led to a better position with one of the smaller Sheffield steel companies, Edgar Allen and Co., which specialised in making railway tracks for countries like India, as well as – or so a giant advertisement stretched across one bridge in the city proclaimed – rotary dryers, crushers, magnets and small tools.

Throughout Michael's boyhood and young adulthood, Ted Palin was Edgar Allen's export manager, only promoted (and then in a minor way) right at the end of his career, rarely given a rise, but famously punctilious and punctual at work. Being the export manager of Edgar Allen and Co., Sheffield, was not, as some might imagine it to be, a glamorous job involving travel to foreign countries and coming home laden with goodies unobtainable in England. Far from it; the grim, provincial, post-war world of Palin's film *A Private Function* would be a vehicle for many of his memories of this period – a time of cod liver oil and tonic pills to bolster poor diet, when a lot of British people wondered just who had won the war. Food and fuel shortages were far worse when peace broke out. Rationing is, for example, a living memory for Palin. His mother would take him to the shops and let him tear out the coupons, whose different colours made a vivid impression on him. He also recalls standing on tiptoe to give the coupons to the shop assistant.

In most important respects, the Palin children had an idyllic childhood. They were not, he has explained, pampered, but were intensely secure in their regular existence, going for walks, playing French cricket in the garden, drinking welfare-state orange juice and – the main shared family activity – listening to the radio, particularly to 'Take it From Here', when all four Palins would sit down to listen together. There were plenty of man-to-man pursuits as well for father and son, cherished moments, in which he recalls his father seeming contented despite all the stress and grind of his underpaid job and a life of keeping up appearances. Ted would take Michael by the hand to go and watch cricket, or wander down to nearby railway cuttings, embankments and tunnel entrances together to watch trains steaming by – a childhood pleasure which was to become one of the cores of Palin's being.

The Palins were not a bookish household but, early in his childhood, Michael did grow to love Richmal Crompton's William stories, which Crompton, at the end of her career, was still writing when he was a boy. Michael remembers being especially intrigued and enchanted by the length of time William Brown could spend just staring at something. He was also tremendously affected by the film of *Around the World in Eighty Days*, although had written his own book by that name before he read the original. Thanks to his juvenile appetite for reading, visits to the library with his father were another feature of childhood and, at Christmas, Michael would always receive books as presents – *Tales of the Arabian Nights*, Keith Miller's autobiography and the *Eagle* annuals stand out in his memory.

The most reliable and regular thing in the Palins' ordered existence were the family's two-week summer holidays, which Ted Palin somehow stretched his pay packet to include. Palin holidays – Michael remembers fifteen or sixteen of them – would be spent habitually at Sheringham in Norfolk or Southwold in Suffolk.

Sheringham in particular left on Palin one of those vivid, if exaggerated, impressions which lodge immovably in children's minds. 'What I remember best about Sheringham,' he has said, 'are the truly monumental toilets which dominated the approach to the firm beaches and rock pools. Probably, they're not as enormous as I remember them, but as a small boy the Gents seemed vast and marbled, a combination of the Taj Mahal and Grand Central Station. Water glugged gently in glass cisterns high above me, the clack of beach shoes on the marbled floor seemed like lese-majesty. One should really have worn evening dress.'

According to Mrs Palin Sr, who gave a rare interview to writer Martin Dawes of the *Sheffield Star* shortly before she died, Michael's first stage appearance dates from one of these holidays. When he was six, the whole family went to see a show at Cromer, in which children were invited to take part. 'Before I knew it,' recounted Mrs Palin in tones which must have sounded incongruously 'cut glass' even in the best residential area of Sheffield, 'he was up on stage. I suppose, now I think of it, that must have been his first public appearance.'

To be accurate, Michael had got his first public laugh at the age of around eighteen months, when he slipped backwards out of his folding pram in front of a crowd of giggling office girls. Additionally, his sister Angela, with whom Michael had a peaceable but distant relationship on account of their age difference, had been tending towards being a little performer long before Michael had. Indeed, friends of the family thought she was the more likely of the siblings to become a Thespian. But, with the help of hindsight, it is Michael whose early theatrical promise has come under the greater scrutiny. As a little boy, 'he was always laughing and joking', Mary Palin told Dawes.

Being a funny family was not, however, what the Palins were really noted for. The principle down-side to life at 26 Whitworth Road, Ranmoor, was Ted Palin's almost legendary grumpiness. He had a dour, disciplinarian exterior which has led ex-school-friends of Michael today to describe Ted Palin as a clone of Victor Meldrew.

'There was always grumpiness and an edge of irritation with him,' Palin has said. 'Once he was apoplectic with rage when I broke a water jug. He chased me out into the garden and took a stick from the hallstand. He couldn't do anything with it because we were in the garden and all the neighbours could see. My father was an angry man, always confronting people – waiters, butchers, taxi-drivers, whatever. He really felt that everyone was out there laying traps for him and that everyone should be treated with extreme suspicion. There was always an air of tension when he was around and I found it deeply embarrassing. With him no encounter ever went smoothly. And I thought, you don't have to be like that.'

Palin has even gone so far as to describe his father as a bully, 'a difficult man who made me very unhappy when I was young'. He was explosive, and would torment his wife: Ted snapping, 'Why isn't tea ready?' or 'Do we have to eat that? We had it yesterday', was the soundtrack for much of the young Michael's life, and it moulded his own character in a predictably reverse manner. In the Python days, when there were rows and disagreements, it would be Palin who tended to be the conciliator. 'I suppose I still am,' he says today. 'I've tended to be the one who still talks to the ones who don't talk to each other, and it was necessary to Python to have someone like that. I hate rows and try to avoid confrontations, you see. I think this attitude comes from my upbringing.' (Always one to look on the bright side, Michael points out that, had his father been a regular Mr Nice Guy, Michael himself could have turned out very differently. 'I might have become an accountant,' he says. 'An angry accountant.')

Yet Ted Palin's behaviour was almost certainly the result of nothing more than a severe stammer with which he was afflicted, the consequence, it is believed by Michael, of a maid having jumped out and frightened him as a small boy. As if unconsciously to exacerbate its importance, the stammer was never referred to by the family despite its noticeable impact on exchanges at table. For years, the young Palins believed, as stammerers' children often apparently do, that it was merely the way some adults speak. 'It was never mentioned at all,' Palin recalls. 'Nobody ever said, "Look, Dad's got this speech impediment, it's called a stammer; we've tried to cure it but it looks as though we're all going to have to live with it."'

It was only when Palin was big enough to bring friends home and observe them trying not to laugh that he even realised his dad had a problem. Many years later, his father's stammer would inspire Palin's performance in *A Fish Called Wanda*, as indeed his whole family's behaviour inspired his play, *The Weekend*.

But, for the years of his childhood, the stammer was to be an embarrassment. 'When I brought new friends back it was obvious he couldn't speak properly. I longed for him to be like any other dad,' Michael says today. 'I remember silently praying sometimes that he would disappear.' Probably rather psychologically damaging to all concerned, the conspiracy of silence surrounding Ted Palin's glaringly obvious speech defect affected Michael as much as anyone else. 'I can't remember Michael ever warning us about his dad's stammer,' recalls one friend. 'It was just one of those things that we just didn't really speak about. It was there, and it was obvious, but in those days, in that sort of society, people just ignored it and pretended it wasn't there.'

There were many aspects to Ted Palin's behaviour which Palin would speak out against as an adult, but he loyally defended his father against the myth that people with a stammer are necessarily solemn, uncommunicative, humourless types. 'That image is bull,' he said quite angrily when opening the Michael Palin Centre, a facility set up in London for stammering children. 'My father had a lot of words to say, but cruelly life frustrated him. We would pray that something would change and the words I know he wanted to say would flow without hindrance.'

Ted Palin's cantankerousness was equally a drawback to visiting the home of the ever-gregarious Michael. When Michael was four and quite a lonely soul, with no other children in the posh suburban street to play with, a family from London moved into the big house next door to the Palins, no. 28. Charles – later Sir Charles – Stuart-Harris was a doctor who, at the age of just thirty-seven almost directly from being an RAMC colonel, came to take up the chair in medicine at Sheffield University. The Stuart-Harrises' son, Graham, was five and, almost instantly, he and Michael became playmates, a friendship which has never waned. Michael and his family still stay with Graham Stuart-Harris and family when they visit Sheffield. And Michael still keeps closely in touch with Graham's mother, Lady Marjorie Stuart-Harris, whom he looks upon as his second mother. As chairman of the Sheffield branch of Save the Children, Lady Marjorie was able with ease to get Palin to come to Sheffield recently for the relatively low-key business of opening a charity shop in Broomhill.

The dynamic of the Michael–Graham relationship was skewed from the start in the matter of whose house the two chose to play in. The Stuart-Harrises, perhaps through being academic and southerners fresh up from London, were considerably more liberal, warmer, and more open, not being dominated by a strict father, as well as being rather better-off. Unsurprisingly, perhaps, Michael chose to be at no. 28 more often than Graham opted to be at Michael's house. It was not just the easier-going atmosphere, either; the Stuart-Harrises had a television, Michael remembers, eight or nine years before the Palins. Not only did they have the TV, but they had it on all the time – and even watched ITV, a sure sign in the fifties either of being working class or of being somewhat radical socially and politically.

'His father was more austere than mine,' Graham, a chartered accountant, explains. 'Mine tended to let the whole family run in remote control, whereas his father was very much an organiser type. Ted Palin seemed to like discipline and everything working properly. The way life was organised, being on time, having tea precisely at four and all that were terribly important. I was really a bit frightened of him. He used to holler, and we would all do exactly what he said. If we saw him coming, we'd be off the other way as quickly as we could. Even if we weren't doing anything wrong, he would find something that we were doing wrong, being overdue for lunch, or anything like that.

'Ted Palin always had some sort of sweets on the top of a bookcase or something in the lounge. Rowntrees fruit gums, they usually were, in those fruit shapes. He was very precise, and at more or less certain times of the day, he would come and put his hand up there. Of course, we used to nick them every so often, and of course, he was the sort of chap who really knew, "I was saving the black one for tomorrow. Where's that gone?"'

While Michael was finding pleasant contrasts between Graham's house and his own, almost inevitably, Graham spotted minor benefits to being next door at Michael's. While Sir Charles Stuart-Harris was zooming off for long working trips and visiting lectureships in the USA, the ordinariness of Ted Palin's provincial, commuting lifestyle had its attractions. 'My father was more or less always absent and he didn't want to be bothered with the house things,' Stuart-Harris says. 'He just spent his time working and working in the evenings and wasn't interested in fruit gums and those sort of things. He had his life to build.'

An important exception, Graham Stuart-Harris points out, to the rule that the majority of playing was done at his house was that those lunches, even if the disciplinarian paraphernalia surrounding them was a bit oppressive, were rather better than his mother had on offer. 'I used to love going to lunch at his house,' Stuart-Harris happily confesses. 'The food was better next door. Sausages and gravy, I remember, were the great favourites, homely cooking with nice thick gravy. Super.'

In Stuart-Harris's view it was not merely the stammer which made his friend's father such an awkward man to deal with. 'He had been to public school, then to Cambridge, I know he rowed there, because I remember in the hall there were oars, all held up with the names of the crew on. So coming from that sort of background in those sort of years, turning up in Sheffield being an export manager for quite an ordinary steel and engineering company – an export manager who spoke no foreign languages and who stuttered anyway – I think he probably had a bit of an inferiority complex, which manifested itself by making him quite dominant in the home environment, whereas he probably wasn't dominant in the commercial environment. I don't think he had fulfilled the ambitions that everyone would have had of him from his earlier years, and I think this had quite an effect on Michael.'

Another boyhood friend, Peter Todd, has similar recollections of Ted Palin. 'I used to be quite frightened of his father,' says Todd, now a Sheffield solicitor. 'You never saw him laughing – he was a very serious sort of man. His stammer was quite noticeable to us and he appeared to be quite a difficult man, a bit bad tempered, and not too tolerant of lads around the place. I remember once going round there, and it was only about six or seven o'clock in the evening, but they were dropping hints that it was time I went. I was obviously not taking the hint, so in the end, they came into the lounge filling up their hot water bottles.'

Yet Palin Sr showed many signs that underneath the crabbiness lay a gentler soul – and one with a sense of humour, the very sense of humour, his mother believed, that Michael (and also Angela) inherited. 'His father had a quiet sense of humour. It's in the Palin family,' his mother often said. 'I remember him as a complex mixture of extreme irascibility and abundant but fairly basic humour,' Palin says. 'Farts and bottoms, he adored all that.'

The best-remembered example of Ted Palin's humour was when he brought home, having presumably purchased in his lunch hour, a fake dog mess. This, he preceded to put down for Mary to find in the midst of preparing for a party. 'He expected me to find it when all the guests had arrived and wonder what on earth it was. It was really terrible because it was terribly life-like dog mess,' Mary Palin explained on a 1983 BBC TV *Comic Roots* programme, which briefly explored Michael's background. 'I remember it was so funny because you discovered it terribly well with a terrible shriek of "What's This!"' Michael added. This incident, according to other accounts, was not just a one-off but was a routine which the Palin parents would frequently do.

The young Michael loved his father for his eccentricity, for the fact that he could be funny. 'There was something anarchic about my father.' He remembers sometimes standing in a room watching him with other men and thinking: they're all doing better than my father, they're much more successful, but they're so dull. Palin says he had inherited a bit of this anarchy. 'It's why I find myself so uncomfortable in establishment company, with people who take themselves seriously, who are self-consciously important. My father never did that, partly because he never was important, but also because he was mischievous.'

It would be wrong to suggest that, because of his formidable normal self, Ted Palin's rarer good-natured side was unknown to friends of the family. 'Ted was quite a humorous man,' Graham Stuart-Harris agrees. 'He could change instantly but he did have a good sense of fun. When it was a good day and things were going well, he used to go out every day and riddle the ashes and bring back the bits that weren't used, and provided he didn't get this stuff flying up in his face, he would come along whistling and it was very much, "Hello, Mikey boy." He would come out and play cricket with us in the garden. Ted wasn't really a words man, but he became jolly like the scout leader going on annual camp, "Come on boys!" He was just jolly and bright like that but he wasn't a conversationalist because of the stutter.'

Ted Palin had another side to his character which was similarly contrary to the impression of dourness he routinely exuded. 'He was a musical man, who loved church music and singing in the choir,' Palin says. 'He was a bell-ringer, too, second in command of a peal of ten bells and once was on the radio on Christmas morning. I was very proud when I watched him. I always felt he was most at ease in church.'

It was almost as if a combination of his stammer and the Great Depression prevented Ted Palin from pursuing some true creative calling. To him, dreams were something one shelved in favour of the urgent job of survival in treacherous times – and even by sticking to the path of righteous conventionality, the prosperity which had followed a major recession and a world war still largely and frustratingly passed him by.

Michael's mother, on the other hand, was an encourager of dreams – a very important thing to be in a household containing a young Michael Palin. Michael was temperamentally closer to his mother, and when his father was out bell-ringing he would get down the family volume of Shakespeare and read the parts – something he could never have done for his father. Later, when both Angela and Michael wanted to act, it was their mother who was by far the more positive of the Palin parents.

'Michael's mum was absolutely terrific,' says Graham Stuart-Harris. 'She was terribly useful to Michael and to me when we were getting into trouble, because she would always take our side. She was a very small lady, but she was like the United Nations between warring parties, and would come and settle the differences.

'Now, if, for example, a few of Ted's fruit gums were missing on our account, Michael's mother would always side with us and help us out, fudge the evidence and negotiate generally. If we wanted to go somewhere and Michael needed some time off, or if we wanted to go out late or go to the pictures or something like that, it would always be a question of getting her to ask Ted. She was a great diplomat. You had to accommodate, you had to play Ted Palin, and she was ace at this. He would come for his supper and say, "Ah, now this is what I want you to do," and she would jump up and get it. She'd almost appear to be sat on most of the time but she was the power really. She came from a better background than Ted in many ways. She would let it slip every now and again, about the staff they had once had in her parents' house. She had certainly been presented at court.'

Angela Palin seems quite a shadowy, indistinct character by the account of Michael's friends. 'I remember once we found some scaffolding,' says Graham Stuart-Harris. 'I dropped a scaffolding pole on my toe and it was all swollen and bleeding, and I felt really wounded. Then Angela came along, and she seemed really older, a more mature sort of girl. I thought I would get a lot of sympathy from her, but she gave me very short shrift and didn't seem at all sympathetic. Angela was more possibly more like her dad than her mum. I don't remember much about her at all; she seemed older and taller and a different generation from us.'

Despite the quite public moments when Ted and Mary Palin would lark about with a plastic dog mess, they seemed, observed the journalist Sally Vincent in a perceptive *Sunday Times* profile, to have a joyless, combative relationship. 'When Michael first learned what divorce meant, he immediately realised it was what his parents needed,' Vincent wrote. 'As he grew older, however, he twigged the nature of their interdependence and thought again.' By the time he was an impressionable adolescent, Michael actually found himself deeply embarrassed by shows of affection between the parents of his friends. To this day, he told the writer, he is wary of what he calls the "darling, I'm home, kiss-kiss, hold hands all the time, lovey-dovey stuff"'.

'If you observe people with a sort of affection meter,' he continued in the same interview, sounding remarkably like his great friend John Cleese in psychotherapeutic mode, 'at the top would be people who are seen to behave in a traditionally romantic way. But you also notice that such couples are less likely to carry on being couples. The ones who appear to be the most diffident are still together.'

The question of male–female relationships and what makes them work – and in particular a rather dismissive attitude to romantic relationships – is a rare area in which Palin ventures into the discussion of psychology, and an indication of how seriously he takes the issue. Generally, he is not a man who likes to bare personal angst, yet most people that know him in adulthood have discerned a dark side, albeit one that Palin keeps well to himself, and feels strongly that it should be kept there.

His parents must have loved each other, Palin has, in adulthood, concluded. After his mother died he found a letter to her from his father which proved they had once been happy. But as children he and Angela didn't feel this. 'When they'd say a kind word to each other it was such a relief.'

'It's funny, isn't it,' he reflects, 'how we struggle so self-consciously to create "family life", when all children really want to know is that two people are living together under the same roof in reasonable harmony.'

As a child, many was the time when, just back from watching trains with his father, Ted would explode with rage at some trivial thing at home. He would long to believe that the cloud of his anger would soon pass, that the happiness they had shared would endure. But the spectre of Ted Palin's unkindness, his unthinking cruelty to the children, diminished all before it. Angela may have suffered most, Palin believes. 'She longed to be an actress and when she failed – "came home, tail between her legs" – there was the shadow of her father saying, "I told you so."'

2

Birkdale

'At the grand age of five,' Michael Palin says, 'I was promptly sent out into the world to be educated.' Both Michael and Graham Stuart-Harris, although Graham was almost a year older, started on the same day at Birkdale, a prep school in the same area of Sheffield as the boys lived. Birkdale was, nevertheless, a stiff walk away from Whitworth Road, thanks to the generous scale of the grand Victorian plan to which the part of the city now designated Sheffield 10 was built. The walk to and from school, sometimes aided by jumping on buses, was to be the arena for much of Michael's dreaming over the next eight years.

The Palin education was conventional, even mundane, with lots of church-going and Bible classes. 'I used to skip down the hill to St John's Church, Ranmoor, for Sunday School each week,' he reminisced in the *Sheffield Star*. Attending services at St John's was, he said, the source of much of his comedy in later years – he was endlessly amused by the ritual and ceremony.

Like most provincial prep schools of the time, Birkdale was something of an educational sleepy hollow, the shambling, slightly eccentric creation of its owner-headmaster, Howard R. Heeley, who was forty-five when Michael and his best friend started school. Mr Heeley had taught at Birkdale since 1923, when he was twenty, and bought it outright in November 1943. A mannerly Edwardian bachelor, he liked to be known as HRH, although was more commonly called 'Tousle' or 'Toozle' by the boys, on account of his rumpled appearance. For the period that Michael was a pupil, Mr Heeley ran the school entirely on his own, both teaching and administering, a task which often left him asleep at his desk in the small hours and waking up without having been home.

He seemed to prefer staying at school after his parents, whom he had lived with, died. A busy school, where Mr Wass, the cook-caretaker was always around, and there were generally a few boys staying late for carpentry, swimming or net practice, must have seemed preferable to a big, lonely house with an overgrown hedge. Heeley ensured that he was busy as late as possible, instituting a compulsory tea 'n' prep for boys of twelve and over. This meant that the school day ended at six, which was unusually late for a predominantly non boarding school (there was a handful of weekly boarders). A keen Christian, Heeley was a Parochial Church Council member and ran a thriving Scripture Union and Crusaders chapter at school as if to keep the place busy even longer; there was also school on Saturday mornings for Common Entrance and Scholarship classes and, of course, games – an activity Michael Edward Palin would have as little to do with as conceivably possible, with the odd exception of throwing the cricket ball, at which he was surprisingly proficient.

Birkdale, according to the report of a school inspector in 1950, when Michael had been a pupil two years, had 207 boys between eight and thirteen, plus ninety-eight between four and eight in Westbury, the adjoining junior and kindergarten department, which the expansionist Mr Heeley had bought in 1946. The inspector's report on Birkdale was far briefer than the lengthy multi-page documents he felt the need to pen on some of Sheffield's more troubled schools. 'Adequate', 'Satisfactory', 'Cheerful' and 'Attractive' may have constituted damning by faint praise, but there was no real note of criticism. Something of an edge may be read into the inspector's comment that 'The headmaster has no formal qualifications as a teacher, though he is clearly an enthusiast for all that Prep School education connotes,' but it is pretty approving on the whole. Of the class which Michael was in at the time of inspection, it was noted: 'They speak clearly, and have confidence and self-possession. Movement is rather restricted in these classes; the classroom furniture consists largely of desks.' Of the classes Michael had yet to reach, the comment was that, 'The teaching is on traditional and rather formal lines. All the classes were well-handled and, in some, good work was seen.' 'There is,' the report concluded, 'no evidence of cramming, and the boys seem cheerful and happy in their work.'

Each member of the eventual Monty Python team had a thorough grounding in the almost studiedly eccentric ways of the English middle class. Howard R. Heeley's contribution to Palin's lexicon of harmless battiness was to have adopted as his own, during a school visit to London, the recorded announcement of the automatic unmanned lifts at a station on the Metropolitan Line. For some unfathomable reason, 'Stand clear of the gates, please' intrigued Mr Heeley, and it became his personal battle cry, which he would call on every occasion that he needed to clear a passage through a clump of chattering boys. Knowing that the headmaster was always around, and could always be relied upon to say 'Stand clear of the gates, please', far from being irritating, was the very kind of comfortable routine which made schools like Birkdale such a calm haven for middle-class boys. Although Palin has kept up some contact with Birkdale it would be wrong to say he has in any way clung to the place, or idealised it. He has been quite critical, indeed, of much about it – and made a point of sending all his three children to state schools.

Much of what went on at Birkdale might raise eyebrows in today's more cynical climate, but by all accounts Mr Heeley's love of the boys in his charge was entirely innocent. 'He had an oldish Standard car which he would put sixteen boys in to go to the football field, and when he came back he would wash you down and nobody thought anything about it,' recalls Graham Stuart-Harris. 'He would come round and pat your leg when you had done well in Latin, and sit on the desk next to you. Indeed he used to weigh and measure you. We used to stand with nothing on up his corridor. But I think he was the nicest man I've ever met. We never ever heard of any actual "incident". Perhaps it was the beginning of what might be; I think he was at the beginning, but there was no might be.'

Howard Heeley was not a financially grasping man, either. He was known as being rather hopeless with and uninterested in money, and the fees at Birkdale were not enormous. A typical term's bill in 1948, when Michael started, would have been less than £15, to include tuition, stationery, swimming, school buses, text books, and even halibut liver oil capsules; games were, conveniently for the notoriously unsporty Palin, an optional extra – albeit for just 2/6 a term. The most luxurious extra available was boxing, which cost a hefty 15/- a term, but was not likely to prove a burden on Ted Palin. As Michael usually made the lengthy trip home for lunch, the bills could be kept down still further by avoiding the 1/9-a-day school lunch charges. All the same, school fees were an additional strain on Ted Palin's horribly creaking budget. 'My father didn't really earn a great deal of money,' he has said. 'I was surprised after he died and I found out how much he had been earning when he sent me away to public school. It must have cost about a third of his income. What I saw as parsimony was really the result of necessity.' He confesses that today, even as a millionaire, his father's example has left him with the tendency to be careful with money, especially when it comes to spending on himself.

From the start at Birkdale, Michael was a bright boy, if a little shy and reserved. Although he and Graham – along with Peter Todd – stuck together, the young neighbours were never in the same class, as Michael was in the A stream and Graham in the B. 'We used to come home for lunch together, get the bus to Ranmoor Church, walk up, then walk down again all in about an hour. It was great sport running back down the hill – it was hell getting up the hill,' Graham recounts. 'Being a stream below Michael didn't really bother me but, since he was doing better, I used to get a terrible time sometimes at home. "Do you realise that you are going to be a bus driver and you are going to be sitting in a town and Michael Palin is going to be coming past your bus as you try and pull out, in a Jaguar." So I was being fed the lines of how successful he was going to be.'

'In the end,' Stuart-Harris jokes at his swish accountant's office, 'I did slightly better than a bus driver – but only just.'

Michael's 'niceness' then and now has become legendary, but it is in these early days at prep school that the real nature of 'niceness' began to be seen. A natural, light diplomacy – inherited, presumably, from his continually peace-making mother – seemed to be the heart of his engaging character. 'Michael is a clever chap,' says Stuart-Harris. 'He never goes too far with anything. He negotiates his way very steadily.'

This meant that, although the boys got up to plenty of mischief, they always avoided serious trouble. 'He got into a fair number of interesting pranks,' reports one ex-Birkdale teacher. 'Once upon a time he fell on some wire netting, and cut his leg on some barbed wire – that scar can probably still be seen today – but he was a red-faced, cheery, well-behaved boy, who always stands out in the memory as being about twelve.'

'We never had real rumpus, although it got a bit dodgy from time to time,' Graham Stuart-Hall says. 'You see, Michael conforms. He bends the rules, but he doesn't break them and generally will conform and try and change things slowly. He certainly doesn't stand up as a leader or an anti. He will be gentle, keep on talking, but certainly he will not confront a situation. He will play people; he is a master at understanding people's reactions. There will have been no master ever at school who will have criticised him; he would have always got a good report for attendance and obedience and all those matters. And there was nobody who didn't like him or fell out with him.'

Diplomacy, then, was an essential part of Michael's armoury of all-round pleasantness, but sheer charm played its part too. A delightful account of what Michael Palin was like as a child comes from the unlikely perspective of his barber, Ernest Hukin, who is now eighty-three, but was in his forties when Michael was first brought by his father into his two-chaired gents' hairdressing saloon (never salon) in a converted house, with its front asphalted over, on Fulwood Road.

'Near to my business there were two prep schools – Birkdale and Westbourne,' he recalls. 'The Birkdale uniform was blue and the other green; they were called Bluebottles and Greenflies and were deadly enemies. Michael came to my saloon for his hair cutting as a boy and a teenager. Of the hundreds of thousands of clients that I had through my working life, Michael as a boy stands out. I will never forget him. Among my clients I had lords, knights, film stars and aristocracy, but Michael's was the one face I shall never forget.

'He used to make his entrance by pushing open my door – sticking his head through the opening and yelling, 'HELLO, Mr Hukin!' looking for all the world like the famous Just William, school cap askew, school bag just hanging on, one sock probably down and he'd hang on to the handle of the door and swing in. But the most important thing about the entry was the great big smile that was on his face as he appeared, the smile that was to become world famous. It was as big as a frying pan and so very infectious. It always made my day – I was so lifted by that grin.

'We'd talk about anything while he was having his sixpenny haircut, but usually about school and what had been going off, and games. He was quite a character even as a boy, stood out a mile. I had a friend who had a son who went to Westbourne and Michael knew him and he'd say, 'Oh, he's a Greenfly'. It wasn't that they didn't like each other, but just friendly competition between two prep schools. I stopped seeing him when he went up to university, so he would have been eighteen. He was still coming to me for haircuts. His haircut had not changed a great deal at all.'

Mr Hukin often used to ask Michael as he snipped away what he wanted to do in life. 'I always got a sort of negative reply, like, "I don't know yet," as though he was waiting to see what sort of results he got. 'I never had a son of my own – just two daughters – and I would have loved a son so much. If I could have picked one,

Michael would have been my choice. He was a wonderful lad. He is still the same when I see him on the TV. That's what appeals to me about the lad – he is exactly the same as I knew him as a little one. His face is exactly the same, his features haven't changed, and the smile is probably a bit bigger.'

There was, of course, another important aspect to Michael Palin's sunny personality, which was to be a not insignificant part of his future. As Palin himself put it, filmed for the BBC's *Comic Roots* programme in 1983, back in his prep school playground, 'Institutions are great breeding ground for humour, and Birkdale was no exception. This is the actual playground where I first learnt the gentle art of playing the fool, as my teachers called it, or avoiding getting bashed up as I called it.'

Michael Palin was a funny boy – at least, quite funny – according to some people. For a man who was to become famous as a comic actor, writer and broadcaster, there is an unusually wide divergence in accounts of how amusing he was as a child. As a rule, humorists were either a hoot as kids or as dull as bran; in Palin's case, there is no consensus.

'Palin? Yes, I remember him,' said Michael's old geography teacher, later Birkdale's headmaster, John Hall, in the *Comic Roots* film. 'Rather a clever boy at Birkdale. He used to be near the top of the class. Quiet, not humorous, really. Of course, we didn't have that kind of humour in those days, did we? Not the sort of humour that appeals to me, but I understand that he has got a certain following, and when I talked to him about coming here [for the filming], I said, "Well, I hope you're not going to try too much of it on here," and he assured me that he wasn't so we were very happy to have him.'

Graham Stuart-Harris says quite candidly – although, it must be stressed, without even a trace of bitterness – that he always thought *he* was the funnier of the duo. 'At Birkdale, Michael began to tell jokes, not manufactured jokes like the one about the Scotsman and the Irishman, but a quickness with general observations and wit, which you see coming through now. I never thought he was funny, but from the age of twelve or earlier, he would *entertain*. He was always quick-witted.'

Richard Heath, now a leading Sheffield undertaker, then a fellow kindergarten entrant at Birkdale school, summed up the young Michael in 1948 thus: 'Affable. Cheerful. But by no means a great wit. I think his humour must have developed at university. He was quiet and quite reserved, as he is now, until people force him to do things. I don't remember any examples of him being funny at school. I always thought of myself as being funny. And Graham *is* funny.'

Peter Todd, another of the class of '48, agrees. 'It did surprise me that Michael became the comic actor and Graham the chartered accountant, because frankly, of the two of them, Graham was the really funny chap. Graham back then was a bit fat and red faced and puffy. He used to get teased an awful lot and was a bit low in confidence, I would think, as a result, whereas Michael was bright and reasonably serious.

'But Graham was a scream, while Michael was quieter and more thoughtful. I suppose he was the ideas man, and he would write things down. The two of them really blossomed in their teens, but it was Graham who made us all laugh. He was a lot more clownish. They used to sing that song together, "I'm Hen-ery the Eighth I am, Hen-ery the Eight I am, I am," and it would be Graham leading it. But Michael was there. They made a very good pair. It would have been nice to see them develop together as a duo. Of course, I always thought on Monty Python there seemed to be a lot of references to chartered accountants being boring and I always thought they were directed at Graham.'

What is mildly curious about these reminiscences – proof, perhaps, that there is a great deal more ego than we might imagine underpinning the benign character we know today – is that Palin's own account of his funniness as a child is perceptibly more generous than that of his friends.

By the time he was eight, he recounts, he could mimic vicars and schoolmasters and get all the admiration and affection he could ever hope for. Then, one rainy break in 1953, he treated his classmates to a rendition of the Coronation, featuring the Duke of Edinburgh being caught short in mid-ceremony, as Palin recalls it, 'how they ran out of toilet paper during the service, silly things like that'. Whenever it rained henceforth, the Palin Coronation was called for, he says, and he was more or less set for life.

'I've always regarded myself as an observer rather than anything else,' Palin says. 'I love watching other people. That's why I started writing and that's why I can act. I've been observing people since I was quite small and could reproduce their behaviour – which is all acting is.

'The first performances I ever remember giving in front of an audience – non-paying,' Michael expounded on *Comic Roots*, 'were during the morning break, or after lunch here in the little place we called The Annexe. I remember doing improvisations in here. I must have been about nine or ten, because it was vaguely satirical material about the Coronation about the Duke of Edinburgh being caught short in the Abbey. More, mercifully, I can't remember. Laughter was all very well as a means of saving my skin in the playground or courting cheap popularity in the lunch hour, but in class it was not encouraged.'

So boys who were with Palin do not remember him being funny, while he distinctly recalls keeping them highly amused. A conundrum in the archaeology of comedy? Not necessarily. What Michael was actually doing was precisely the same as one John Marwood Cleese had been doing at his prep school far away in Weston-super-Mare four or five years previously – pitching his comedy at a level where it was, for much of the time at least, tantalisingly beyond his contemporaries' sense of humour. At the infant Cleese's school, there was a buzz that the boy was funny, but nobody – not boys or staff, in Cleese's case – quite understood why; at Birkdale, Palin provided a light distraction, but did not generally impress his pals as funny in the aisle-rolling sense, and certainly did not touch his teachers particularly.

None of this, however, is to suggest that Michael Palin wasn't funny. At home, before the far more sophisticated audience of his parents and – more importantly still – the worldly Stuart-Harris parents, he had something approaching the public he deserved. He had a set-piece about a lady on a beach being stung by a bee. Whenever two or three people were gathered together in the Palin parlour, young Michael would leap into action. Even his father found his impromptu shows at home funny, although for the most part, father and son did not share a sense of humour, and Ted Palin could be deeply scathing: 'Is that supposed to be funny?' he would often demand.

In a set piece interview around the Stuart-Harris breakfast table on *Comic Roots*, Sir Charles told Palin, 'You'd have been about eight years of age, and one of you took the part of the BBC Home Service and the other used to chip in with remarks all the time. You had a wonderful time. I always thought you would do something in the entertaining world but never what you are doing now.'

'Your mimes', Lady Stuart-Harris chipped in, 'were really rather funny and we all found them rather amusing. The odd one, we thought, was rather rude, but I don't think they would be considered rude today. Mrs Simpson, our char lady, was very interested in you all, and often she rings me at Christmas. I said once, "Do you see Michael, Michael Palin?" and she said, "Oh, yes." I said, "Do you watch him?" and she said, "Oh, no I don't bother. I've seen it all acted in your kitchen."'

Palin's humour wasn't entirely inaccessible to his pals. Peter Todd recounts, 'I remember going to Crusader camp with him down at Studland Bay in Dorset. This was really our first time away from home, and we slept in these bell tents on palliasses. These camps were run very much on military lines. They had a commandant, whom we were told to call affectionately Commie, and an adjutant, whom we were to call Adjie. There was also an Assistant Adjutant, called Stadjie.

'We were quite homesick to start with. Now, this field that we were in had been previously occupied by cows, and it had an electric fence around it. I remember Michael's imagination went wild. We were in this place surrounded by an electric fence, with a commandant called Grunberg, who sounded just like a German. So he had this idea that we were actually prisoners of war and there was no escape, and we had to plot how we were going to get away. Then we used to have our walk, come back and drink cocoa out of these horrible soft plastic mugs which ended up tasting more of the plastic than the cocoa, and be put to bed fairly early.'

Another highly significant parallel between Palin and Cleese was that both, to the virtual exclusion and bafflement of their parents and teachers, were fanatical followers from 1954 onwards of The Goons. 'For someone like me with an absurd sense of humour and nowhere for it to go, The Goons was like manna from heaven. The day when it was *The Goon Show* kept me going for the entire week. Sometimes, if I missed the bus home from school, I would run the entire two miles to be sure of catching *The Goon Show* on the radio.'

Generally, radio was a shared family activity, particularly shows like *Take it From Here*, when all the family would sit down to listen together. *The Goon Show*, however, drew a line directly between parents and their children. Radio comedy in the early fifties was infinitely more inventive than anything on the television.

'It was very exciting,' Palin explains. 'I saw The Goons as companions of Elvis Presley. I'll never forget the first time I heard Elvis singing "Heartbreak Hotel" on *Family Favourites*. My father got up and began fiddling with the radio. He thought it had gone out of tune. Then I heard "Heartbreak Hotel" again and realised that there was nothing wrong. It was supposed to sound like that.

'The Goons were quite inexplicable to my parents, they were my discovery. I had found them. They were my heroes. Of course any thought of emulating them was quite out of the question, but on my solitary bike rides in Derbyshire, I could always dream that one day perhaps something quite out of the question might possibly just happen.'

(Many years later, Palin briefly met Peter Sellers, who was his greatest comic hero. 'I passed him in a studio, and the only thing I could think of to say was, "Ah, hello Peter." I just did a Goon voice, instantly because I recognised him from *The Goon Show* and I felt such a fool afterwards.' Spike Milligan, when Palin related this story to him on TV, mischievously replied, 'That's right, he told me. He said, I passed a chap today who looked such a fool afterwards.')

Obviously television too was a vital part of Palin's initiation into comedy. And watching television in the Palin household was an event in itself for an observational comedian in the making. 'We got a television set in 1958, a KB New Queen, quite a handsome little set, but my father kept it covered up most of the time with a sort of knitted antimacassar,' Palin explains. 'He'd go through the *Radio Times* and circle the things he wanted to watch. 'We'd turn the armchair around, then there would be the warm-up time, about a minute and a half, and he'd wait. And then, finally, the programme wouldn't be on. That always used to throw him. The previous programme had obviously overrun. "What's this? This isn't the *Festival of Nine Lessons and Carols*, is it?" he'd say, when it palpably wasn't, probably somebody showing their bottom on a nature programme. "Mother, get the *Radio Times*." '

By the time the Palins had their own set, ITV had upped the ante immeasurably, and no longer did BBC radio have the monopoly on high quality comedy. 'I recall one episode of *Hancock's Half Hour* where I couldn't stay in my chair,' says Palin. 'I slid all over the floor; I clutched myself; I howled. I was thirteen or fourteen. It was just a very silly thing, really – about this sort of sad bloke who lived in a little suburb of London and got a bunch of friends together to do a remake of *The Vikings* on the local common, like a home movie. It was daft. Buses would pull up and Vikings would run off to catch the bus to go shopping with people pursuing them. I don't usually get off on jokes, as such. I need something more than just a man up there saying gags. Really it's situations, incongruous situations. We are a truly very silly species – the absurd things we get ourselves into. And that doesn't have to be gleaned from joke books. Read Kafka.'

With a shared delight in comedy now cementing the original infanthood relationship between Michael and Graham Stuart-

Harris, the thought even entered their heads that they might one day become professionally involved in the stuff. 'Graham and I were very keen on becoming scriptwriters for comedy series, like Galton and Simpson and Barry Took. We thought we would be very funny scriptwriters. But that seemed to be a world from which we would always be excluded.'

In terms of official, rather than impromptu, performance at Birkdale, Palin's mother's principal memory of Michael was of him falling off a rickety stage in a production of *A Christmas Carol*, in which Michael was playing Martha Cratchit. But this was far from his sole distinction. 'I remember his sketches very well, and they were good. But we used to do form plays and that sort of thing, and Palin always took the lead with those,' says John Hall, who is now seventy-six.

Just as a modest helping of ego seems to make Palin's own account of his early comic success that touch more impressive than his Sheffield friends recall it, there was another strand in his developing persona of the kind of steel a glittering career would inevitably require. This was that virtue of virtues (for the successful) – competitiveness.

Palin confesses that he always wanted to be the centre of attention. Even as a perfectly behaved, Identikit little prep-school boy, he found it quite hard to accept that anyone might pay more attention to Graham or Peter or Richard than to himself. He wanted to be at least as good as, preferably better than, others. But even early on, there was a strong sense of this accomplishment needing to be his own; Palin was no cribsheet addict. When visiting lecturers came to the school, he has often explained, the more reliable boys such as himself would be primed with clever-sounding questions to ask so that the traditionally embarrassing silence at the 'Any questions?' prompt could be avoided. But he hated the deceit of such a set up. 'He still gets "hot under the collar" – Palin-speak for angry – when he thinks about it,' reported one journalist with whom he had discussed the practice. 'The attention he won had to be based on something true, something of his own making.'

A significant gap in Palin's childhood, which will always be cheering to those who were not sporty at school, is that he was rather chubby, not very well co-ordinated, and hence very much among the boys who straggled on cross-country runs, and tried to make themselves invisible when games loomed on the time-table. It was common at the time for games teachers to feed boys the line that they stood little chance of success in life if they did not at least try, and that the ranks of adult failures were peopled mostly by chaps who didn't put their back into school sports. Palin, Stuart-Harris and Peter Todd too, for that matter, could be used as evidence for the defence – that early pre-eminence at sport has little bearing on anything much. In various of the slightly hokey 'polls' that today are puffed in the media, Palin frequently emerges as a most favoured male role model. In one poll, carried out for *She* magazine, Palin, with eighteen per cent, was second only to Richard Branson (twenty-two per cent) when 1004 men were asked with whom they most identified. Gary Lineker came third, with ten per cent, Arnold Schwarzenegger seven per cent and Paul Gascoigne just four per cent. So much for games teachers. (In the female category, by way of comparison, the favourite women nationally were Goldie Hawn, Cindy Crawford, Felicity Kendal and Princess Diana.)

Not that Michael was in the least bit persecuted by that peculiar tribe; he was lucky to go to schools where a relaxed attitude was taken to sport. 'We avoided anything that was sporty,' confirms Stuart-Harris. 'Sport to me – perhaps a *bit* less to him – was always a bit of a punishment, so rather than volunteering for football on Saturdays or anything like that, we made our own entertainment, we made our own fun. The worst time was on Mondays when there was always a school run after school. It wouldn't have been so bad if it was in school time, but it was about four p.m. You used to hear Mr Heeley coming up the corridor, and this was the chance for Michael to suddenly be taken by a call of nature and disappear to the lavatory. He was always very much a lavatory man, was Michael. But never smoking in the lavatory; at Birkdale, I don't think I ever saw anyone smoking. It was terribly innocent – I don't think there was any alcohol or anything.'

Todd has memories of the time the boys' disappearing act failed. 'I was inclined towards the skivers, too,' he says. 'We used to have to do the Monday run round Ranmoor and back. Mr Heeley used to follow us round in his car to pick up any stragglers, and certainly Graham was always towards the end of the field and Michael and myself were well towards the back as well.'

Michael and Graham, singularly unenthused by the actual doing of sport or any physical activity, were nevertheless characteristically amused by its concept. Of the cricket games organised in his garden by Michael's father, Graham recounts: 'The bowler had a huge advantage because of the slope – if ever you lost control of a sledge or a pram or anything it went crashing down. I was pushing Michael around one time in this pram – I had younger brothers and sisters, you see – and we went off to the top of my garden, and it went over the rockery and crashed down the drive into the road just in front of a passing car. Yes, I nearly got rid of him that time.'

Palin also found the slope at Birkdale's football pitch a matter of enormous amusement. 'No wonder I went in for comedy, because the football pitch was on a ninety-degree slope up Hagg Lane, and if you kicked the ball out, it fell two hundred feet and bounced into the river. Then we would disappear abseiling down the rocks, off to find the ball.'

Against the run of things, perhaps, Michael was a demon at conkers, one of those school sub-skills which – like throwing the cricket ball – often blesses the less physically talented. 'Preparation of the conker was the key element of success,' he explains. 'We kept them in dry cupboards in the dark, sometimes from one season to the next, and put them in vinegar. This was all quite legitimate and above board. It was perfectly acceptable, in fact it was all part of it.'

Michael Palin's was, then, by and large a relaxed, torpid, friendly, skivy childhood. Graham Stuart-Harris still puzzles over the question of what the friends actually did with the expanses of free time at their disposal.

'There wasn't much to do really if you didn't want to go and play football and you didn't like sport. We weren't very interested in anything terribly much. We never volunteered for anything, apart from the fact that on Sundays we did go to Crusaders. But we thought this was a good keep-in because it was run by Mr Heeley and his deputy Mr Hall and various other masters. But the odd thing is that, in fact, we were busy all the time.'

The pictures took up a lot of spare time. So did eating sweets, an activity about which both boys were most enthusiastic. Music was not an issue for either boy. Michael had a solitary piano lesson with somebody who placed her hands above his and rammed one finger down on top of the other, which was supposed to pass for tuition. It was not until his own children turned out to be musical that any glimmering of musicality was seen among the Palins – although Michael used to love watching and listening to brass bands.

When he got a little older, Michael, usually accompanied by Graham, would slope off from dancing classes or golf lessons as often as possible to watch films at the Gaumont cinema in Sheffield, and at the less well-remembered Palace in Union Street, which has long since been replaced by a Town Hall car park. He would go to the cinema as often as three times a week. The boys would be driven into Sheffield in Ted Palin's A50, and either drift off to the cinema afterwards, or not go to dancing at all. The cinema tickets were often paid for, Michael has admitted, by 'borrowings' from the charity box in the Palins' front hall. Although they were not aware that the League of Pity box was being raided on a regular basis, both sets of parents were well aware of the boys' love of the cinema so, when punishment was necessary, the right to go to the pictures was withdrawn.

'The Palace was one of the smaller cinemas and there was never anybody there in the afternoon,' Palin recalls. 'There was that rich smell of cigarette smoke which characterised cinemas then, and when the film was in 3D they never had enough glasses, so we would get in on the cheap.' He always remembers a film called *The*

Charge at Feather River with Guy Madison and Vera Miles as the archetypal 3D epic of the time.

Palin's apparent languidness in this easy, sunny portrait of a middle-class suburban youth is just a little deceptive, however. On the quiet, he was developing into a remarkably keen young man. It was not just the drama at school and the comedy both at Birkdale and at home. He was also extraordinarily fond – for someone who had never been abroad or at that stage been presented with much prospect of so doing – of geography. 'It almost goes back as far as crawling around the house as a toddler,' he says. 'That feeling that what's behind the sofa must be different and more interesting than what's in front of it. And what's behind the radio, with all those wires, was even more unexplored and fascinating.'

Although he jokes sometimes about a love for foreign places being a natural consequence of coming from Sheffield, he had a great affection for his home city, which he assiduously retains, to the extent of remaining a devout Sheffield Wednesday supporter even though he has for his entire adult life lived in north London; he watches Wednesday whenever they are playing in London, and will even go to see Sheffield United too, he says, when they are doing well. Indeed, apart from the family holidays in East Anglia, he did not venture abroad very much or very far before his mid-twenties. 'I'm still very fond of Sheffield,' he explained recently. 'I'm oddly sentimental about my home town, and I feel an affinity for anyone I meet who comes from Sheffield. I don't regard myself as a Londoner – I still consider that I come from Sheffield. Your past isn't something that's ever forgotten, or dies easily. Sheffield has a particular proud and independent character quite unlike anywhere else in Britain. I remember the huge foundries like Hadfields and Firth Brown which flanked Attercliffe Road and the Don. You felt really proud. You felt that here was being produced something which couldn't be produced anywhere else in the country. There's a distinct definition to the Yorkshire character,' he goes on to explain. 'Yorkshiremen are particularly arrogant about their county. They have a great sense of belonging.'

'I suppose I associate Sheffield with innocence and fun,' he explained to a Sheffield University publication on the occasion – by which he was notably touched – of receiving his honorary doctorate. 'For instance,' Palin continued, 'I miss the hill we used to walk up to get home, even though it was probably a real nuisance when I was a child. I like the memory.'

'He was very interested in geography, and bright, very bright,' confirms John Hall, then the geography teacher at Birkdale. 'We used to have a special room in which I would put a sand model of a country like India, or of somewhere like Sheffield and its surrounds, all built on a big table, about standard billiard table size. The sand would be coloured for the different types of vegetation, showing mountains and lowlands, with white for the Himalayas, and Monopoly houses and hotels for towns, that sort of thing. I made them myself. I used a lot of coloured chalks and powdered paints. The models would dry out and crumble and then we would make another one. The sand was just held together with water. This was in the days before there were a lot of visual aids. Like everybody else, I went on to slides and videos, but this was before that time, and Michael was one of the boys who used to get round the table with my models on it. He mentioned them at a function he was at not so long ago as being the inspiration for all his travelling.'

Unusually, perhaps, for post-war Sheffield, there was, even at 26 Whitworth Road, the occasional connection with foreign parts, a whiff of the exotic. Ted Palin, in one of his rarer duties as export manager of Edgar Allen, would very occasionally bring foreign customers back to the house. The odd Indian, Dutchman or Malay would thus occasionally be found struggling up the steep front path to take a sherry with Ted and family. 'Every Christmas for quite a few years,' Palin says, 'he received a box of dates from Algeria with his name misspelt as E. M. Palm. When eventually he put them right, they stopped sending the dates.'

The first sign that Palin might be an habitual, even a professional, traveller came in train spotting visits to Retford in Nottinghamshire, just a few miles from Sheffield, when he was still a child. 'I loved the idea of travelling, which was why I was a railway spotter. I can remember the excitement of that journey. I still get quite excited by trains and I think a good train journey is absolutely the best. I prefer to be on the ground than in the air because I like to see things and I like to be able to move around. There's a certain romance and glamour to a train journey.' Palin also liked to read Biggles and other adventure stories: 'I got a whiff of exotic places. I have an insatiable curiosity. Even just travelling into central London is fresh and exciting to me. Never dull.'

Train spotting was originally important in that it was an interest he shared with his father. But the father's interest was, typically, colonised, then eclipsed, by the son. As late as 1982, when asked what his favourite possession was, Palin replied, with only the slightest pause for deliberation, that it was his 1955 Ian Allen *Train Spotters' Book*, with the names and numbers of hundreds of engines neatly underlined in red and blue. 'It would be absolutely awful to lose that,' he said. 'There was a time in my life when it was never out of my hands.'

In 1980, Palin made a delightful documentary called *Confessions of a Train Spotter* for BBC 2, in which he was filmed riding the 785 railway miles from Euston to the Kyle of Lochalsh, the Scottish terminus just 400 yards from the Isle of Skye. The ultimate purpose of the journey was to take home an enormous platform sign from the remote station for his railway memorabilia collection. He positively cooed with delight ('the start of a train journey ... one of the great sensations of life') as he indulged his lifelong passion for steam, timetables and railway gossip. The enthusiasm he transmitted was infectious too; train spotting does not have the best image as a pastime, yet he managed to make the whole subject attractive, engaging and even quite exciting. It must have made millions of people wonder whether steam trains and railway buffs were that bad after all.

Interestingly, Palin as a boy was not at all evangelistic about his train spotting. To some of his friends, he barely mentioned it, and none ever remembers accompanying him to one of his train haunts.

'Oh, yes, he was a great one for train spotting,' says Peter Todd. 'He had these books. He used to go down to the Midland station and put the numbers in when he had seen particular trains. I don't think I ever went, because I was never keen on train spotting. He used to get covered in grime because they were all steam engines in those days.'

'It's odd, isn't it,' says Graham Stuart-Harris, 'that he never asked me to go with him, and hardly even mentioned it. I certainly wouldn't have wanted to go – it sounded so boring. I don't know how he found the time to go train spotting, actually. As far as I remember, we were always together.' Richard Heath adds: 'He didn't try and talk about train spotting with me. He certainly didn't get any enthusiasm from me about it, so perhaps that would lead him not to mention it to me. I think it's pretty much something you do on your own, anyway.'

It was clear even to a schoolboy, however, that train spotting might be a fine hobby, even a minor calling, but it was hardly a profession.

'My earliest ambition,' as Palin has explained, 'was to be an explorer. I loved all those tales about crossing the Australian desert or the North West Passage, people like Hudson and Cabot having to eat each other to keep going. I used to look at photographs of Southern Railway locos and they would seem as remote to me as Tierra del Fuego. The first really big voyage of my life was to Manchester. By the time I was eight I remember telling people I wanted to be an explorer. "It's all been explored," they'd say, in that tone of lofty imperial dogmatism which had a ring of confidence well into the 1950s. So I eventually shut up and decided to be something more mid-twentieth century, like an airline pilot or racing driver.' The phrase, 'It's all been explored,' was in fact Ted Palin's, rather than an unspecific 'they'.

'Then I wanted to be a test pilot, until I discovered you needed O-level maths and I knew I wouldn't get that. I suppose about twelve, I realised I'd better think of something realistic.'

'Though I affected other ambitions,' he told the *Observer* in 1992, 'the desire to explore continued, steadily and subversively, to run my life. I collected stamps, not for the endless tedious heads of Hindenburg and Queen Elizabeth but for Nyasaland and its water-falls or Mauritius and its sugar plantations. I went to church every Sunday, not so much for the "Te Deum" and the long rambling creeds but in the hope that the visiting preacher might be a mission-ary – a lean, sun-pickled, steely-eyed macho man with hair-raising tales of Africa and half an arm missing. Once a month we had to suffer talks from guest speakers, and the ones I always liked were the missionaries – bronzed men who would grip the sides of the pulpit and tell terrible stories of how they were captured by natives or escaped from piranha fish. I thought they were very romantic figures.'

Palin enjoyed listening to the visiting missionaries because they talked about other countries and travel in a very theatrical way. 'That mixture of travel and religion was a heady concoction when I was young,' he remembers. 'Not for nothing was geography my favourite subject or Biggles my favourite fictional character. With him I could sniff the Gobi Desert (though his tobacco tended to get in the way) and fly to the shores of the Baltic. I followed cricket largely for the Australian tourists, bringing with them their funny accents and oddly shaped caps and the almost unbearable lure of a massive island on the other side of the world full of coral reefs and bizarre animals. I became a train spotter because beneath the oil and grime of the locomotives that pulled into Sheffield Midland were nameplates evoking a world of exotic possibilities: "Palestine", "Sarawak", "Tasmania" and "New Hebrides".

'It made little difference that as a family we never once left England. This only intensified my curiosity and strengthened my appetite for whatever exploration meant. It didn't necessarily mean going somewhere exotic. I could get quite excited by a day trip to Doncaster. But deep down my heart was anywhere that was "bleak", "remote" or "inaccessible". One thing you could say for Doncaster, it was not inaccessible.'

Curiously, Michael's parents never encouraged him with talk of their own travels, though both had been to India in the 1920s. After they died, he found a box of old photos, not of the great tourist sites of India, 'but of my father in various theatrical costumes on a beach in Bombay'.

It was one of the sparse but most precious pieces of evidence Michael Palin ever had that underneath his father's testy character, with his dismissive attitude to his son's wackier ambitions, the heart of an original, unconventional, theatrical man might actually have existed.

3

Shrewsbury

At thirteen, Palin followed his father to Shrewsbury. The Revd Edward Palin – Michael's great-grandfather and the subject of his film *American Friends* – sent his sons to the school, starting a tradition which had already spanned three Palin generations. Michael as a parent would be the first to halt the custom; his three children went to the local state school. 'One thing I didn't like about Shrewsbury was the elitist assumption that you had more money than anybody else,' he has said.

That assumption was extremely flawed in the case of Ted Palin, even if, ironically, Michael now has more than enough money to have sent his children to private school. His father, he says with much pride, never made him feel the school fees were a sacrifice. 'He was just very proud that I had got in, and we were probably at our closest during my teenage years when he could relive his years at Shrewsbury through me.'

Because of the struggle his father was going through to make Shrewsbury affordable, Michael suffered, 'moments which no child should have to go through. For instance, I was embarrassed that my parents had such a small car when they came to speech days. And it seems to me terrible that any place should foster that kind of feeling. My parents just didn't have that sense of innate superiority that the successful parents had. When he came to visit, I used to hope he would park the car around the corner.'

The massed ranks of Jaguars in the carpark at the beginning and end of term at Shrewsbury must have made Ted Palin, in his old Austin A50, feel every bit as miserable as Michael. But it was the son rather than the father, so far as can be discerned, who went on to develop political misgivings about the system rather than merely suffer its multiplicity of embarrassments.

Palin is no fan now of the British private education establishment: 'It's an education system that doesn't make it easy for people to talk to each other. It produces a certain mind-set, a "them and us" mentality which is not helpful, and the result for the country as a whole is that a lot of good work just doesn't get done because people are so awkward with each other.'

'It was at public school,' he explained in an interview many years later with a Sheffield magazine, *Westside*, 'that I learned the idea that money could buy you status. The school had its own peculiar privileges and rituals. That was all part of the class system at the time, which we accepted. The British class system,' he continued, a little surprisingly, although there was doubtless a good deal of irony in what he was saying, 'is still the best in the world – eccentric and outdated, but still very effective. But it's becoming more like the American system now, based on money rather than breeding.'

Palin does not deny having enjoyed going to such an elite and elitist school, and emphatically denies that it did him any psychological damage, but when he had his own children and the wherewithal to send them anywhere he liked, he sent them to local comprehensives. 'They never make judgements on grounds of class,' he says. 'They never change as I had to. That's why I like them.'

When he was a teenager, however, he readily admits to not having been quite so opposed to the system; rebellion was hardly part of Palin's make-up anyway and, with parental and peer pressure combining, it was hardly likely that any but the most unusual adolescent would have fought against the status quo from inside. Rebellion – and even then of the gentlest sort – was not sparked until he had conquered the summit of educational elitism, at Oxford.

For the moment, in attitude he was like any other prep school–public school product of the fifties: 'I became a bit of a snob,' he confessed readily to Minty Clinch of the *Observer*. 'I made judgements about people who hadn't been to public school. I suppose it was encouraged at home, not positively or aggressively, but we talked about tradition a lot. What they did to you there was to make you feel rather special because you were at Shrewsbury, pumping it into you that you were among the country's elite. It stays with you for life. Grammar school boys – the term 'grammar school' was so derogatory – were so absolutely beneath you. That was the way they wanted you to think.' He agrees that he has sometimes found it hard to shake off all the resonances of such an education, even later in life.

'I remember being permanently cold and short of breath, and carrying vast amounts of books from our house to the main school buildings, taking care not to walk over certain parts of the grounds you couldn't step on until you had been there for four years,' Palin has said of Shrewsbury. Yet it was an institution which, despite appearing to epitomise the stuffiness and nonsense of the public school, seemed at the same time to foster a culture of informed, gentlemanly subversiveness. It was distinctly non-oppressive, many of the masters were original and eccentric men, and the grounds were beautiful. Whether as a result of some devious educational plan cooked up by masters – to provide an environment so full of pomposity and meaningless tradition that any intelligent boy would rebel against it – or whether Shrewsbury boys were their own inspiration, the school had established a slightly seditious tradition.

Not long before Palin came to Shrewsbury, Richard Ingrams and Willie Rushton had been there, and would within a few years be starting the epicentre of establishment subversion, *Private Eye*, which at times would resemble a sort of *Old Salopian* magazine in exile. Palin was also at Shrewsbury at the same time as the older John Peel (John Ravenscroft as he then was), a wealthy boy from Cheshire who, with a restored Merseyside accent – almost ironed out for good at Shrewsbury – would become a leading icon for another sixties youth rebellion, pop music.

The mischievous ethic of what would be *Private Eye* was not regarded at all as an embarrassment by Shrewsbury, as it would unquestionably have been at the majority of public schools. Palin remembers being shown copies of *Mesopotamia*, the *Eye*'s Oxford precursor, by a history master. 'It was certainly a cut above the *Salopian*, our school magazine to which I contributed the occasional match report,' Palin recalls.

Another peculiarity of Shrewsbury, which indicates to a mild extent that a quietly radical approach to education may have underpinned the place's superficial formality, was that the school was renowned as a home for elaborate practical jokes. Even the masters would play complicated tricks on one other. Palin recalls his house, Riggs, as a very happy place, largely due to a wonderful housemaster, Revd R.H.J. Brooke, known only as Brooke, who was, as Palin puts it, 'very silly, full of jokes. He kept us full of laughter, and enabled us to cope with the awful food and waking up in winter with six inches of snow on the beds.'

Palin did not, as it happens, take to satire or to counterculture, preferring instead to write some rather serious short poems for the school magazine. The strong conformist streak in Palin led to him even becoming a colour sergeant in the school CCF. Still a rather shy boy, the corps helped him come out of himself: 'You got to shout at people. It was very reassuring to be part of such tradition,' he has said.

As another method of going with the public school flow, he became keen on the idea of excelling at sport, of which there was a great deal at Shrewsbury, even if no greater kudos was attached to sport than to acting or to being a musician. 'Unfortunately you couldn't just sit and read a book in the afternoon. That was right out,' he says. So, as his father had done before him, he began rowing.

Palin's sporting campaign may have been mistaken, unless he was determined like his father one day to have a front hall hung with notable blades. 'He left a lasting impression of being distinctly non-sporty,' recalls one contemporary. 'Michael rowed on the Severn, but I don't think he was particularly accomplished.' Michael was lucky enough to be the first Palin qualified – by virtue of being born there – to play cricket for Yorkshire, a qualification of little use to him, since cricket at Shrewsbury required a few skills beyond that at which he had shone at Birkdale – throwing the cricket ball.

'It was very unpleasant at first,' Palin says of rowing. 'You had a fixed seat so you got nothing but blisters on the bum.' Later on, he graduated to a moving seat, a blisterless bum and, true to form, a place in the school Second VIII. It became fun.

The unlikely sight of Palin the footballer could even be seen on the playing fields of Shrewsbury. 'I longed to be really good at sport. I was good enough for the Second XI but I only made the First XI on a bad day, when nine had gone down with pneumonia,' he says. 'I always wanted to be better co-ordinated. I wanted to move round the world like Fred Astaire, instead of knocking things over all the time. I used to be quite chubby, but it never worried me.'

It would be wrong to assume that public school was entirely to the young Palin's taste. He was never bullied, he says, but adds: 'It was a fierce regime. Seniority made people superior. They ignored you.' Once he was sitting in the lavatory when he overheard two senior boys in the urinals. 'What do you think of that Palin?' said one. 'He's mad,' replied the other. 'Yeah,' said the first, 'he's mad, but he's quite nice.'

Older boys may have thought he was mad, but anyone seeking evidence of a continuation at Shrewsbury of Palin's dabbling in comedy back at prep school would find it surprisingly thin on the ground. Whereas John Cleese had regularly caused convulsions of laughter at his public school with precise and utterly corrosive sketches about masters, Palin's humour was more in the line of being wry, witty and amusing in an everyday way, which was very much the accepted mode at Shrewsbury.

Humour was regarded as being all very well in its place, but a mature, responsible person would know when jokes had to stop. Young Palin was regarded as a potential head of house but believes that he was thwarted in this by virtue of having been the cause of laughter beyond the properly defined boundaries. Something – a certain smugness, an unsettling quietness, perhaps – seemed at last to be bringing about a reaction in the few more rigid, authoritarian personalities around him. Almost accidentally, the idea of Palin as a subversive was beginning to form, even if his subversiveness had just the kind of affectionate, harmless turn to it which would one day help inspire him to write and act in his public school pastiche, *Ripping Yarns*.

The sense that Palin, M.E., was not quite serious enough for high office meant he only made Vice Head of House. The Vice Head of House title was a banner under which he was to enjoy the delight of power without responsibility. Palin seems to have discovered something of an aptitude, as he puts it, for 'being consistently good at being second'. (An interesting point of Monty Pythonic history, although of quite what significance it is a little hard to judge, is that, of all the five British members of the team, only Palin and Cleese failed in their youth to make head of school.)

Of his time at Shrewsbury, Palin has said, 'I suppose sometimes I felt, "This is it, I'm here, I've read all the right books. I'm all set up." But then something totally absurd would happen and I could never take it too seriously. I could always see a lot of absurdity in some of the traditions. I still do. I was the court-jester figure who used humour to face the world. But I don't think I was a rebel. I remember a school report which said, "Michael sits at the back of the class and says little."'

Francis Ravenscroft, younger brother of John Peel, was a direct contemporary of Palin in Riggs. The Ravenscroft brothers were the sons of a prosperous Liverpool cotton merchant. (John Peel himself was a couple of years older than Palin, and recalls him only as 'an impertinently clever younger boy, who shot into the school above me'.) 'Michael was very amusing, very well-liked, but he wasn't one of those people who achieved great things at public school and then had loads of silver cups on mantelpieces,' Francis Ravenscroft says. 'But then I never got the impression that he was ill at ease in a public school. His father was an old bloke here too. He spoke the Queen's English, without any accent at all. At public schools you get some people who are great mixers and doers and movers and shakers, and some who aren't. In a way, he ploughed his own furrow, as it were.'

Ravenscroft believes that the happy accident of Palin being placed in Riggs House, under the benevolent wing of Brooke, a man who rarely took anything seriously, was a key element in his friend's social and, possibly, comedic development. 'How happy you were at Shrewsbury was very much dependent upon the house in which you were resident, and Brooke was, for most of his pupils, a hero in real life. He was a really brilliant teacher, who encouraged everyone to make the best of their talents and never imposed discipline of any kind. It was implied that indiscipline would have let him down.'

It was Brooke who encouraged Palin at Shrewsbury when he began to write what he now calls 'self-conscious humorous pieces'. 'Brooke only took Holy Orders half way through his time as a house master,' Ravenscroft remembers, 'which was a source of much merriment to his pupils. The main thing that I remember him teaching was called Cultural French, a subject which had nothing whatsoever to do with either French or culture. It was called Cultural French because something had to go on the timetable. It consisted of Brooke throwing into the maelstrom some fairly provocative remark, and then encouraging everyone to discuss it at length. This was nothing like a public school is now. It was much more a rounded education.'

It would be misleading to suggest that Palin became in any way more religious under the housemastership of the charismatic Brooke, yet Palin, who would some years later be defending – and doing so with great intellectual force – the arguably anti-religion film Monty Python's *Life of Brian*, was by no means anti religion as a teenager. He has described himself at this time as 'an agnostic with doubts', but his home background was surprisingly churchy. As a teenager, he had been through the mill of Sunday school, regular church attendance and the highly propagandistic Crusaders, and as a result, knew his Bible and the routine of religious observance pretty well. Palin's father was fascinated not only by trains, but by looking round churches too, an activity Palin the boy was not particularly inspired by, yet at the same time, one suspects, found quite a comforting routine, if only because of its familiarity.

Even if his distaste, or perhaps just disillusion, with organised religion had not yet formed back in Sheffield, at Shrewsbury, the preposterousness to his mind of orthodox Church of England Christianity was confirmed. 'We were in the chapel every hour on the hour,' he says. 'It was like a barrage of belief thrust upon us. Some things were thought of as too sacred to be laughed at. I couldn't accept it at all. I could always see a lot of absurdity in some of the traditions. I still do.'

While formalised religion was so much part of the structure of Shrewsbury school, the more agreeable matter of house plays was central to life at Riggs, even though Palin did not particularly dominate them. He was obliged by his parents, who were deeply unhappy about both Angela's and Michael's growing interest in acting professionally, to keep his interest in the theatre low key. 'He saw acting as a way to total moral compromise and financial despair. Within his particular circle, acting wasn't the right thing to do. He didn't see it as a man's job,' says Palin.

Thus did it become a virtually illicit pleasure, not least because it was thought to be a distraction from work, something Ted Palin would not countenance, and Michael, being such a good boy, went along with it. At least, he almost did. He turned down a big part in one school production of *The Applecart*, but nevertheless took a small one, in the hope that his parents might not notice he was in it at all. The ploy worked; his father, he claimed at the time, slept through all his lines.

House plays were easier to get away with. 'They were regarded as an enormous joke, as an opportunity for a laugh,' Ravenscroft explains. 'School plays were taken more seriously because they were Shakespeare, because it was done for O level. In one house play I particularly remember, I played one prostitute and Michael played another. It was called *Two Gentlemen of Soho*.

'Michael was a very malleable person. He was totally unthreatening, which is what made him such a nice guy. I actually went over to Sheffield to see him. I spent a couple of days there. His mother was a very charming, unobtrusive sort of person. Michael and I went out to Blue John Mines at Castleton on my motor scooter with Michael on the back. I think I saw him once at Oxford, but I haven't seen him since. People who go on to university develop a different life there, and people who don't, as I didn't, miss out on that.'

Going to Shrewsbury did not mean that Michael's friendship with Graham Stuart-Harris back in Ranmoor was in any way on the back burner. Palin's first loyalties to his past have consistently been to Sheffield and Sheffield people, with Oxford second and Shrewsbury, it sometimes seems, almost a minor interlude. He had, after all, spent nine years at Birkdale, more than twice the time he was at Shrewsbury. In his *Comic Roots* film, Palin dwelt only briefly, if with characteristic benignity, on his second school. 'I spent four happy years at Shrewsbury,' he summed up, 'doing Latin unseen, cleaning monitors' football boots, blistering my bum rowing up the Severn and reluctantly respecting parental restrictions on my acting activities. Thus, doing the decent thing, I worked my way through O levels and A levels.'

While Michael surged ahead academically, Graham Stuart-Harris had considered himself well out of the Shrewsbury league, and had tried – unsuccessfully – for Repton, eventually setting for a boarding place at Trent College. At home, however, Michael and Graham were as inseparable as ever.

What did boys of fifteen, sixteen and soon eighteen get up to when they got together in the holidays? 'Well, we didn't have girlfriends and nobody seemed to be concerned or worried about it,' says Graham. 'We knew girls but they didn't like going out to have six pints. That was the trouble with the girls. People now would think we were a bit odd. Michael certainly never had a girlfriend, although he might have tried once or twice rather unsuccessfully. I tried once or twice. And of course, both our parents tried quite hard to get us girls, but the trouble is they always wanted us to go to dances. We had been to dancing lessons, you see. I certainly remember Mrs Palin and my mother ringing up neighbours round and about saying, will you take our boys to the whatever it is.'

Michael actually was pursuing some notion of sex, but that side of life was strictly concentrated into holidays, which the Palins were still taking every year in Suffolk, and during which, as he puts it, 'the damp-palmed quest for true love began to shape my holidays'.

'The two holiday weeks were a vitally important part of the process of getting to know girls,' Palin admitted in a 1987 *Daily Mail* article linked to the screening of his nostalgia BBC 2 drama, *East of Ipswich*, made the year before, which borrowed heavily from his own family seaside holidays of the fifties. 'These were the two weeks when you could be different from what you were the rest of the year,' he wrote. 'The normal rules were relaxed, you were in a sort of social limbo land. Holidays were when "It" might happen if "It" was ever going to. To a public schoolboy in the 1950s, women were like newspapers are to Rupert Murdoch,' he says. 'You wanted as many of them as possible, and there the comparison stops. There was an enormous gap between hope and reality. This was filled with things like yearning, true love, romance and other bad habits.'

He went on to recall much of the angst of the teenage pursuit of sex, especially for a still notably shy young man when it came to the matter of speaking to girls. In particular, he recalls how minor decisions about minuscule matters of personal appearance – choices over how to wear your shirt collar, brush your hair, apply Valderma to a particular pimple and so on – became imbued with huge, disproportionate significance, 'as if getting the right combination of them would suddenly unlock the doors of desire'.

He managed quite brilliantly to rediscover that adolescent male bafflement over whether the female of the species was or was not interested in sex, and how the question re-opened in his mind each summer as he arrived from sexless Sheffield in hormone-laden Southwold, which from 1958 had been Ted Palin's holiday resort of choice: 'The perceptions of girls which whirled confusingly in my head, as our car drove along the front to the familiar brown-painted guest house, were of two kinds: the Ideal, represented by my mother, the Queen and Jane Russell; and the Available.'

Impossible as it was to envision the 'Ideal' type of woman being in the remotest bit interested in sex, it would surely have to fall to the 'Available' to initiate the likes of him into whatever it was that there was to be initiated into. 'The idea that girls had similar or even greater, sexual curiosity about men seemed as likely as Doncaster winning the F.A. Cup.

'I hearten myself,' Palin concluded, 'by remembering that the girl I eventually plucked up courage to speak to on a beach in Suffolk in 1959 is still my best friend twenty-seven years later. She's my wife. Perhaps it was worth all the agonising.'

Helen Gibbins was a Cambridgeshire farmer's daughter, a couple of years older than Michael, whom he met – or rather engineered a meeting with – when he threw a beach ball at her and knocked her hat off. He alluded to the story of the romance in *East of Ipswich*, although the film stopped well short of revealing the real genesis of Michael and Helen's relationship, in keeping with the care with which he has always maintained his wife's privacy. The hat incident does not occur in the film, although a wide-brimmed straw hat belonging to the girl Palin's character longs for does have a small part. As to the full details of the real-life couple's meeting, Palin told questing journalists at the time of *East of Ipswich*, 'That is a secret. It was osmosis, a natural process. It seemed natural that we should spend time together.'

He did not draw directly on his own sexual awakening in *East of Ipswich* – the Michael character, Richard Burrill (played with perfect awkwardness by Edward Rawle-Hicks) actually ends up having sex in a field not with the sweet and beautiful Helen (or Julia as she is in the film) but with a stroppy and sexually rapacious Dutch exchange student.

What did inform large parts of *East of Ipswich* were the other details of his own adolescence. The Burrill family's car, an Austin with a roof rack, is similar to the Palins'. The film is set and filmed in Southwold. Like Michael, Richard is, by the age of seventeen, holidaying alone with his parents – Angela Palin was, of course, by this time living her own life, as she was several years older than Michael.

Above all, Richard's father in *East of Ipswich*, Harold, appears to be Ted Palin in dozens of respects. He does not stammer, but works in engineering, is stiff, formal, snobbish and rather old. He often refers to Richard as 'the boy'. He is not very well off, scoffing at the idea of taking a beach hut as a waste of money. He is obsessed with organising activities, especially that of looking round churches.

Other details, we can only imagine, are on permanent loan from the Ted Palin collection. He insists on taking lengthy back road routes to get to the family's holiday destination. He has a thing about men driving Rovers having declined in social status from what they once were. He faffs about on the beach, the family trailing behind him, in the search for the perfect spot, rejecting proposed locations one by one – 'Too close to the steps', 'Too many dogs', and so on. He sits on the beach in his jacket scanning the horizon with field glasses and pointing out, to his wife's total lack of interest, passing ships and identifying them as oil tankers or bauxite carriers en route to Sunderland. He is concerned with his bowel movements and the lack of Grape Nuts among the selection of breakfast cereals on offer at the gloomy guesthouse the family is staying at.

Palin also, however, touches on the more playful, naughty side of his father. He cheats outrageously at Scrabble, and tells the guesthouse landlady a lie about Michael's grandfather having died, as an excuse for the Burrills to go home early without having to pay for the remainder of their stay.

The overall picture of Palin's teenage years is a curious mixture; on the one hand, it seems to have been fearsomely stuffy and bleak, on the other, comforting, gentle and mannerly. He portrays himself as quiet and rather moody, a bit stuffy himself, but anxious to be less so despite his deeply bred instincts for correctness. Interestingly, he is shown as having quite a sharp temper, something he has insisted over the years he really does possess, despite the unshakeable received wisdom that he is the nicest man in the world.

At one point in the film, Richard Burrill complains that he 'doesn't like being organised'. Any man who believes that, whether he likes it or not, he will eventually turn into his father will be interested to note that during the making of *East of Ipswich* in 1986, Palin was never happier than when busying himself organising day-off activities for the entire film crew. 'He was very excited about being in Southwold,' explains one crew member, 'as not only was it terrifically nostalgic for him, but his mother was still living close by. One Sunday, Michael put on a champagne breakfast in Southwold to which everybody had to turn up dressed in white. After that, he had organised a whole day of rowing, to which his mother came along, and treated him like a child the whole time, which was very sweet and funny to see. And most evenings, he was delighted to go out drinking with us all. He made it one of the most enjoyable shoots I've ever been on.'

Some of the detail in *East of Ipswich* is personal but not obviously so. In one brief glimpse, a group of young Christians is seen on the sea front singing a hymn. Only a few seconds of this is heard, and could easily be missed: 'Waft, waft, ye winds, his story,' the youngsters sing, 'And you, ye waters, roll, Till like a sea of glory, It spreads from pole to pole.'

Palin did indeed borrow the name – and perhaps the concept, too – of his second TV travel series, *Pole to Pole*, which he made in 1992, from this favourite hymn, 'From Greenland's Icy Mountains'. The hymn is about missionaries – the tanned macho men whose lectures so inspired him as a boy in church in Sheffield. This was not the only time it had surfaced in his work, either. In 1983, Palin opened his film *The Missionary* with a 1907 scene of boys at an English public school singing the opening lines of 'From Greenland's Icy Mountains'; they soon mutate into African schoolchildren, but never quite get to the crucial 'pole to pole' line. (The more frequently borrowed line from Bishop Reginald Heber's early nineteenth-century hymn is the early environmentalist observation, 'Though every prospect pleases, and only man is vile.')

The fateful meeting with Helen Gibbins in the summer of 1959, part two of which was played out the following summer back in Southwold, took place towards the end of Palin's time at Shrewsbury. By the time university entrance was being talked about, he and Helen were exchanging letters regularly.

By 1961, Michael was striding towards the singularly unimaginative goal Ted Palin had had in mind for his son all the time – a place at his old college, Clare, Cambridge. He went for an interview and exams there and failed. He finally got into Brasenose College, Oxford, but only after a considerable palaver, at least for a young man who was still clever, if not quite as pre-eminent as he had been at Birkdale. He makes a point now of speaking a little dismissively of the achievement of getting into Oxford. 'Brasenose is like a railway waiting room,' he says. 'Anyone can go in.'

Palin was not considered scholarship material, but Shrewsbury thought that he should try for an award, since it might help him get a regular place. He went to Oxford initially for the Magdalen and Worcester exams; the trips were not much of a success either, the interview at Worcester providing Palin with confirmation of his idea of himself as being an expert at being not quite good enough. He still sees the Worcester interview as one of the most embarrassing moments of his life.

He wanted at the time to read English, and had carefully swotted up on his favourite author then and now, Graham Greene. One of the first questions at the interview was which authors he read; he replied Graham Greene, and from the answer – 'No, which authors on the *syllabus*' – it was clear that he might as well have listed which plumbers he preferred to use. He attempted to use poetry as an escape route. Not unnaturally, the interviewer asked which poets he liked. Realising that he was on the run, Michael's mind obliged by completely stalling; the name of any poets he did know escaped him, and eventually he blurted 'Wordsworth'. 'Name six of his poems,' the don asked. After a period he remembers as being 'forty seconds', he recalls mumbling, ' "Daffodils" '.

At Magdalen, things went better, superficially; at least Michael did not dry up. On a general paper, there was the well-worn question, 'A house is a machine for living in – Le Corbusier. Discuss.' He replied with a fluent discussion of how this notion had indeed applied in the sixteenth century, back in Le Corbusier's day, but that now things were naturally very different. Needless to say, Le Corbusier was, in fact, still alive, and Michael Palin did not join Magdalen College.

Michael left Shrewsbury with two terms and the summer holidays to kill before going up to Oxford, a delightful break for any young man, especially with the hardest job of his life, that of getting into the university, done. Curiously, perhaps, for the famous traveller to be, he did not, as he puts it, 'go to Morocco, cross the Sahara, cycle round France, hitchhike through Mongolia or become an au pair in the Yukon like everyone else'. He took instead a temporary job at the Sheffield steelworks where his father worked, mucked around in his home town and enjoyed a golden few months in reassuring, familiar surroundings.

'I wasn't doing anything butch like forging hot steel,' Palin hastens to point out. 'I worked in the publicity department, the arts side of the steel industry.' What Palin had found at Edgar Allen was an outlet for his second choice career after acting – journalism: 'I was involved in interviewing people about racing pigeons against the noise of a ten tonne steam hammer,' he recalls. 'The only man who was interesting swore so much, I could use nothing he said.'

The *Edgar Allen Magazine* was a quite extraordinary institution in that anything so literate and glossily presented should have been produced as a works newsletter, and by such a relatively small company. In the style of an exceptionally up-market school magazine, it allowed Edgar Allen employees to see published practically anything they cared to write, draw, paint or photograph, and they seized the opportunity with relish. Yet the magazine was very much in the spirit of the kind of enthusiastic, bounding Englishness Michael Palin himself exemplifies.

Its pages in the back issues file are filled with essays on everything you would not expect in a steelworks' publication. Articles were not just work related ('Interesting Facts About Heat Exchangers') or DIY oriented ('The new Marley ceiling tiles are a top favourite with the lady of the house'). All interests, hobbies and down-right obsessions were amply catered for: 'Blackbeard: the Terror of the Seas', 'Giving Up Smoking', 'The Magic of the Close-up Photograph', 'Bowling – The New Craze', 'Gliding'; and a contribution of Olympian eccentricity, 'Housebuilding on Tristan da Cunha', this last article appearing with several black and white photographs.

On the news pages, other wonderfully Monty Python-esque touches could be found at every turn. The annual competition for the title of Miss Edgar Allen (a curious enough name in itself) would inevitably produce a glamour puss winner from the typing pool, who would be shown in a fuzzy photograph in a one-piece bathing suit pouting voluptuously – from behind thick, upswept spectacles of the kind that Dame Edna Everage would one day immortalise. Many of the newsy articles and company personality profiles appeared unsigned, and some seem to have a suspicious touch of Palin about them: 'On Saturday nights, you will invariably find Susan at the City Hall, twisting and shaking with her friend Marlene Myers of the Publicity Department.'

The *Edgar Allen Magazine* would, throughout Michael's university years, be the recipient of several of his earliest attempts at travel writing; pieces he would have known instinctively were far too middlebrow for weighty student publications such as *Isis*, could nevertheless see the light of day in the obscurity of a private publication in his home town. Among these articles are to be found such inspirational titles as 'Surviving in Scotland' – an account of Michael's first visit north of the border, and 'Try Germany this Summer!' a quite funny essay on his second trip abroad – the first had been a skiing trip to Austria in the same year, 1963, and on which he does not seem to have written anything.

Within the confines of the *Edgar Allen Magazine*'s readership, his articles served the triple purposes of making his father proud (Ted Palin did not retire from the company until 1966), of giving Palin a chance to try out some funny semi-journalistic writing, and of giving vent in a less intellectually critical arena than Oxford to the young man's considerable desire to teach and instruct, or if that suggests too bossy a character, at least to share his experiences with a wider audience, albeit as yet not much wider. Then as now, describing his experiences was almost as great a motivating force in Palin as performing.

There was something about taking such a funny little job in such prosaic, yet potentially amusing, circumstances which seemed ideally suited to the eighteen-year-old Palin. Comedy in general, and Monty Python in particular, would require him to have a highly developed, and above all, informed, sense of not only the absurd, but of the utterly everyday and banal. The most junior job in the most pointless department in a minor provincial factory in the becalmed middle of a particularly inward-looking and introverted period of British history was almost certainly a far more useful grounding for Palin than the more butch – and, it has to be said, conventional – pursuits for young men in his position. Babysitting in the Yukon be blowed; this was practically vocational training for a comic writer.

The spell at Edgar Allen also provided Michael with a chance to work on the very much unfinished business of growing up. 'When I was a kid I thought I'd grow up at eighteen but it didn't happen,' he said in 1979. 'Then I thought, "Wait until twenty-five" – and I'm still waiting. Growing up to me is a tired cluttering up of one's life. Filling it with forms. Going off to studies and writing dull letters. It's like when someone says to you, "This isn't funny. Not funny at all," and you stop yourself from giggling because you're supposed to be grown up. I like giggling.'

Hanging out in Sheffield with three meals a day provided by his mother, the company of old friends and regular letters from Helen in Cambridgeshire was the perfect way, it seems, for Palin to prepare for the really big step of going to Oxford. It was also an ideal way to appease his ever anxious parents who, thanks to him having such a safe-sounding temporary job, were now starting to get ideas about Michael eventually going into the advertising industry.

There was at the same time something else highly significant going on for Michael during this pleasant, if at times slightly hopeless, time. 'My father didn't want me to be an actor, apart from very small parts in school plays,' he explains. 'I think he thought it would interfere with my work. My sister joined a professional repertory company, and I knew he would have preferred her to be a secretary. But he didn't mind me acting after I had left school because I had got my place at Oxford.'

One of the people at Edgar Allen discovered Palin was interested in theatre, and introduced him in turn to Jack Parkin, who in his spare time was a leading member of an amateur theatre group, the now defunct Brightside and Carbrook Co-operative Society Players. And it was Parkin who first brought Palin to a stage outside school. He took Michael along to rehearsals and soon realised, as he explains, 'that potential was there'.

Unlike at school, however, he played no comic roles at all. 'I played lots of serious roles, very tragic, very moving, but I was always more ham than Hamlet,' he confessed in a recent *Sheffield Star* interview.

All the same, when he shot to fame in *Monty Python's Flying Circus*, the Brightside and Carbrook Players told a local reporter they thought it was a waste of a good serious actor. 'We did heavy acting,' Palin says, as if it were somehow in tune with a city known for heavy industry. 'I played gritty, serious roles that made *GBH* look like music hall,' Michael has said. 'In a play called *The Woodcarver*, about a realist carving of a statue of Christ, I was a moody agnostic who seduced Audrey Greenslade on a couch. She was seven months' pregnant. Her husband did the lighting. What he made of all this I don't know.'

The young man's abilities were recognised in the next production,

Exit For Seven. 'We were political prisoners waiting to be shot. We took it to the Bradford Co-operative drama competition. I won Best Perf (gent) and Doreen Barrowclough won Best Perf (non gent). I won Best Perf (gent) solely on the strength of my scar make-up, which made the audience gasp.'

Palin did not seem to blanch in the least at not doing comedy – there was quite a serious part of him which the Brightside and Carbrook Players encouraged. 'I always thought you would make something of it but I never thought it would have been comedy,' commented one fellow actor to Palin on the BBC film *Comic Roots.* 'But thinking back on it, there was that twinkle in your eye that should have told me.' Another female actor from the group concurred, 'The only thing I can remember going all that way back was that you were very easy to act with. But I never really thought you would branch off into the comedy line.'

The experience in Sheffield amateur theatre seems not only to have stimulated his desire still further to be an actor, but left him longing for more in the way of serious theatre. 'One thing that I really have missed and I haven't done since Sheffield,' he has since said, 'is doing a sustained, a complete, play. The Python and all that was a bit bitty and tends to be short sketches, and the film acting again is something that is done in short spurts. But I have not done any theatre work.'

For a man who has done nothing to attempt to cover up or forget any part of his roots or upbringing, and has positively revelled in publicly celebrating his family history, Shrewsbury school seems, from the little it crops up in his writing and performing, to have made far less impact on Palin than almost any other time in his life. Even his brief interlude between school and university provided various rich seams to mine for material in the future. Some of Palin's attitude to public school has undoubtedly been influenced by his political and moral opposition to the private school system.

However, in the same way that the Church of England, with which he similarly lacks much sympathy, has nevertheless done much to shape the Michael Palin of today, so did the public school experience do its bit to shape the adult Palin. Several decades after he left school, he was in New Zealand, being inducted for the cameras in a Maori ceremony. As part of the proceedings, he was required to sing a song.

'I was fed up with doing my normal party piece, the "Lumberjack Song,"' he relates, 'so I gave them my old schoolsong, "*Floreat Salopia*". The Latin all came back to me – and they all applauded.'

4

Oxford

With the difficulties and embarrassment he had encountered on the way, Palin had been relieved above all when the good news came through that he had got into Brasenose, the college his great-grandfather had attended, as well as, he jokes, the only Oxford college named after a part of the body – the Brase.

Brasenose was renowned for having something of a 'good chap' policy, preferring to choose people who were not necessarily going to turn out to get firsts, 'but showed some sign,' as a contemporary of Palin puts it, 'that they might contribute to the general sum of human happiness.'

One of the first congratulations Michael received on being accepted by Brasenose was a note from Cambridgeshire, from his sort-of girlfriend, Helen Gibbins. It was a charming little piece of sarcasm, to the effect that she had heard he had got into Oxford, and that they must have lowered the standards. She for her part was going to do teacher training at the Froebel Institute, a progressive college at Roehampton, in south-west London. The ways between the two seemed to be parting, not that they had been particularly convergent at any stage. Realistically, it seemed unlikely that they would have much more contact.

Oxford was a revelation for Michael, a completely new environ-ment, where kindred spirits abounded, he could muck about to his heart's content and still come away with a reasonable degree. He was there ostensibly to read history – 'in the evenings', as he puts it – and by day could indulge his growing love for acting in any one of dozens of college drama productions and revues. 'Provided I did my history essays on time,' he recalls, 'I was allowed to join the dramatic society and write revues and perform them at the Union Cellars. It was tremendous, a time of golden opportunities.'

He met his tutor in the first couple of days, a delightful man called Eric Collieu. Collieu had what his students called 'the last one-bar electric fire in Oxford', and had some important advice for his new tutees. 'Don't work too hard,' he would say. 'Enjoy yourself.'

Palin was at Oxford from 1962 to 1965 – a time of sex, drugs, rock 'n' roll and great optimism. 'There was a feeling that good times were ahead, that you were lucky to be there and that we were all very much in control of things,' he has said. 'I don't like the *Brideshead* image of Oxford. I think it does an immense disservice to the place. I enjoyed my three years there enormously because of the opportunities it gave me – I came out with an odd sort of a degree in comedy-writing rather than modern history. But I always felt excluded from the senior common room side, which didn't see undergraduates as part of the place – they thought it was for postgraduates and academics – which is probably why my view of it in *American Friends* is of a dark, enclosed, almost clandestine society.'

Palin reminisced about Oxford in a 1986 book called *The Gradu-ates* by an Edward Whitley, who, as a student three years previously, had done a round of fascinating interviews with prominent Oxford graduates. 'Oxford was a wonderfully liberating experience,' Palin told Whitley, 'because I suddenly found myself being able to choose what I wanted to do, rather than being forced to read Latin and French all day. It was also the first time that I mixed with boys from a non-public school background.

'Since the time I left my Sheffield prep school, from the age of fourteen to nineteen, I had only met the same sort of person as myself – tentative public school boys. Oxford was an introduction to lots of grammar school boys, where things like background, parents, parents' cars and money no longer mattered.

'At Shrewsbury, everyone had been so conscious of the ritual of being at a place of tradition that a horrible sense of privilege dominated the school. This I didn't see at Oxford. I was aware that places like Christ Church might operate like that, but Brasenose had a genuinely wide social mixture – bottles of Merrydown on the lawn at Magdalen was the closest we got to Evelyn Waugh's Oxford.'

Bizarrely, perhaps, Palin's first instinct as a fresher was to go in for sport rather than drama, as if his natural ability may have improved by virtue of coming up to Oxford. It is not uncommon for public school boys, who a few months previously were forced to take part in games and disliked the pressure, promptly to volunteer for more of the same as soon as they get to university. A few sessions of being terrorised by more talented lads from tougher schools usually puts paid to any hope of finally making it as a sportsman, and Palin for one soon realised that playing football, especially in the autumn run up the coldest winter since 1947, was a miserable experience even if you were doing so at Oxford with the future leaders of the country. So after a few weeks of trailing off to football matches, he started going AWOL from games as had been his wont at Birkdale.

So the theatre beckoned – and how. Palin's triumph that spring with the Brightside and Carbrook Co-operative players had left him hungering for more theatre, even despite Angela's unfortunate experience in rep, which had so vindicated Ted Palin's unshakeable view that acting was not a solid person's vocation. Angela was by now working as a radio studio manager with the BBC World Service – a perfectly pleasant job, but not one which satisfied her theatrical ambitions, or brought her particularly closer to her little brother.

There is a view that Oxford is not quite the place for the comedy-minded student; yet although the Cambridge Footlights Club has always attracted most of the media attention – Footlights was indeed recognised newspaper shorthand for undergraduate comedy – there was also a strong comedy tradition at Oxford, which encompassed both the Oxford University Dramatic Society and its sidekick, the Experimental Theatre Club. There was also a distinctly Oxford tradition of summer revues, which were normally transplanted to the Edinburgh Festival Fringe in August.

Palin's first venture into theatre at Oxford was far from a comedy. He played Third Peasant out of four in Lope de Vega's *Fuente Ovejuna*. As he was later to explain, 'I never had the feeling that comedy or cabaret was definitely what I wanted to do. It was a nice process of discovery'. Nevertheless, the role in this first serious undergraduate production led directly to Palin's most important social and career breakthrough at university.

The *Fuente Ovejuna* company spent months learning about the life of fifteenth-century Spanish peasants only to end up in a splendidly disastrous production. Stage machinery failed, a fountain – always likely to cause trouble – was capricious in the extreme, and went on and off each night apparently at will. Terry Jones, without yet being known to Palin, said it was the funniest play he had ever seen.

The Fourth Peasant in the show, however, was a history classmate of Palin's, Robert Hewison, now an author, journalist and cultural commentator as well as being the Professor of Literary and Cultural Studies at Lancaster University. Palin and Hewison had met on their first day at Brasenose; they were the only two of the group of nervous young men not wearing ties.

They got talking, and discovered by some wonderful symbiotic chemistry that not only were they both funny, but they were even funnier together. Their impromptu – and soon written – routines played well in front of informal audiences of friends, and in a very short time the idea struck Hewison that they could perform together.

'Robert was from London and very cosmopolitan,' Palin records. 'He said that if we could make people laugh in class, we could earn thirty shillings a night doing it in the Oxford Union cellars. I found I had a streak of sheer, naked exhibitionism. Robert channelled this very well.'

After Graham Stuart-Harris, Hewison would be the person who influenced Michael most powerfully. In an odd echo of the way the Stuart-Harrises and their London ways had come as a pleasant discovery to Michael as a very young boy, Hewison too lifted the Sheffield lad's horizons a rung higher. Palin remembers him as urbane, sophisticated, smooth, even, and above all funny, a raconteur and brilliant at the vogue Goons gag of adopting funny voices.

Hewison insists today that the social gulf between them was negligible: 'Michael always makes a great joke about the fact that he was the rough northerner and I was the great sophisticated southerner,' he maintains. 'The truth is that we have almost identical social and educational backgrounds – and of course that includes our cultural formation, in that we both could recite the entire *Goon Show* backwards. Even today, if we speak on the phone, immediately it is exactly the same as that first conversation, in that you suddenly find there is a kind of peculiar parlance based on public school joshing and the *Goon Show*.'

There were, in reality, both great similarities and great differences between their backgrounds. Hewison had been to Bedford school, which is of similar ranking to Shrewsbury, although differs in having a strong military tradition and a lot of Forces boys. Hewison acted at Bedford with one Jeremy Ashdown, who went on to the Navy, and then, as Paddy, to lead the Liberal Democratic Party. Hewison's father was a senior civil servant, and while he was a boy, the family had lived in Paris, where Hewison Sr worked for NATO, and later in Ceylon. By the time Hewison went up to Oxford, he lived nowhere more exotic than Weybridge, although his father had a pied-à-terre in Chelsea, where Hewison and Palin used to spend time and write some of their comedy material. Another possibly significant connection between the two was that both had a much older sister with whom they had less contact than they would have liked.

As most of his friends have noted down the years, food is often the route to Michael Palin's heart; his mother cooked well, and his father ensured that meals were eaten on time; consequently, Michael has never been a man who appreciated missing meals. Hewison opened Palin's eyes to the exciting new cuisines which existed beyond Ranmoor and public school. The Hewisons' flat in Chelsea was opposite a Polish delicatessen, and Michael developed a love of such rarities in early sixties Britain as Polish sausage. 'He very much appreciated being introduced to such exotic things,' Hewison notes.

There was one slight difference between the new friends. 'Michael was,' Hewison recalls, 'a bit more of a hearty than I was. He was a good sportsman, and was fit; he would always run when we went up to Brasenose. I am a terrible sportsman, and I am certainly more of a public school rebel than I think Michael was.' It is interesting that Palin's own account of his youth, and those of his early school-friends, while concurring on the question of Michael's innate con-formity, emphasise his averageness at games. Perhaps Palin has simply been modest and was a late developer; his father was, after all, a rowing ace, his son Tom has grown up to be a black belt at hapkido and a keen rock climber – and Palin himself remains a disciplined runner, his regular jogs having become one of the sights of north London's Parliament Hill Fields.

Hewison was a young man who seemed to have an extra helping of confidence in his nature, which some saw as bumptiousness but, whichever, was to be of untold value to the more diffident Palin. Naturally, there was a element of competition, from Palin's point of view, at least. Palin has admitted to Hewison that he was a little threatened by him at their first meeting because he was funny. But the two became inseparable friends, and have remained so – Hewison is godfather to Palin's third child, Rachel, twenty-two. Both Hewison and Palin – no real surprise here – had listened to the great radio comedies from early childhood. Graham Stuart-Harris had been in no position to realise Michael's dream of their writing comedy, whereas Hewison boosted Palin's confidence with a loan of some of his own, and appeared to open up to him a perfectly realistic path into the top flight of comedy. There was, he made Palin realise, no reason why he could not join the ranks of his heroes; he had done the difficult stuff, by getting to Oxford. Hewison had the ambition Palin had not dared admit to, plus the essential social, networking instincts to guide Palin in the direction of the university's successful, influential undergraduates.

Finding themselves at the same college doing the same subject, they went to drama auditions independently, and it was largely as a shared reaction to the intense seriousness with which Oxford undergraduate theatre treated itself that they took to comedy.

'Along with *Fuente Ovejuna*, we went in for what was known as drama cuppers. In the first term, every college does a short play in a competition – there are also sporting cuppers. We were both in this little one-act farce by Chekhov, so, as we were finding our feet academically, which we soon sussed, we were also both rehearsing immediately in two productions.'

In the autumn of 1962, Hewison and Palin additionally started writing comedy improvisations, almost always in Hewison's room at Brasenose. Palin's room was modern and in a basement buried deep in the middle of college, while Hewison's was more of a suite, with a living room as well as a bedroom, and was hidden away high up in what was known at Brasenose as the Arab Quarter. 'At the same time,' says Hewison, 'we could actually sit up here by the table and look out of the window and see life passing by, you know, not undergraduate life, but real people.'

Together, they used to speak in the inevitable Spike Milliganesque funny voices. Together, they sighed about the fact that Oxford didn't have its Cambridge Footlights, but they knew by now that this lack was a mere inconvenience.

Having injected Palin with masses of confidence and ambition, Hewison then initiated the idea of a formal comedy performing partnership. 'I do remember saying, "Michael we have this very funny relationship – sorry, we have this comic partnership. Why don't we structure it in some way and go and do a twenty-minute or half-hour cabaret!"'

Hewison and Palin duly paired up on stage under the name of Seedy Entertainers and quickly got the job of performing at the 1962 Christmas party of the Oxford University Psychological Society. In the same year that Michael had been meandering away in the publicity department of Edgar Allen Engineering, he became half of the act which rapidly became known university-wide as the favoured Oxford student cabaret of the year.

The new partners wrote together, but Palin also liked to write his own stuff, and impressed Hewison from the start with not only his talent but his work rate. 'Sometimes I would say, "Come on, Michael, we've got to produce some more material." So we would sit down and write in the evening. I would finish about midnight, and he would then climb out of college for more cigarettes and a hamburger from the High Street – in those days, we were locked in at twelve, but we had these hamburger vans wafting their slightly dubious gastronomic scents into the colleges – and when I came back in the morning, he would have written, damn it, two more sketches in one of his spiral-bound notebooks. He just couldn't stop.'

The Palin–Hewison act, although tame and a little raw, was not entirely derivative, either. 'I had a theory.' Hewison says. 'This was just after Beyond The Fringe, so there was a certain type of comedy which meant undergraduate comedy, and which had all been done. So we had to do something like that but different – in fact we wrote a terrible song called "We'll Never Go Beyond The Fringe".'

There was a strong element in Hewison's and Palin's material of the surreal and absurd, and an equally clear thread of the then new idea of 'taking off' television programmes. Both these concepts, needless to say, would be central to *Monty Python's Flying Circus*. 'We did a sketch which was a documentary about banana addiction,' Palin says, 'which ended up with the presenter eating more and more bananas to illustrate his point, and gradually his eyes becoming rather set and fixed. Whoever did that part had to eat about twenty bananas in fifteen seconds, which was a most horrible thing to do.

'We also did a little quickie, involving somebody with a big packet of Tide (the washing powder), advertising it in foreign gibberish; then saying "Tide, lovely Tide – very good", pouring it into a bowl and eating it. Blackout – laugh, you hope; whilst the performer retires behind screens to regurgitate Tide.'

One of Hewison's sketches for the Psychology Society party would have been considered disgraceful today, although Hewison points out that he did, in fact, steal it from the trendy dancer and director, Lindsey Kemp, whom he had met in London. 'It was a terrible, un-PC sketch called "Automobile", which was about teaching a spastic to say the word automobile,' Hewison recounts. 'It was one of those dead simple transition sketches, where you have the man in the white coat with the terrible spastic trying to teach his patient to say the word. By the end of the sketch, which can last from anything from thirty seconds to half an hour, the patient says the word automobile perfectly, but the man in the white coat is a gibbering spastic wreck. We used to have great fun doing that but it was a terribly naughty sketch one couldn't do nowadays.'

Seedy Entertainers also did sketches spoofing Armand and Michaela Denis, at that time popular presenters of television nature films, and others parodying another butt of jokes common at the time, wartime RAF briefings, all moustaches and lunacy. Another regular Hewison–Palin routine involved the pair being silly with a bucket of water – stepping in it, spilling it, throwing it, or looking into a bucket to the background of a tape of different noises: of enormous quantities of water, plugs being pulled out of baths and so on.

The partners did not agree wholly on what constituted a comedy sketch. Palin admits to being the more conventional. To him, a sketch required a dialogue between two people. The rather more existential bucket sketch, actually a mime, was Hewison's. Both traditions would be central to Palin's later work on Monty Python and, for the moment, the writing and performing partnership was perfect for both Palin and Hewison. 'We have this fantastic mental communication,' Hewison says. 'We always knew what the other person was going to do or say. It's telepathic in some peculiar way, not to do with talent; it's a gift which somebody gave us.'

They do not remember disagreeing over anything much other than intellectual questions of comedy. 'I can't remember any clashes at all,' says Hewison. 'Occasionally he might get fed up with what I got up to in my private life, but if there was anything else, I've erased it. The point is we were lucky people for whom work and play and life were all the same thing because we were together constantly, apart from the fact that we never shared digs.'

If Palin's first term at Oxford sounds in retrospect as if it was altogether too crowded and busy for one man, the examiners in his Prelim papers seem to have agreed. The Prelims are the first-year exams which you need to pass to avoid being thrown out; many students would try to get the exams out of their way by taking them in the first term. Palin, however, clearly following Eric Collieu's advice a little too closely, failed. As a result, he had to move out of his college room and go into digs with an old lady in the Iffley Road.

Typically, Palin was not especially depressed about failing his Prelims. 'I think it was a nuisance,' says Hewison, 'but actually he had a wonderful old landlady, very funny, and he had quite a good time.'

Where the remnants of Michael Palin's shyness disappeared to in the autumn of 1962 was anybody's guess; perhaps it had never really been anything other than a childish trait exacerbated by his father's crushing lack of encouragement for all but the most humdrum of ambitions.

Heady stuff as it was, Oxford life for Palin wasn't all theatre. A résumé of his Oxford experience suggests that that was all there was, but he also managed to find time with Hewison to write a column called Percy Flage for *Cherwell* (under the editorship of Nicholas Lloyd, one day to edit the *Daily Express*) – and even to have a social life. For one thing, Oxford offered the chance to meet women. 'You'd perhaps meet them at parties,' he says of his social life in Sheffield, 'but never get to know them. You just wanted to have a few drinks and get your hand down their jumper. At Oxford there were these very intelligent girls whom you could talk to.'

Despite the existence of all these new women, Palin was, of course, already more or less spoken for romantically. He alludes in general terms to having had the odd fling back then, and friends recall him 'having the odd snog', but his relationship with Helen managed to survive his going to Oxford and her to London. It was an exceptionally stable coupling for the student milieu. The letters and phone calls to and from Roehampton built up not dramatically, but steadily throughout his first few weeks at university. His developing friendship with Robert Hewison meanwhile had a remarkable co-incidental spin-off; 'Robert said that I must meet his girlfriend, called Piglet, who was in London at a teachers' training college, and it turned out to be the one at which Helen was also studying. So the girls came up to Oxford together. We saw each other most weekends after that.'

Piglet – whose real name was Heather – was Hewison's girlfriend from Bedford. She and Hewison broke up during the first year but a year of coming up to Oxford on the coach with Helen was enough to cement Michael's relationship with her. The affectionately mocking card Helen had sent Palin when he had been accepted by Brasenose had had an enormous effect on the young man. 'That card showed a sense of humour, which of course is what helps keep you together ... we could always make each other laugh,' he explains. Helen being slightly older also seems to have had a strong influence on Michael; even now, he talks of her having educated him.

After a very short time, Hewison was virtually family for Palin and, from the second year, would often go and stay in Sheffield for what the young men would call 'writing weeks' which could be for academic work or, more often, to brainstorm over a new revue. 'Michael's mum was astonishingly sweet, loving and kind, a wonderful, gentle, funny woman, very small and hunched,' recalls Hewison. 'The father was obviously deeply difficult. He had had his life blighted by the war and had ended up a man disappointed in his hopes and imprisoned in his stutter. He certainly was a fairly angry man, but he obviously didn't say much, because of this dreadful stutter. We kind of worked round him, as a couple of adolescents would.'

Although the friendship and comedy collaboration between Palin and Hewison was both immensely productive and a source of great pleasure to the two of them, it has to be said that it baffled many of their acquaintances. As one contemporary Oxford student, also at Brasenose, recalls, 'It was always a mystery to everyone that Michael was so talented and so funny and Robert Hewison was much less obviously so. So those who didn't know how much they relied on one another always found it quite odd that they were a partnership.

'But they were right through their time at Oxford,' he continues. 'Robert Hewison was at that time very handsome and cool with the birds, and Michael Palin wasn't, or at least didn't seem to consider himself to be. I am sure he saw Hewison as somebody more sophisticated and probably more pushy. It was certainly Hewison who got them bookings and all the rest of it. But it didn't prevent everyone from gossiping, a bit cruelly, perhaps, along the lines of "Why does that brilliant Michael Palin stay with that not so brilliant Hewison?" All it was that he wasn't really very engaging on stage, whereas Palin always was. It was that tendency to confuse what they saw on stage with what they were like in reality.

'Palin not only came across as very nice and sweet in his stage person, but he was well known at Oxford for being as nice and sweet as it was possible to be. He really was a very nice man, whereas Hewison rather fancied himself and he gave the impression that he thought he was the bee's knees and terribly attractive and all the rest of it. I think what was going on was that Hewison was tagging along on Palin's talent and popularity, while Palin was, in a way, using Hewison's charm, ambition and sophistication. So, in that symbiotic way, it was a creative and successful partnership.'

Palin was always considered a delightful man by his contemporaries. One English student at St Anne's, the writer Lynn Barber, became one of the finest interviewers in British journalism but, even in recent years, has sometimes held off from interviewing Palin because he is 'too nice and honest and straightforward'.

'There is now, and was then, simply no mystery about him,' she says. 'He really is and always was as nice as anything, and nobody ever had a bad word for him. His talent was obvious right from the beginning. There used to be these little smokers where people would get up and do a few sketches or something. His and Robert's weren't necessarily the funniest that anyone did, but they always had a charm about them and Michael in particular is a really charming man.

'I remember once at Oxford, I did a disastrous thing which I thought was a bright idea, which was to have an all day At Home. I sent out invitations to people saying I am having some wine and just drop round at any time on such and such a date, and it worked as badly as possible because people came in pairs and left, and then somebody else would come and it was awful. But Palin was one of those who came when nobody else was there. He was absolutely sweet and was as entertaining as if it were a glamorous party. He is a totally, totally nice man.

'He wasn't,' Barber continues, 'really attractive, other than in that he was terribly nice. That was the difference between him and Robert Hewison. Robert was cool and trendy, whereas Palin, apart from anything else, had a girlfriend almost from day one, who became his wife. So he wasn't available, but he also had that trademark thing of being rather like a 1940s schoolboy, with a distinctly un-sixties haircut. He was a bit trainspottery, or at least conveyed that impression. But anyway, one knew that he was seriously attached to his girlfriend. I must have met her, but I only remember her as being very pretty.'

Content to while away his time back in Sheffield during his gap year (or eight months as it actually was), and to keep up a long-distance relationship with a schooldays sweetheart Palin may have been, but he was by no means a complete stay-at-home. Occasionally he will suggest today that he did not travel at all before his mid-twenties, but it would be more accurate to record that he did not travel extensively. During his first vacation, aged nineteen, Michael had saved enough money from performing to go on his first journey abroad – a fateful moment, had anyone realised it – on a skiing trip to Austria, to which he and some new friends travelled by train. Flying was still a little beyond a healthy student budget.

In the summer vacation at the end of his first year at Oxford, in 1963, there was a more ambitious trip. He took himself off rather impressively on three-month working holiday in Germany, having gone, as was not uncommon at the time, on the pretext of 'selling Bibles and encyclopaedias' to American servicemen. However, for the most part, as hundreds of British students used to find when they got to the American bases on these jaunts, the kind of Yank who felt he needed a Bible invariably already had several, and there were precious few who wanted an encyclopaedia. The replacement Bible business was hence a bit limited in scope, which was how a severely broke and increasingly hungry Palin – he had been planning to join Hewison and some other friends in a villa in Greece on the proceeds of his book salesmanship – came to get a job as a kitchen helper in the Officers Mess at Robinson Barracks, a US Army installation in Stuttgart.

The star of the Oxford cabaret scene started work at 5.30 in the morning on a sweltering late August Tuesday. His boss was the head cook, Hermann, a hot-tempered Wehrmacht veteran of Stalingrad. ('He once threw a toaster on the floor,' records Palin; 'it didn't break, so he threw another one.') Other workmates included Montes, a Spanish chancer trying to con as much money as he could from the Americans and Germans so he could start a fish-and-chip shop on the Costas; Emilio, a singing Italian; Frau Olga, a hardworking salad maker; Emmie, a sixty-year-old German warp-speed washer up; a morose Greek married couple; Jimmy, a Rhodesian in crisp khaki shorts; Max, a muscular German with a booming voice, who had greatly enjoyed his time in a British POW camp; and Jakar, a jocular Pole who told jokes all day in Polish, at which everyone charitably laughed.

Typically, Michael had a ball as a kitchen helper. 'We all got on like a house on fire,' he said. The kitchen gang would gather for breakfast, after which his first job was to help take out and then wash the dustbins with a high pressure hose. Then the local German dustmen would come and be invited into the kitchen for tea and a smoke; when the dustmen found out that he was English, they were extra friendly, and asked once if he did this kind of work at home. 'I thought of my six months in the publicity department at Edgar Allen, paused a minute, but said no.'

His late morning duties would include peeling several hundred potatoes, at which he would continually cut his hands. The crew would then have lunch at 12 with the cleaning girls, after which Michael had to mop the floors and knock off work to take a bus back to the centre of Stuttgart, to spend the afternoon doing very little.

In his second year at Oxford, Palin put the comedy to some extent on pause to pursue some more straight acting and to try to catch up with his academic work, with which he was badly behind. He played McCann in the Experimental Theatre Club's production of Harold Pinter's *The Birthday Party*, and had a stab at political theatre with an anti-capital-punishment piece set in a circus ring, and called *Hang Down Your Head and Die*. This show, which was a huge hit at Oxford, even played in the West End for a limited run at the Comedy Theatre. *Hang Down Your Head and Die* was a musical, featuring such songs as 'All That Gas' and 'The English Way To Die', and attracted a glowing review from Harold Hobson, the *Sunday Times* theatre critic. Palin's Shakespearean debut, on the other hand, as Petruchio in *The Taming of the Shrew* was thwarted to his irritation when the production was cancelled with him already having learned half the part.

Even with so much work to catch up on, the second year for Palin was a satisfying, productive time. 'It was the first time I felt there was a chance that after Oxford I could earn my living as an actor or a writer, or both,' he later reflected. It was also the period during which he developed his friendship with Terry Jones, at the time a famously admired and influential English student in the year above him. Having laughed heartily at Michael's serious stage debut, the Welshman had seen him again in cabaret and commented that 'Michael came across as very warm,' which may sound backhanded, but was a compliment none the less.

'I was in the audience the first time I saw him, and then we met up,' Jones recollects now. 'I suppose I must have met Mike and Robert, because they were always going round in a duo at that time, so I got to know them together. He and Robert were doing a cabaret at the Oxford Union Cellars, and I just thought it was very funny stuff. I thought, wow, this is new and I particularly liked what Michael was doing. He just seemed to have a gift.

'He was a really funny bloke. He was a friendly, great man to have around except when he hadn't eaten. He still gets a bit shirty when he is hungry – I remember him getting very cross once when we were in Paris and we were trying to find somewhere to eat and he started getting grumpy. It's a food deprivation thing I think. But other than that, he is the best company you could possibly want.'

Terry Jones, who came from Colwyn Bay in north Wales but went to school in Guildford, was an imposing, tall, dark figure whose trademark, according to Palin, was 'an amazing dark-brown, hairy check coat'. Jones read English at St Edmund's College ('tantamount to reading nothing, really'), worked on *Isis* for a bit and got involved with the Experimental Theatre, doing a Brecht play, which led curiously enough to comedy revue, because the ETC always did a revue in the summer term.

At the end of Terry Jones's second year at Oxford, while Palin was peeling spuds in Stuttgart, he appeared in an Oxford revue which went to the Edinburgh Festival. 'We always felt we were a bit ahead of the Cambridge revues,' he has said. 'They were always very slick, it was all part of a formula, I suppose. At the Oxford revue, there was no organisation at all. How they decided who did the revue, I just don't know.' The show, with the daft but doubtless trendy title '****', was a success at Edinburgh, and ran for two weeks at the Phoenix Theatre, in the West End, where it gained Jones a second special mention from the formidable Hobson as 'a first class mimic'.

The first time Palin and Jones – a partnership which would extend long beyond Monty Python – wrote together was for a show in a marquee called *Loitering Within Tent*. Neither student imagined their collaboration would be very long lasting, but it threw up some promising material. Most famous, and still being performed late into the 1970s, was an extended joke about joke-making, which Hewison also had a large hand in. This involved a university lecturer with a trio of laboratory assistants expounding on the origin and technique behind various slapstick routines – custard pie throwing, banana skins, hitting each other with planks of wood and so on. The idea for the sketch actually came from Chris Braden, son of the Canadian TV star Bernard, whose ITV show *The Braden Beat* was the precursor to the tackier *That's Life*.

The 'Slapstick Sketch' received the considerable accolade of being greatly admired by Jones's and Palin's peers in the Cambridge Foot-lights revue, *Cambridge Circus*, who got permission to borrow it for their revue – in which John Cleese and Graham Chapman were leading lights.

Terry Jones now sees *Hang Down Your Head and Die* as the real start of his and Palin's close friendship. 'After we met, I was doing a play which was basically just me droning on – I can't even remember the name of the guy who wrote it. Mike and Robert played a couple of policemen who came in and took me away at the end, or something. Then we did *Loitering Within Tent*, but, for me, it was only really when we started writing for *Hang Down Your Head and Die* that we started working together. I remember being up all night one night in somebody's room, and Robert, Mike and me going through *Hang Down Your Head and Die*, because we just thought it was such a disaster. It was a week before we were supposed to be doing the dress rehearsal, and it was so cumbersome that we were trying to put some shape on to the show.'

Jones starred as the central figure, the condemned man, in *Hang Down Your Head*, but it was really only in the summer of 1964, at the end of Palin's second year, that his own big breakthrough, a starring role in *The Oxford Revue* at the Edinburgh Fringe, came about.

Immediately before that, Michael was in another often overlooked production, the summer revue at the Oxford Playhouse, a show called *Keep This To Yourself*. Palin played a man called Smart in a theme revue based on a secret institution to produce conformists. Although the show was a little unpolished – indeed, according to Hewison, was staged unfinished – it was unusual in that it made a profit.

In Edinburgh, Michael appeared with Terry Jones and a cast of three others – Doug Fisher, Nigel Pegram and Annabel Leventon – in *The Oxford Revue*. Palin and Hewison wrote much of the show, some in almost recognisably Monty Python style. Although, in the life-cycle of Python, the cross-pollination between Ox and Bridge was still in its earliest stages, the Python style of comedy was clearly developing out of the mists from both universities as something of an antidote to satire, which was so much the rage in the early sixties. Jones's '****' the year before had been firmly in the *That Was the Week That Was* satirical-comment style. 'This one,' Jones says, 'was more like antecedents of Monty Python – "zany", people were calling it. It was more bizarre. One had the feeling one was doing something new and slightly different.'

The retreat from satire was, perhaps, in some sense in keeping with the imminence of the end of the famous 'Thirteen years of Tory misrule'. Harold Wilson was highly likely to become the first Labour Prime Minister since 1950 – he did so six weeks after the end of the Festival – and it was still too early to predict whether or not the radical new socialist PM would turn out to be any less worthy of satire than the discredited old Conservatives. Whether it was Harold Wilson's fault or not, within a couple of years, Jones and Palin would be required to write some satire again for the BBC; the death of the genre, not surprisingly, hit mainstream entertainment some time after it was felt in fringe undergraduate theatre.

The Revue and a straight play were rehearsed simultaneously and staged, as had been the Oxford shows of the previous six years, in the Roman Eagle Masonic Lodge on Cranston Street, a peeling mausoleum of a place hired out to the students 'for the purveyance of comic entertainment' by the Parks and Burials and Allotments Department of Edinburgh City Council. The thirty-six students also slept at the hall, men downstairs, women in separate meeting rooms. For Palin, it was the happiest time of his performing life. 'The world of entertainment which seemed so utterly remote to me in Sheffield came a lot nearer in Edinburgh.'

In a quite wondrously dull piece he wrote for the *Edgar Allen Magazine* back in Sheffield between the end of the festival in September and the start of the new term at Oxford, he detailed everything that was tangential and uninteresting about this, his biggest break in showbusiness. Why Palin was still writing travel articles for his father's steelworks magazine when he was a star Oxford University character, and also beginning to make a mark on a national stage, tells us a great deal about the man, much of which still very much applies.

He is loyal to a turn, never neglecting or forgetting any part of his upbringing, with the possible exception of Shrewsbury school; his political opposition to it seems ever so slightly to have soured his memory of the place. He is entirely lacking in pomposity; it would have seemed quite natural to him to sit down for several hours – unpaid, of course – to pen an article which would be read only by the narrowest circle of steelworkers and colleagues of his father. Terry Jones has been known to rib Palin gently for his lack of focus and penchant sometimes for giving unnecessary attention to projects which do not strictly deserve it. He points out that Palin effectively drifted into both acting and comedy: 'Michael has always been attracted to somebody with strong ambitions, and been pulled along in their wake,' Jones says. Palin also has a train spotter's eye for detail – in some cases for terrifically tedious detail (delivered ironically, but delivered none the less) – allied to the assumption that the reader requires such schoolboyish precision.

It was thanks to this appealing lack of direction that Edgar Allen workers learned in the autumn of 1964 that an Oxford University theatrical assault upon the Edinburgh Fringe Festival consisted of: 'A business manager, ultimately responsible for everything from press releases to buying haggis, a bookings manager, two props girls, two electricians, a carpenter, half a dozen stage hands, two wardrobe mistresses, and then, of course, the actors: four men and a girl for the revue, four men and four women for the play.'

Everyone in the company did everything we also discover. The equipment needed to build a stage arrived in a special British Railways truck from Oxford, which carried 'over thirty floodlights and spotlights, thousands of feet of cable, four lighting control boards (huge cast iron monsters, that the Foundry would be proud of), enough wood to make a stage, three heavy black curtains, 25 feet by 30 feet, rope, steel clamps, and scenery, which is kept to a minimum. The vast amount of scaffolding required to hang the curtains and carry the heavy floodlights is hired in Edinburgh – it just wouldn't fit in the truck. Everyone helps unload – I've still got the marks to prove it – and then, for two weeks, the transformation from bleak hall to comfortable theatre begins.'

There were ten student revues competing with the Oxford show that year, but Palin's got the lion's share of the attention. Items about it appeared on regional and national radio and TV programmes, and the show also went down exceptionally well with the press. 'It had a tremendous effect on the papers,' Jones says. 'The critical reaction was "Wow! Something new has happened!" The difference between doing a revue in Oxford and in Edinburgh was that people in Edinburgh noticed you. David Frost would come back stage and talk to you, and people from London would take notice. You got the feeling it was going in your direction.' (Frost had indeed come to see the revue, said how much he had liked their act and promised to 'be in touch'. He was not for over a year, but had far from forgotten Palin and Jones.)

Typical of the laudatory press reaction was that of the *Scotsman*'s critic. He wrote of *The Oxford Revue*: 'It is much more than a stimulant for culture-sated minds or a pleasant night-cap. It is proof that a new generation of satirists with fresh style is arising fast through the debris of mediocrity left in the wake of those now rather passé sub-culture symbols, Beyond The Fringe.'

Even the *Daily Mail*, not renowned for patrolling the undergraduate humour beat, was sitting up and taking notice. 'We are against attacking people,' Hewison told the paper's reporter. 'We want to build up something that is funny in itself. No satire, no mention of the Prime Minister. We want to avoid the idea of being clever young men in suits being witty.'

He went on to describe a recent sketch by Palin: 'A seedy entertainer comes on stage and starts to sing a song. He is terrible. In the middle of the song he suddenly becomes aware of a box on the side of the stage. He stops to look at it. It's a present from the audience. He thanks them profusely, puts it in the wings, then goes on with his song. Suddenly there is a great explosion and bits of shattered box fly on stage. End.'

The result of all this exposure was that every one of the twenty-two performances of *The Oxford Revue* was a sell-out, with 228 seats, as Palin helpfully pointed out in his article, selling for up to 8/6d.

The August of 1964 in Edinburgh was Terry Jones's farewell to Oxford, but Palin still had another year, one which culminated in *The Oxford Line*, a show largely written and directed by Palin, which advanced the genre of surreal comedy even further, and again went to Edinburgh.

In his third year, however, Palin was suddenly preoccupied with matters aside from both his cosy romance with Helen and his burgeoning comedy career. 'I was still supposed to be being educated,' he says. 'I was at Oxford to study history not comedy – in those days the two were not as inextricably linked as they have recently become. So in a burst of solid and carefully selected cramming in the college library, I did three years' work in three months, and much to my surprise and everyone else's, I emerged with a respectable second class degree in modern history.'

He had, indeed, impressed and surpassed most of his fellow university Thesps. Hewison, who was always more academic than

Palin, and is now a full university professor, got precisely the same degree, effectively a 2:1. A contemporary, the journalist Janet Watts, remembers dropping in on Michael Palin when he was supposed to be in the midst of the final agony of his final year, the Modern History Examination Schools. 'But the pale and anxious Palin I had feared (hoped?) to find was nowhere to be seen,' Watts wrote in the *Radio Times*. 'The familiar rosy face beamed with joy as he capered about his flat in a German fireman's brass helmet circa 1870, his latest acquisition.'

'That helmet was important,' Palin confessed later. 'Keeping it polished was certainly more important than the history syllabus.' Lucky fireman's helmet or not, Palin believes his degree was boosted substantially by a finals essay on Hegel based entirely on reading about him, for the first time, on the bus taking him to the Examination Schools.

Palin left Oxford in the summer of 1965, having been in full time education since 1948. 'I couldn't stall any longer. It was time to take a decision and be serious and frustrated or funny and poor,' he says. 'I was terribly busy at Oxford, busy just *being* at Oxford. I acted and I wrote, and never thought of the outside world or what I would eventually have to do when the three years came to an end.'

He has always maintained his gratitude for the opportunities the university gave him, despite its lamentable lack of a Footlights equivalent. He is a gregarious being and by no means lacked poise, and he thoroughly enjoyed the social side of Oxford life.

For a Sheffield lad, Palin found himself rubbing shoulders with some extremely well-connected people, too. In another of his extraordinary missives to the *Edgar Allen Magazine*, this one very amusingly written under the by-line 'M.E. Palin,' he described an afternoon with an unnamed friend in London.

'Let's go and see Viscount Montgomery,' his pal had apparently said, as the two students, in £4 Army and Navy Stores donkey jackets, were wandering aimlessly along The Embankment.

'Very funny,' Michael had replied. 'Yes, and we'll drop in on Jackie Kennedy while we're at it.'

'No, seriously,' Palin's friend explained, 'he's a friend of mine. I've stayed at his house before now, and he said, if I'm ever in London, I was to come and see him at the House.'

Ten minutes later, he reported, the pair were at the Peers' Entrance to the Palace of Westminster, asking to see the great Monty – and being asked politely if they were autograph hunters. When all was explained, they were allowed in. The Masters of Arms 'looked at my coat with the expression of one who has swallowed stewed plums with no sugar. "Er, shall I take your coat, sir?" I told him I'd rather keep it on; my jacket underneath looked even worse.

'He took us along oak-panelled corridors fitted with plush red carpets and silence, drawing closer and closer to the heart of the British Empire, or at least to somewhere we could sit down.' Montgomery welcomed the bedraggled-looking students (who were at least wearing ties) warmly. They were introduced to Black Rod. 'My donkey jacket,' Michael wrote, 'seemed to be burning a hole in my back; I felt as if I were sinking into the thick pile of the carpet – this was no joke, I *was* sinking!'

Monty then arranged for them to occupy two seats in the Peers' Visitors' Gallery to listen to a defence debate. Feeling more relaxed about his horrible jacket now, Palin took it off and hung it on the golden rail which surrounded the Gallery. 'Below me, the House assembled,' he wrote. 'It was quite fascinating – in fact, one uniformed official was actually beckoning to me from below. Did he want me to open the case for the government? I nodded back amiably. No, he continued pointing, he seemed in some pain.'

It turned out that the official was asking for the donkey jacket to be removed. Lord Hailsham arrived after half an hour, 'with the air of one who is a special attraction', winked at his colleagues and put his feet up against the table which divided the parties. 'He was not the only one who had his feet up; Tory shoes faced Labour shoes across the House.'

Palin and his friend stayed for forty-five minutes, until Michael began to nod off – although, as he noted, 'several of the Honourable Members had beaten me to it'. On the way out, they bumped into Montgomery again in a corridor. 'He was off to a meeting . . . goodbye . . . goodbye . . . keep on the straight and narrow . . . Whatever did he mean by that?' Soon afterwards, the students were back on the street, amused and not a little bemused.

'There is such a thin line between what is constructive and destructive about the freedom of Oxford that it is difficult to make the distinction between those who are elitist, dabbling dilettantes and those who are genuinely trying to experience something,' comments Palin in reference to the entire Oxbridge phenomenon. 'Some of them are going to fail hopelessly and some will appear awfully arrogant and pretentious but, by the same token, others, and I feel I was one, will benefit from being able to do what was probably awfully pretentious nonsense in the Union Cellars for thirty bob a night.'

Was it an unfortunate setback for British comedy that there was no Footlights at Oxford, or that he failed his entrance exam for Clare College? Could Michael Palin have been better employed than traipsing through some fairly obscure and self-consciously serious drama?

There was clearly an inner desire in Palin, going right back to the amateur dramatics group in Sheffield, to be serious – a desire John Cleese was entirely immune from at the same stage of his career. There may be an argument for getting such seriousness out of one's system earlier; while Cleese became more serious later in life, Palin, in so far as his work and public utterances are concerned, seems to have shed all the baggage of solemnity. Had Palin been at Cambridge and joined the Footlights, it is quite possible that he too would have returned later in life to serious drama – a prospect which strikes today as being peculiarly uncomfortable, even embarrassing; one of the delights of Palin is his undiminished, schoolboyish mischievousness, a charming puckishness Cleese can summon up only, or so it appears, with some effort.

There was another hidden benefit to Palin being kept apart, as it were, from the Footlights men, Cleese, Chapman and Eric Idle. This was the creative value of the difference between Oxford culture and Cambridge culture, a warp and weft which, it has been argued, helped the development of the Pythons as a team. In the writing of Monty Python, there was a clear division, which seemed natural to everybody concerned, that Palin and Terry Jones did their thing together, Cleese and Chapman theirs, with Idle tending to write and contribute ideas on his own. Palin usually strikes people as the nicest of the Pythons, the conciliator in the case of dispute, a fact which Cleese, discussing the Oxford–Cambridge split in the team, concludes is down to there being something 'woollier' about the Oxford side. Palin, Cleese has often noted, even seems to wear softer clothes. Jones acknowledges the division, 'There was a different feel and different sympathy as well. What one lot found funny the other lot often didn't. The Oxford people tended to be a bit more sympathetic and woolly, while the Cambridge lot were much more caustic and intellectual.'

Palin agrees, explaining the causes of the difference by use of a travel writer's perspective. Discussing the divide with Janet Watts, he attributed the cultural differences to geography: 'Cambridge is set in flat, bleak lands and, whenever I've been there, I've found it a chilly place where you have to stay indoors and read a book. Oxford is set in pleasant, leafy countryside and seems more of an outdoor city, warmer and friendlier.'

Typically, for Palin clings loyally to every physical place he has contact with, from Birkdale school to the north London street where he lives, he has kept up contact with Brasenose. His middle son, William, went up to the college to read English, prompting Palin to enthuse at the time, 'I'd like to read History again. I might understand it. It would give the old brain a bit of exercise.'

He has also returned to work in Oxford a number of times. Part of the BBC's *Comic Roots* film was shot there, for which Brasenose 'had the nerve to charge us two hundred quid for half a day's filming of my own memories of it'. He says that this affected his decision to film *American Friends* at another college, although it was set at

Brasenose. 'I should have told them that an ancestor of mine, George Pay-Linn, was a generous benefactor of the college and that it was time to repay,' he joked.

Palin and Hewison left Oxford on the best of terms. The college was, says Hewison, 'rather proud that Michael and I became stars in the university theatrical firmament or whatever. When I went back in 1969, I saw Eric Collieu, and he said, "You are the last generation that enjoyed themselves." But the interesting thing is that when Michael and I went back to a college reunion in the early eighties, I think we both hated it. We found it very uncomfortable, although perhaps only because the people we really wanted to see weren't there.'

Despite the astonishing success he had had at Oxford, Palin still failed to get on to the BBC's general traineeship scheme ('They should have a special tie for those who failed to get on,' he says), and left university sure only that he wanted to write, and did not want the kind of 'proper' profession his father had in mind for him. Michael would still unquestionably have made a splendid and successful nine-to-five copywriter in an advertising agency, but had no intention of doing anything as routine. His orderly, rule-bound upbringing left him much happier doing things unconventionally, even a little haphazardly. In the closing moments of *Comic Roots*, he parodied his feelings at the time; like most parodies, it contained a germ of reality.

In a funny *Brideshead* voice, he expounded, 'As the dreaming spires slipped away behind the scrapyards of Botley, I decided that there was very little future for me in any respectable profession. I was one of that cursed generation doomed to take nothing seriously at all. Not for me the management training scheme, the marketing course, the promotion, the annual bonus or the works outing. After seventeen years of the finest education the country could afford, all that lay ahead for me was the silly walk, and the funny voice, the zany costume, the wacky one-liner and the false breasts. Where had it all gone wrong?'

The last question was one which Palin could legitimately have asked himself, perhaps. David Frost's promise the previous September to keep in touch had not necessarily expired, but the phone clearly was not ringing yet. So Palin's first 'real' job was a most unlikely one – working for the Bristol-based ITV contractor, Television Wales West (TWW, long since defunct), presenting a low budget teenage pop programme, *NOW!*, which was broadcast to Wales and parts of the west of England for a few months. He had been put up for the job after managing to get two weeks as a DJ for a BBC children's programme, thanks to his sister, Angela, who was continuing to carve out a quiet career for herself at the BBC.

Why a provincial pop programme could have imagined it needed an Old Salopian with a decent Oxford degree in modern history (with special reference to Hegel) to introduce Eric Clapton, The Toys and Patti La Belle and her Blue Belles, and appear to know what he was talking about as a disc jockey, is one of the mysteries which only television companies, obsessed now as then with taking on over-qualified people, could explain. His finely honed Oxford intellect was doubtlessly no obstacle to passing informed comment on such matters as the colour of pop stars' socks, but it cannot have been enormously helpful, either. Perhaps it was his young, healthy, almost clear-cut appearance which persuaded the producers that he was their man. And they had a point; it is not hard to imagine Michael Palin, handsome in a homely kind of way, with these alert, honest, interested eyes, having pursued a straight TV career: reading the local news, presenting chat shows, and perhaps now hosting an afternoon studio discussion programme. Much of his genius at parodying ghastly TV shows rests, after all, on the fact that he looks just like the people who do them in real life.

Anyway, *NOW!* gave Palin some useful experience in appearing before television cameras. Michael imagined his father would be furious at seeing his son in such a flyweight job after having scrimped and saved from the age of forty-seven to sixty-four to put him through the most exclusive education possible. On the other hand, Palin's contract, which ran from October 1965 to June 1966, offered him a handsome £35 a week – the same as many middle management executives were earning in industry at the time. There is a lot of vicariousness involved in parenthood, and one of the greatest thrills of it must be to put your child in the position where his first wage packet is almost the same as yours at the summit of your working life. Ted Palin was a year off retirement when Michael left Oxford; the fact that his son was, at last – and at such a convenient point, financially speaking – off the family payroll was a matter of great joy to him, even if the job Michael got was not quite the sort of thing he would want to brag about to his colleagues at Edgar Allen.

It seems unlikely that Ted Palin would have gone out of his way to mention to his work mates, for example, Michael's attempt during the run of *NOW!* to ride a pantomime horse along Hyde Park's Rotten Row. He had hired the horse outfit from a West End costumiers and decided to stage the stunt with two scriptwriters inside. They had gone ten yards when a policeman told Palin to dismount. 'He took it all rather seriously,' Palin explained at the time. 'He said that people rode real horses in the Row and wouldn't want this sort of thing.'

In a way, because he was already such a polished performer, Palin found the transition to life after Oxford easier than his friend Hewison. Hewison was the first to get a job, as a graduate trainee at Southern Television in Southampton, but found both the job and the city uninspiring. 'The period Michael and I had been writing together had ended more or less at the end of university, because I knew that I wasn't going to be a comic actor or a comic writer,' Hewison reflects. 'I suppose I could have hung on, but there didn't seem to be any point. I wanted to be a TV director which I also never became.

'Then, through Michael and his sister Angela, I started doing work in radio for the World Service. I remember Michael went off and did an interview with the Moody Blues, and I did a programme on Swinging London in French for the French Canadian service.

'The last ever appearance on stage of Palin and myself was the most horrendous disaster. It was absolutely wonderful, at a holiday camp in Bognor Regis where there was a gala at the end of the season. The son of the owner had seen us at Cambridge, and wanted us to go and do the cabaret. But of course with three bars open in this room and no mike it was hopeless. But it did pay better than anything we did in Oxford.'

In April 1966 when Michael was just twenty-two, he presented his father with another pleasant retirement surprise. Not only was he now financially independent; he and Helen married and bought their first home, a small terraced house in Gospel Oak, a not-yet fashionable enclave of north London, close to a railway line between Hampstead and Kentish Town.

Michael's marriage was marked by an extra treat for himself and Helen. Now that he was earning good money, it was decided to go to Dublin – by air. Such a trip was still a positive extravagance in 1965, and it was Michael's first flight. 'It was on a Viscount, but I can't remember anything about the flight,' he says. 'We just wanted to get to Dublin and get into the hotel.' Marriage and a mortgage was, Palin thinks – and not controversially – the end of childhood.

Ted Palin's retirement ceremony, the end of another era for the Palin family, took place in the boardroom of Edgar Allen a few weeks later, on 19 June. He was photographed in the *Edgar Allen Magazine* being presented with a cheque and surrounded by the company bigwigs. Michael's father appeared older than his sixty-five years, a slightly doleful look in his eyes as he received the envelope. 'We understand Ted intends to move to Norfolk, where we hope he will enjoy a long and happy retirement,' the half-page tribute in the magazine read.

Correct as ever, Mr Palin wrote a letter to appear in the same edition of the magazine.

May I take this opportunity of expressing my sincere thanks to all those who so generously contributed to my retirement present which, in the form of a cheque, was recently presented to me, in private, by the Chairman in the board room.

I have spent the money on a new watch in replacement of

one that has already served me faithfully for thirty-three years. I consider this a happy choice because, a) it will improve my time-keeping (not that I have any reason to be ashamed of that!) and, b) it will remind me, whenever I look at it, of my friends at Edgar Allen and the happy times I have had with them in the course of nearly twenty years at Imperial Steel Works. Best wishes to all and, again, many thanks for your kindness.

Yours sincerely, E.M. Palin.

5

London

The modern expression for where Palin found himself immediately after leaving university would be 'in the loop'. All the connections were made to keep him in work, as indeed they have, for a lifetime. In the classic Oxbridge style, he had made it. He was young, talented and sought after, a more or less fully-fledged member of what has been described as 'the post-satire Oxbridge comedy mafia'. The choice as to how he used the enviable position he had fashioned for himself was his – and typically, he missed hardly a beat in taking advantage of every opportunity in which he soft-landed. They were, says Palin, exciting times.

Terry Jones, a year Michael's senior, proved to be a trusty friend. Jones had joined the BBC, which was almost insatiably hungry at the time for bright graduates, despite having turned Palin down for a formal traineeship. It was the anarchic – and employed – Jones who cleared the path for Palin's progress, getting him in here and there, introducing him around London. Even while Michael was doing his strange pop programme in Bristol, Jones, who was on a directors' course, was roping Palin in to help him with his training film, Sarah Miles having turned him down. They wrote some gags together for the likes of Russ Conway and Billy Cotton – 'You get pretty good after spending a morning thinking up a joke for Russ

Conway,' says Jones – and were approached by William Donaldson to write what turned out to be an abortive musical, *The Love Show*, which was a revue based on little more than the trendy title, the only parameter being that it should exclusively concern the hot topic of the day, the sexual revolution.

Palin got himself some publicity in the national press when the Lord Chamberlain cut one of his sketches from a Plymouth Arts Festival because an actress was required to impersonate the Queen. The sketch was about an attempt to steal the Crown Jewels and at one point the Queen was to have been seen reading a gas meter. Michael also appeared fleetingly in Ken Russell's television film *Isadora*; he and Eric Idle were cast as jazz musicians on the roof of a hearse. And, one of the more remarkable quirks in the history of comedy, Palin did several TV commercials, which he characterises as 'appalling, such a waste of time, except for about three notable exceptions. I was at an audition for a Maxwell House ad once when I had to shake the jar and say, "Listen to the sound of Maxwell House". I said to the director that people wanted to drink the stuff not listen to it. He said, look here, you may think it's funny, but there are people out there who'd be glad to do your job, so get on with it. So I got on with it – and I never got the job.'

The Love Show did not happen, but it did contribute towards establishing Palin and Jones in London as a post-varsity writing team. Jones was assigned to the arts magazine programme on the new BBC2, *Late Night Line-Up*. The producer wanted to dip his toe into the satire pool, a little late in the day perhaps, and Jones was asked to write the jokes – of which, as he later joked, 'there weren't many so it wasn't exactly arduous'. To assist him, Jones naturally called on the skills of his Oxford friends, Robert Hewison and Michael Palin. Barry Cryer joined the group, and they wrote sketches for a month or so until some internal political wrangle halted the project for good.

'One night Michael and I did a sketch for the programme dressed up in Batman suits and jumping off chairs,' Jones says. 'We recorded our bit and then went home and sat by the set, surrounded by admiring or just amazed relatives. Anyway, our sketch came on and then after it they started one of those *Line-Up* discussions about the future of the arts or something, and Dennis Potter said he hadn't come all the way from Gloucestershire to take part in a programme which could include such idiots as us.'

Jones's next placement was in an office, he says, next to the man who used to write 'Pinky and Perky'. 'There I sat trying to think up jokes while all the time I could hear the typewriter banging away next door as another 'Perky' sketch hit the paper.'

Neither Palin nor Jones was wasting his time, however, as jobbing gag writers. Although it was perfectly possible to drown in the BBC, Jones, playing the role Hewison had done at Oxford in egging Palin on to more ambitious targets, ensured the pair were performing cabaret spots in various clubs. As a result of their TV and cabaret work, their activities had for the second time attracted the interest of David Frost, who was the effective wholesaler at the time for a warehouse full of young comic talent.

It is worth noting that the concept of middle-class comedy as a commodity for general public consumption, as well as a respectable profession for fearsomely bright young chaps down from Oxbridge, was truly established by this time; Peter Cook had blazed the trail for the first generation of non-working-class comedians – The Goons, of course, although appealing to clever young people, were not strictly a proletarian phenomenon. Beyond the Fringe cemented the concept of the Oxbridge revue being thrown open to a wider audience, but it was the strangely classless Frost who was the impresario, practically, who opened television up to the likes of Jones, Cleese and Palin, and beat the path which would soon lead to Monty Python's Flying Circus.

When Frost reappeared in their lives, Palin, Jones and Robert Hewison were doing two weeks with a revue at a small theatre club, the Rehearsal Club, above the Royal Court Theatre. They were paid £10 a week each, plus a free dinner, for which they had to wait – and here was the catch – until 2 a.m. The show was sparsely attended although Paul McCartney turned up one night. But the following night David Frost came along. Frost was scouting for writers for his new BBC series *The Frost Report*, which turned out to be the meeting place of all the future Pythons, Terry Gilliam, the American artist, included. He was impressed by Jones's and Palin's new work, and offered them work on the *Frost Report* team, neglecting to quite explain that their material would all be credited as having been written by David Frost, although such was the man's kudos that they would not have minded too much, even as almost established TV people themselves. An invitation from Frost was the comedy equivalent of being signed for Manchester United, even though in a way *The Frost Report* would represent a retrograde step, as it was very much a return for them to straight satire.

Although their role on *The Frost Report* would be quite junior, and was indeed paying only £14 a week each, there was no doubt that Jones and Palin were already extremely prolific and successful when Frost picked them up. They were everywhere in 1965 to 1967; in the business of tracing the roots of Monty Python, comedy family trees are every bit as complicated as those of rock groups. They authored and performed a few short film inserts for *The Late Show*, which ran for six months from October 1966, as a late-in-the-day *That Was The Week That Was* style satire.

Their first *Late Show* appearance was in a samurai spoof called 'Hibachi'. Later, they wrote and performed a sketch about fantasy commuters fighting their path through a jungle to work. Another rather less accessible sketch was a pastiche of the foreboding, menacing style of the film director Antonioni, whose films such as *L'Avventura* and *Blow-Up* were very in vogue in the mid-sixties.

In 1967, Palin and Jones worked together on 'additional material' for *A Series of Birds*, an eight-episode comedy series starring Cambridge's John Bird and John Fortune. The producer of the show was Dennis Main Wilson, who went on to produce Monty Python. One of the things about *A Series of Birds* which played rather badly with the public, critics and, to some extent, the BBC, was its slightly surreal style, involving seemingly unconnected stories. A further strand of Python was also forming quietly within the Corporation;

a method was being pioneered in the *Birds* series of showing the audience the backstage construction of what was seen front stage. The 'see-through' notion, with its somehow democratic overtones of 'involving' the public in a process traditionally secret to them, of destroying the mystique of outward appearance, would before long seep through into every field, from the design of consumer goods – transparent watches and the like – to architecture, in the form of buildings which wore their inside on the outside, or at least seemed to, to the famous first behind-the-scenes BBC TV documentary on the Royal Family. Although the product of elitism, Monty Python and its immediate comedic predecessors were part of the irreverent, equalising momentum of the sixties; comedy shows may not seem to have had much to do with the Summer of Love and all that, yet these were broadly part of the same movement in society.

In one episode of *A Series of Birds*, viewers saw the highly surreal sight of apparently straightforward actions like pouring a cup of tea having to be done repeatedly until they look right to an audience which already knows that they are not strictly 'honest'. In another episode, the viewer is asked to believe that the BBC has decided to make a documentary about an unemployed man, the publicity for which results in the subject being offered a job. The BBC is consequently obliged to employ him to stay on the dole, and thus confirm the film's integrity.

'It gave Terry and me some of the best writing opportunities we'd had since we started,' Palin has said of the *Birds* show, 'It was an attempt to break away from sketches and write narrative. And learning to work with people like John Bird and Dennis Wilson was good experience.'

But most important for Palin and Jones of all these career breaks was *The Frost Report*, which ran for twenty-six editions in two series of thirteen, starting in March 1966 and April 1967. The programme's writers were led by the astonishingly influential, yet sometimes overlooked, Marty Feldman, who was considerably older than the likes of Jones, Palin and John Cleese, whose own invitation to join Frost came in a phone call from the Great Man in a callbox at Kennedy Airport. Feldman's background in comedy was very different from that of his younger writers. He had written for radio shows such as *Educating Archie* in the 1950s, been in variety as a third of a music-hall act called 'Morris, Marty and Mitch', and had also written a lot of *Round The Horne* with Barry Took. He had lately been a major performer in the TV show *At Last The 1948 Show*.

The other writers on the *Frost Report* team comprise pretty much a roll call of the top available talent in London in 1966. They included Antony Jay, Keith Waterhouse and Willis Hall, Frank Muir and Denis Norden, David Nobbs, Dick Vosburgh, Peter Tinniswood, Barry Cryer, Barry Took, Tim Brooke-Taylor, Tony Hendra, Herbert Kretzmer, Peter Lewis, Peter Dobreiner, Bill Oddie, Graham Chapman (in between breaks from his medical school finals), Eric Idle and – with maximum billing next to Frost – Cleese, who has pointed out how, 'At the end of the show, before this huge list of names, the credits always used to say "Written by David Frost", which was really a bit naughty. Chosen by David Frost, fair enough.'

Each *Frost Report* had a more or less news-based theme, which would often be introduced, in the show's meteorology-inspired phrase, as Frost *over* 'Class', 'Youth' or 'Women'. Apart from the filmed inserts, most of the show was performed live, making it probably the last live comedy show to be done on TV. The sketches, the writing of which tended to be the job of the more senior team members, were linked by what was known, peculiarly again, as the CDM – Continuing Developing Monologue – which was often Jones's and Palin's territory. They occasionally had a hand in sketches; one of theirs, based on how karate experts (a vogue subject in the sixties) would cut a wedding cake, was in the edition which won the Golden Rose at the 1967 Montreux Festival. This sketch also began to establish Palin's and Jones's reputation at the BBC for outdoor-filmed, rather than made-in-the-studio, comedy sketches.

Terry Jones probably made slightly more impression than Palin during the *Frost Report*'s first series; at Christmas 1966, a Parlophone compilation record was released called *The Frost Report on Britain*, on which Jones but not Palin is listed as a writer. By the time of the second series, in 1967, Palin and Jones both moved up in the pecking order, taking part in the programme planning meetings and developing a proper niche for their sketches. Typical of these, and almost transplantable into Monty Python had they wished, was a sketch broadcast in *Frost Over Christmas*, a one-off outside the main series, on Boxing Day 1967. Cleese and Ronnie Corbett played strangers who meet a party. Cleese was a world-travelling, suave expert on everything, James Bond character, while Corbett was a very boring and tedious chartered accountant from Hendon, which was chosen as the archetype of suburbia. Corbett is determined to find something in common with the exotic Cleese, while Cleese is anxious to seem polite, but nevertheless better everything Corbett says with mention of some rarefied exploit. The sketch is really a mini dissertation of non communication as a great deal of Monty Python would be. (Chartered accountancy was, of course, the profession beloved of both *Frost Report* and Monty Python sketches, and may well stand as the lasting legacy to British comedy of Palin's boyhood friend Graham Stuart-Harris, who had, of course, become a chartered accountant.)

In the same period as *The Frost Report*, Palin and Jones also worked on *Twice a Fortnight*, a show dominated by ex-Footlights men such as Bill Oddie, Jonathan Lynn and Graeme Garden. *Twice a Fortnight* was effectively a television adaptation of the BBC radio show, *I'm Sorry I'll Read That Again*, and was the brainchild of Tony Palmer, who went on to become a highly regarded film director (in 1983, Palmer made *Wagner*, the movie, a five-hour biopic with Richard Burton, John Gielgud, Vanessa Redgrave and Laurence Olivier). In these less ambitious days, Palmer's comedy show ran on BBC 1 for ten weeks in 1967 without attracting a great deal of attention.

Neither was *Twice a Fortnight* marked by a great chemistry between Palmer and his principal talent. Bill Oddie in particular tended to be at odds with Palmer over differing ideas on comedy.

Palin and Jones were careful to stay outside the fray, writing film inserts which were made away from the studio, where much of the creative tension on the series was felt. Jones is on the record as being quite positive above *Twice a Fortnight*. 'I think those films were the first time I realised how much good filming could add to comedy,' he has said. 'Palmer wasn't very sensitive in a way to what we were doing, but he had a tremendous visual sense – he knew how to get a good picture and it looked terrific. I became aware then that you could marry beautiful pictures to comedy and get something really amazing.'

Indeed, Tony Palmer seems to have left quite an impression on Palin and Jones. Paying detailed attention to what comedy scenes looked like, to treating the aesthetic as more than a mere backdrop for script – perhaps even for the general 'atmosphere' of a scene to be almost as important as the comedy – was to become a hallmark of the films of both the men, as much when they worked on their own as together.

Oddie, Garden and Co. would always be a different comedy stable from the Pythons, and the split between the two camps was evident to Palmer during *Twice a Fortnight*. 'You saw within it,' Palmer says, 'very clearly and within quite a short space of time, the flowering of two quite different kinds of humour, which clearly would never be in the same bed together again.'

It was during these prolific post-university years too that Terry Jones was invited by Humphrey Barclay to contribute to *Do Not Adjust Your Set*, another wacky, pre-Python series, ostensibly aimed at children, but in reality a cult show for young and not so young adults, with people rushing home from the office to catch it. The show was the concept of Jeremy Isaacs at Rediffusion. Barclay, a Footlights man who had been recruited into BBC Radio as a writer–producer direct from Cambridge in the same intake as Cleese and Oddie, was determined not to fall into the common trap of patronising children. Passing over the regulars of *I'm Sorry I'll Read That Again*, which he produced, he looked instead to the talents of Eric Idle, who was regarded as a little under-used at the time in major roles, and Jones, whom he had seen in the Oxford revue, '****'.

Jones naturally leapt at the offer, but insisted that Michael Palin, whom Barclay did not know, also be brought in. The two of them were teamed up with Eric Idle and deliberately non-university performers in David Jason and Denise Coffey to form a flourishing comedy team, which was working almost at the same time, and to some extent in competition with, *At Last The 1948 Show*, which was Graham Chapman's and John Cleese's vehicle at this point on the journey towards Python. *Do Not Adjust Your Set* ran for two series, beginning in January 1968.

Palin, Jones and Idle did not have a child between them or have much idea of what sixties youngsters would enjoy. On the other hand, they had all been children relatively recently, and youth was still something of a novelty in the old man's business of comedy at the time. The influence of such a simple and obvious attribute as youthfulness can never be emphasised enough in trying to work out what it was that made Monty Python and its immediate ancestors so fresh and novel. Python was intellectual, it was undergraduate, it was elitist, it was middle class ... but above all, it was *young*. It was no wonder that *Do Not Adjust Your Set* was a children's show. Python's middle-aged detractors would regard it above all as childish comedy, but Michael Palin, who even in his fifties retains both a schoolboyish appeal and a great deal of schoolboy humour, prefers to describe it as child*like*.

So, without much up-to-date experience of modern children, the writers launched with some trepidation into what they found funny a decade or so earlier, and they discovered that jokes about school subjects, fantasy sketches about history and school games played just as well in 1968 as in 1958. So a sketch in which Jason, as James Watt, notices (as in the school history and science books) the power of steam in a kettle, and goes on to imagine the kettle becoming a major method of transport, was perfectly calculated, if to some extent by accident, to work. Musical interludes in *Do Not Adjust Your Set* were provided by the Bonzo Dog Doo Dah Band, whose chaotic visual lunacy was a stab at not the middle-aged estab-lishment, but at the growing solemnness and self-reverence of the new pop genre. Eric Idle was quick to acknowledge that the Bonzos paved some of the way to Monty Python.

In 1968, by the time a second *Do Not Adjust Your Set* series was called for, Thames Television won the weekday ITV franchise for London from Rediffusion, and London Weekend Television inherited Friday evenings to Sundays from ATV. Humphrey Barclay was hired by Frank Muir, as Head of Entertainment at the new LWT, and in 1969 *Do Not Adjust Your Set* lived again. Under LWT's control, moreover, its adult following was acknowledged, and the show was repeated in the evening. And another development – a young American artist John Cleese had met in the States, Terry Gilliam, was brought in to the show to do animated cartoons.

At Frank Muir's behest, Barclay went on to produce a parodic history series, *The Complete and Utter History of Britain*, which was, more than any show previously, Palin's and Jones's baby – even to the extent that they could have a say in casting. (They did not, for example, want to use David Jason and Denise Coffey.)

They both wrote and performed in *The Complete and Utter History of Britain*; since a famous extended filmed sketch in *Twice a Fortnight* in which the Battle of Hastings was presented as a home movie, Palin and Jones had virtually cornered the market in funny historical material. The device of mixing ancient and modern, which would become familiar in Monty Python, was still a rev-elation in 1968. 'We used modern television techniques to look at a historical period, but as if those techniques had been invented then,' Palin explains. 'How would a television company of the Middle Ages have dealt with the Battle of Hastings, or Richard I's arrival from the Crusades?' Another sketch in a similar vein had Palin as an estate agent trying to sell Stonehenge to a young couple, the man being Jones. William the Conqueror was seen being inter-viewed *Grandstand*-style after the Battle of Hastings ('King William – congratulations on a wonderful victory.' 'Thank you, David').

It was only unfortunate that *The Complete and Utter History* was not networked; Palin felt that resentment in the regional companies over the strength of the new independent contractor, LWT, was behind this neglect of the series, which ran for six Sundays at the beginning of 1969. There was, however, a feeling at LWT that some of the material was not quite strong enough for broadcast; one distinctly clever sketch – but hardly very suitable for ITV; it was dropped – concerned a husband and wife trying to get used to speaking Latin after the Roman invasion ('Where been have you?' 'Ah! Flosburga (vocative)! Well I, a cup of mead, with Egfrith, having been enjoying, I his place was about to having been making the action of being about to go, when . . .'). A sketch about St Augustine trying to introduce Christianity to heathen Britons was lost, as was one about a caveman trying to patent the chair as a device to enable one 'to sit down higher up'.

The first episode of *The Complete and Utter History* earned some rather bad reviews, which inevitably hinged on the show's 'undergraduate humour'. Thereafter, it was largely ignored. Great as their capacity was, the young men were beginning to suffer from a touch of work overload. Palin's cigarette intake had increased from twenty a day at Oxford to forty and more. At one point late in 1968, in addition to their own show they were writing for Feldman's own show, *Marty*, for *Frost on Saturday*, and undertook two pantomimes – *Aladdin* and *Beauty and the Beast* – for the Civic Theatre, Watford. 'Because of all this we really weren't able to clear the decks and concentrate as much as we needed to,' admitted Palin. Speed was working to the detriment of quality. The augurs were suggesting the pair were not ITV naturals. Something new was needed to channel Palin's and Jones's prodigious talents in a more unified project. And, in 1969, that something happened.

It started with – or at least, could not be started without – John Cleese's decision to concentrate on television as his mainstay. The BBC was extremely keen for him to have his own show. Chapman and Idle were busily separately writing material which Cleese admired; Terry Gilliam had made a minor mark as a wacky animator. Somewhere along the way, Barry Took brought an idea for a John Cleese show to Michael Mills, the BBC's head of comedy, and the idea culminated in the birth (after several extremely well-documented changes of name) as *Monty Python's Flying Circus.*

'It was like being back at university,' enthuses Palin. 'We made each other laugh. We had a mutual disrespect for authority.'

6

Shepherd's Bush

Michael Palin has been described as the very backbone of the Python team – wry, versatile, tolerant and born funny with the sort of rubbery, anonymous face that lends itself to infinite roles. He will always be known as the Python with the knotted hankie on his head – he even calls his company the Gumby Corporation Limited, after Mr Gumby, the moron he used to play, with his rolled-up trousers, braces, spectacles, small moustache and handkerchief with the four corners knotted as a headpiece.

Today, he still uses a discreet drawing of a knotted hankie as his corporate image. But he is remembered in Python for more than just Mr Gumby. He will equally be known forever as the pet shop owner who tries to persuade an incandescent John Cleese that a parrot is not really dead, just a Norwegian Blue pining for the fjords and resting.

It is often overlooked that Palin was just twenty-six when Python finally evolved. He actually wanted the series to be called Gwen Dibley's Flying Circus, rather than the ecologically unsound Owl Stretching Time which was the show's name up to a very late stage of its development. With his characteristic reluctance to consign any part of his past to history, it is not surprising that in his fifties

Palin is the most comfortable of the five surviving performers about having been a member of the Monty Python team.

Although in middle age, he has triumphantly combined a continuing presence in comedy with a complete reinvention of himself as a modern (although softer and less waspish) Alan Whicker, he shows no sign at all of being embarrassed by the work he did in his twenties. John Cleese, on the other hand, does. Cleese would be appalled to be asked to do a silly walk today; Palin is happy to use that hankie as a trademark, and happily lapses into Pythonisms if some occasion (opening a charity event or whatever) demands it.

After the first Python series, during which Palin recalls the six were 'rather polite to one another', they became quite an argumentative group. Palin (known much of the time as Chunky, owing to his slightly chubby physique at the time), however, largely avoided confrontation with the famously candid Cleese; if there was arguing to be done on behalf of the Palin–Jones axis, the more excitable Jones (the 'fat Welshman' as he was called) could be relied upon to do it, and with some gusto.

The freedom Monty Python offered the team was like oxygen to Palin, whose brand of child-like anarchism had got him and Jones nowhere in *The Complete and Utter History of Britain*. Now, the same concentrated silliness was being given *carte blanche*. 'We could do whatever we wanted, anywhere and everywhere – on film, in the studio,' Palin has said, 'We could turn the screen upside down if we wanted to, or have a blank screen for a minute and a half and just have voices in the background. We could take the BBC symbol which normally goes on at the end and stick it in the middle ... It's a way of looking at the world through humour-tinted spectacles.'

When Monty Python was first broadcast on 5 October 1969, having been recorded a month earlier at BBC studios in Shepherd's Bush and East Acton, Michael's first appearance was as a Frenchman discussing with Cleese the phenomenon of flying sheep which nest in trees under the impression they are birds – in nonsense French. Although their material was used less than that of Cleese and Chapman in episode one (which as a matter of detail was the second recorded), within a short time Palin's and Jones's sketches were getting a generous airing. Their shared historical obsession, their tradition of fusing incongruous elements into one sketch – plus another trait of imposing a cosy Englishness on to the most exotic of scenarios – were central to the Monty Python culture, which within months had become a major youth cult. 'A lot of people simply couldn't see the appeal of Python,' Palin has said. 'They found it all extremely silly; a waste of public money and university degrees. But at the same time we'd hear about pubs going quiet for an hour in the evenings and pop groups refusing to go on stage until the programme had finished.'

Incredibly, with only forty-five episodes to its name over a four-year period, Python continues to be a cult world-wide nearly thirty years later, much of its continuation due to a massive amount of interest in the series on the Internet.

There were distinct areas in which the two principle Monty Python writing teams, Palin–Jones and Cleese–Chapman, specialised. The latter loved superficially serious TV studio discussions, with some insane spin, such as all the participants being cardboard cut-outs. They also were the masters of what Palin called 'Thesaurus sketches' – long diatribes stuffed with kaleidoscopic verbiage and ridiculous restatements of the same thought in increasingly pompous language. Meanwhile, Jones's and Palin's predilection for filming historical sketches on remote and uncomfortable locations (Palin's particular enchantment being Arthurian legend, Jones's with anything Chaucerian) unexpectedly found a fellow spirit in Gilliam, who was also fascinated by the past.

According to Cleese, quoted in Roger Wilmut's definitive 1980 book on sixties and seventies comedy, *From Fringe to Flying Circus*: 'Most of the sketches with heavy abuse in them were Graham's and mine; any sketch that started with a slow pan across countryside and impressive music was Mike and Terry's; and anything that got utterly involved with words and disappeared up any personal orifice was Eric's.'

Palin and Jones sketches were frequently not just shot on location, but were also long and involved. They wrote the first of the lengthy sequences, 'The Funniest Joke in the World', about a joke so funny it is lethal, and was secretly developed for use in the Second World War. For safety's sake, the writers did not include the joke itself in the script – only its German version: Q: *'Wenn is das nöd-schtuck git und slottermeier?' A: 'Ja, Beigerhund das oder die Flipperwaldt gerschput.'*

A type of sketch whose appeal was universal among the team members was not original to Python, and had been a mainstay of *That Was The Week That Was*. This was the notion of reversing a cliché media subject; where TV and newspapers would frequently carry features along the lines of the confessions of a homosexual, drug addict and so on, Python would show people dramatically confessing to mundane or harmless 'problems' – 'I was a heterosexual', or the confessions of a cheese addict.

A further, and in this case more original, area which united the (broadly) Oxford and Cambridge factions was another manifestation of the 'see-through' sketch, which gave the (entirely fallacious) impression of letting the audience in on the backstage workings of television. A couple of months into the first series of Python, in a sketch written by the unusual combination of Palin and Cleese, both the 'silly' joke and the innovation of ending sketches halfway through were born.

In this doubly novel sketch, Chapman played a colonel interviewing Eric Idle, as a soldier scared of fighting because it's dangerous. Palin and Jones intervene, as mafia men offering for fifteen bob a week to 'protect' the battalion. 'No, this is silly,' Chapman barks; 'What's silly?' asks Jones. 'The whole premise is silly,' replies Chapman, 'and it's very badly written. I'm the senior officer here, and I haven't had a funny line yet, so I'm stopping it.'

On certain broad themes within Monty Python, all the six members of the team are agreed. All, for example, recognise that there is an element of their own mothers in the ubiquitous middle-aged ladies in the sketches. Palin's mother commented once that when Michael was in drag, 'People say he looks like my sister.' (She added that Michael looked the image of his father in his film *The Missionary*.)

On the question of what might be described as the series' political angle, Palin almost certainly spoke for the team when he said: 'Pythons are not anarchists by any means, but when we get together and start assembling material, the most fertile ground for our comedy is the follies of the people we see around us, and it is even worse when we feel that those people are in a superior position over most people and are still more stupid ... That is where our area goes, and that can go through from merchant bankers to doctors or actors – wherever we see any sort of pomposity or pretension. If we feel that, when somebody unsuitably in authority is telling people to do something, it is gratifying to be able to deflate them by humour.'

What, then, was Michael Palin's particular contribution to Monty Python? What might have been different had he not been in show-business at all, but writing advertising copy in an agency, or hacking away interviewing prominent steelworker for the *Edgar Allen Magazine*?

Palin certainly had a huge stake in the Pythonic silliness – the words to the 'Lumberjack Song' were his, after all, as was the 'Sperm Song', which, as a matter of historical record, was written with Terry Jones at a table at Michael's parents' retirement home in Southwold. Silliness aside, here is also an ever-so-slightly serious edge underlying some of Palin's comedy, a certain down-trodden-ness among the characters he created for Python. While the other Pythons' fathers were rather successful provincial middle-class men, the overriding theme of Ted Palin's life was one of crushed hopes; the experience of seeing his father's struggle seems to have influenced Palin quite profoundly.

Palin himself says his characters were 'marginalised by history'; the wimpish, mustachioed Arthur Putey, whose beautiful wife makes love with their marriage counsellor during a session, the pet shop assistant yearning to be a lumberjack, the accountant who longs to be a lion-tamer and Reg Pither, the bobble-hatted hero of the cycling tour of north Cornwall, were all, it is not too fanciful to suggest, reflections of life as a mild English failure. Mr Pither, the invention of a Palin–Jones half-hour script which had been earlier rejected with some force by the BBC (but lived again as a rare one-sketch Python episode), has been described as a super-intelligent Gumby. Some Palin characters were hopeless, unrequited dreamers, others dim-witted, ordinary little men, others still naive, overgrown schoolboys.

'I do like playing rather gullible characters like that,' says Palin, 'but I like giving them that extra dimension. Pither is a simple-minded chap, really, and yet awfully aggressive in a way – he won't let you go. I don't actually like bright, sharp, clever, pushy people, so I tend to go for the sort of characters that would infuriate them; those are the sort of characters I like to play.'

Although he was equally capable of playing such Python staples as flashy quizmasters and television interviewers, wistfulness was, and continues to be, Michael Palin's signature. His comedy has little to do with jokes, a genre which, like a fair proportion of comedy writers, he is a little snobbish about: as Robert Hewison says, 'Michael and I don't make jokes, we *have* jokes.'

'I don't know any and can't write any,' Palin says. 'I'm most concerned with writing that arises out of character.'

It is easy to see, then, the process which led to creations of his such as the two most famous Monty Python sketches – the 'Ministry of Silly Walks' and the parrot sketch. 'Silly Walks', which John Cleese has grown to loathe since it typecast him (or at least his legs) for the following thirty years, was written by Palin and Jones. The parrot sketch, although written by Cleese and Chapman, was based on a character observation and original idea of Palin.

He had acted in a show with Cleese, and written by Cleese and Chapman, called *How To Irritate People*. He had told Cleese about his conversations with a local garage owner who had sold him a car. 'He was one of those people who could never accept anything had gone wrong,' Palin explains. 'I was telling John that the brakes seemed to have gone, but when I told the mechanic this, he said,

"Oh, well, it's a new car, bound to happen." He had an answer for everything. I'd say the door came off while I was doing fifty mph, and he'd say, "Well yeah, they do, don't they." '

Cleese also saw the potential of the character, and Palin played his local garage man almost line for line in *How To Irritate People*. When Cleese and Chapman were on the hunt for material for the first Python series, Chapman had the inspired idea of transmuting the garage man into a pet shop owner trying to justify having sold a customer a dead bird, and what is almost certainly the world's most famous comedy sketch was born. It was hardly Cleese's, Chapman's or Palin's fault that in the ensuing years the parrot sketch would come to be a mite overanalysed. One overexcited critic has in all seriousness interpreted the parrot sketch as a parody of the Christian belief in eternal life.

'A lot of people in America seemed to think we'd written them under the influence of drugs,' Palin told the journalist Mick Brown in an interview which appeared in *Penthouse* magazine in 1978. 'They'd say, "You guys musta bin outta ya minds when you wrote this." But just because *they* were out of their minds when they saw it, it doesn't mean we were when we wrote it.'

In fact, Palin confided, a little surprisingly perhaps, that he had actually given up smoking cannabis by the time he was working on Python. 'Not,' Brown added, 'that he had ever been an inveterate user. "I'd never been to art school, you see. That was the trouble. I dabbled. But generally speaking I could get into any state I wanted on three glasses of wine. I don't like getting out of control. I've found it very difficult to write while I'm high; with comedy it's absolutely impossible." '

His method of dreaming up Python ideas was very much to let his (undrugged) mind freewheel. While Cleese favoured a highly systematic approach to inspiration, with charts, diagrams and flow charts to ensure the 'internal logic' of even the most absurd sketches (a guiding principle of his comedy, which Cleese had been taught by Marty Feldman) Palin has explained how stream of consciousness was his basic method – yet another example, perhaps, of the 'organic'

Oxford approach to the analytic Cambridge tradition. 'Sometimes in the morning, when I'm half awake, or just when I'm about to go to sleep, all sorts of strange thoughts will come into my mind,' Palin says.

The famous Spanish Inquisition sketch was the result of such drifting thoughts. He recounts starting with a northern joke, in which Chapman comes home to his wife and announces there's 'trouble at t' mill'. She fails to understand his accent, and gets him to explain what the problem at the mill is, whereupon he gets irritated and complains that all he wanted was to say there was trouble at mill without going into any great detail, and that 'I didn't expect a kind of Spanish Inquisition'. 'I wrote that line just as it was, and thought, "Great, what we must do here is bring the Spanish Inquisition into it." '

(On the subject of stimulants, since he raised it himself in his *Penthouse* interview, it is worth noting that, in fact, Palin had not only given up dope by the time of Python; he had also ditched his forty-a-day cigarette smoking following the birth of his and Helen's first child – the first Python baby – Tom, who was born during the run-up to the first Python show in 1969. 'At eight months, he started to climb on to my knee for a hug, and it was difficult to keep my fag out of his face and impossible to keep Tom out of the ashtray, so I gave up,' he recounted recently.)

After finishing the second series of Python at the end of 1970 (which included, from Palin's pen, 'Silly Walks' and 'The Spanish Inquisition'), the team started on a cinema version of material from the first two series. The film was called *And Now For Something Completely Different* and was made over five weeks in a defunct United Dairies depot in Totteridge, a handy twenty minutes' drive away from Palin's house. The film was a quite calculated method of cashing in on a most unexpected audience which had been discovered for Monty Python in the USA. Before the first series of Python had garnered much press attention in Britain, a *Washington Post* writer called Fred Friendly had somehow caught up with Python, and declared it in the newspaper the most wonderful thing ever. Students who had seen the show in Britain spread the word, and it was decided, four years before the series was tentatively shown on television in the States, to attempt to exploit the market for such lunacy via the cinema.

As things turned out, the American campus audience for Monty Python was not only unexpected – it was practically non-existent. *And Now For Something Completely Different* was not a great success. But the triumphant progress of Python was not disrupted by the film's slightly limp reception; in a sense, Monty Python was the comedy which made occasional failure acceptable. Had a Hancock or Eric Sykes turned in a dud episode, audiences would soon wither. In the early seventies, if this week's Python was disappointing, you looked forward all the more to the next.

A further unexpected medium by which Python expanded towards North America was the stage show. A show in 1970 at the Belgrade Theatre, Coventry, had been successful, and a tour of one-night stands around the country followed. Next, the team went on tour across Canada, opening in a small theatre in Toronto, and then in successively larger venues as they travelled west – through Winnipeg, Edmonton, Calgary and Vancouver. They were soon playing to audiences of three thousand and more.

For Michael, the return to theatre had a particular drawback. The manic parts he had created needed a great deal of shouting. He enjoyed being a Gumby on television but, live, found it strenuous: 'It was very therapeutic – lovely to be able to stand there and just yell. Until I had to do it in the stage show and then I realised the disadvantage – six weeks with laryngitis.'

The third series of Python was recorded from December 1971 to May 1972, and transmitted from October 1972 to January 1973. Cleese was starting by this time to get sick of the Pythons, and has often said that he feels that the quality was already tailing off during the third series. Towards the end there is a tendency for some of the material to become weird rather than funny and Cleese's presence was less in evidence – he took part in every show, but there were far fewer of the typical Cleese–Chapman confrontation sketches than previously.

Conflicts among the group also erupted along the pre-existing fault lines during the writing of the third series. The Python working method had always been that sketches were subjected to group scrutiny; everyone respected everyone else's opinion, and thus was a high standard maintained. The old problem, however, of Palin and Jones being more interested in the overall shape of a show, while Cleese and Chapman were insistent on sustaining the 'internal logic' of sketches, became less of a source of creative tension and more of an obstacle to producing a top-rate finished programme.

'It wasn't as if we were just happy with a successful television show, it had to be something more,' Palin has said. 'What it was about, and what each of us was expressing of ourselves, was also important. I don't think the show would have been successful if people hadn't been pulling in various directions.'

Having grown over the past twenty years to become rather less the conformist than he was at prep school in Sheffield, Palin was beginning to find the BBC bureaucracy stifling. 'During the third series we had a list of thirty-two points presented to us, which they wanted changed and which we fought, and I think we got it reduced to about ten. This involved having meetings with the BBC in which we would discuss whether we should say "masturbation" or not – with six of us and one of the BBC, they were bizarre meetings.'

(In Palin's and Jones's 'Summarise Proust Competition' sketch, Graham Chapman, as one of the contestants, was to list his hobbies as 'golf and strangling animals and masturbation'. The BBC succeeded in getting masturbation cut, but lip-readers could still apparently appreciate what the huge studio audience laugh was for.)

Passably bolshie though Palin had become, he still possessed in spades the quality of boyish enthusiasm, and this prevented him from becoming as bored with Monty Python as the saturnine Cleese, who has always been inclined to get bored with projects when he has exhausted their intellectual potential as far as he is concerned. In the summer of 1973, during a flight to Canada for another Python tour, Cleese announced to the group that he was quitting. He explained that he could not understand why they, too, were not bored with the show. The five remaining Pythons became convinced that Cleese was becoming increasingly obsessed with money, and was leaving them in (or near) the lurch for his own financial benefit.

The press immediately speculated that Cleese's departure would be the end of *Monty Python's Flying Circus* – and even the BBC considered cancelling the planned fourth series. They were, bar a little jumping the gun, accurate. But the fourth, Cleese-less, series went ahead, after a long stage tour which Cleese stayed with all the way.

The absence of Cleese prompted a great deal of thinking among the remaining Pythons about just what his role had been. 'That was when I slightly felt that perhaps he did over-dominate it,' said Palin. 'Although a vital element was missing, I would have felt a vital element was missing if Graham, Eric or Terry had left. *Monty Python* is by no means John's show. Although he came up very strongly in terms of the influence he had on us, it is really a genuinely combined influence.'

Palin was asked a few years later if he found it frustrating that Cleese was perceived to be the moving force of Monty Python. 'Not any more,' he replied. 'It maybe did at one stage, but I've always found that it's completely understandable that John should stand out from the rest of us. For a start, physically he stands out in any circumstance. For instance, John would be the first to admit that he's not the world's greatest character actor because he can never submerge himself and disappear inside a role. He tends to play John visually, so the public always has a very clear view of him. John tends to be fairly dominant, but that all goes with his height and size and imperial bearing. In fact, it is not something which worries me any more.'

Transmission of the series minus Cleese began in October 1974 – a truncated run of six programmes, now called simply *Monty Python*. There is, inevitably, a revisionist movement among Python fans to suggest that the fourth series was better than its adverse press reaction suggested but, overall, Palin is the first to admit *Python* had lost its way as a TV programme. 'There was an ingredient missing,' he admits. 'The sort of middle-class ferocity that John could express so well wasn't quite there; also Terry Gilliam wasn't able to do much animation and Eric wrote very little.'

Certain aspects of series four pleased Palin enormously; he was delighted by Terry Gilliam's efforts at acting, into which the American was thrown and landed a little reluctantly. Some of the material, Palin regards as good as the best of the full-deck Pythons. He is especially fond of a sketch entitled, 'The Worst Family in Britain', which featured Gilliam, as the worst member of the Garibaldi family of Droitwich, stuffing himself stupid with baked beans. 'I liked that. John Cleese was never totally comfortable letting himself go like that,' he says.

Paradoxically, the audiences for the fourth Python series were the highest yet. But with Cleese absent, Idle becoming more interested in doing his own series and a general feeling that the team was breaking up, it was decided that it was time to stop the television Monty Pythons altogether.

'Doing the Pythons was like a good summer,' Palin was later to say. 'It can't be like that all the time. I miss it like I miss picnics on the grass at Oxford – I don't miss it in the sense that I wish I were still doing it. The nice thing is that it still goes on in reruns.' He loves to remember the good times: 'We were filming one day and we all needed to cash cheques. So we converged on this bank, all dressed as Long John Silver, and each of us with a parrot on our shoulder. The cashier looked up without blinking and said, "Do you have a Barclaycard?"'

In the same way as, in 1975, the glory of Cleese's *Fawlty Towers* would be seen as the fact that there were only ever twelve episodes made, Palin regards the shortness of the life of *Python* as a TV series as one of its great strengths. 'That sort of burst of creativity is like a sunspot,' Palin told the Python specialist author, Kim Howard Johnson, in his comprehensive 1979 Python almanac, *The First 200 Years of Monty Python*. 'It flares up, very intensely and brilliantly for a very short period. If it lasted any longer, it would never have been as brilliant in the first place.'

And what was Michael Palin's favourite Monty Python sketch? 'The fish flapping dance,' he replies without hesitation. 'John Cleese and I were dressed in solar topees and long shorts. We dance. I lightly slap him on the face with two pilchards. John produces an eighteen-inch salmon and knocks me into the canal. It's almost glum-proof.'

7

On Location

Monty Python fans who thought their weekly fix since 1969 (at least during times when the show was running) was over for good in 1973 had a delight – several, really – in store when the disunited Pythons started uniting again on a regular basis throughout the mid- and late seventies to make a series of films, some of them incorporating material every bit as sublime as the original TV show.

Palin has always seen the development of the team into a coalition of individual Pythons doing their own thing around the world and getting together occasionally to make a movie as a deliberate policy. 'Somehow the coincidence of this strongly creative group, each of us bringing different things to the series, allowed it to work,' he says. 'There was nothing much left for us to do,' explains Palin. 'So we went on to the films.'

Monty Python and the Holy Grail was the first true Monty Python film, as opposed to *And Now For Something Completely Different*, which was merely a television spin-off. *Holy Grail* was also a huge breakthrough for Michael Palin. At the age of thirty-two, his personal fascination with Arthurian legend had given birth to an entire feature film, with a proper, if modest, budget of £229,000, which was put together by the Python-friendly impresario Michael

Whitworth Road, Ranmoor, Sheffield: Michael was born in the top front bedroom.

On the beach, aged six.

At Birkdale Prep School, Sheffield: Palin is top right.

In *The Woodcarver*, an amateur production in Sheffield. A pensiv Palin is far right.

The *Edgar Allen Magazine* – unlikely recipient of some of Palin's earliest writing.

EDGAR ALLEN

magazine

JUNE 1963   NUMBER 86   THREEPENCE

The Internal House Journal of Edgar Allen & Co. Ltd., Sheffield. Steelmakers and Engineers

Ted Palin receives his retirement presentation cheque at Edgar Allen, 1966.

Michael Palin with
his mother, Mary,
at a family wedding.

Locker room humour: Michael at his old prep school during the shooting of BBC TV's *Comic Roots* in 1983 *(BBC Picture Archives).*

Dressing up always appealed to Michael – never more so than during LWT's *The Complete and Utter History of Britain*, 1969 *(LWT).*

He was a lumberjack – and he was OK. From *And Now For Something Completely Different*, 1971 *(BBC Picture Archives).*

'Welease Wodger? Why should I ... welease Wodger?'
Michael in *The Life of Brian*.

Palin in philosophical mood as Mr Gumby.

In *The Testing of Eric Olthwaite*, one of the finest *Ripping Yarns (BBC Picture Archives)*.

LEFT In *A Fish Called Wanda* –
with the star.

RIGHT Pole position: Michael Palin
at the North Pole, 1992. During *Pole
to Pole*, his second world travel series
(Basil Pao, BBC Worldwide 1997).

BELOW Playing his own ancestor, thinly
disguised as the Revd Francis Ashby in
American Friends, 1991.

Michael and Helen Palin at a BAFTA
Awards ceremony *(Alan Davidson)*.

Michael and eldest son Tom, Hampstead 1997 *(Tim O'Sullivan*

Michael Palin owns several homes but, unusually for an international film star, they are all
stuck together in the same north London street *(Mail Newspapers)*.

White. White persuaded a diverse group of fellow Python admirers to put up money, including the pop groups Pink Floyd and Led Zeppelin.

Palin also emerged, perhaps a little reluctantly, as the organisational inspiration of the film, leaving the directing entirely to the two Terrys; the evaporation of the Pythons as a group which could be called on at all times certainly tested his people-skills further than they were used to being stretched.

'The organisation of the shows and the engineering of the product took over, leaving less and less time for writing,' he explains. 'That, in fact, may also be one of the problems with the *Holy Grail* film ... so much of our time was spent organising and arranging and financing that there was very little left for the actual filming. I used sometimes to get very cross privately at home that everyone wasn't pulling their weight when things like finishing off a record or going to see a bit of dubbing came along, things that didn't need everybody. The only two who could ever be contacted were Terry Jones and me because we were at home.

It wasn't just the occasional elusiveness of Cleese, Idle, Chapman and Gilliam which made his biggest project to date an organisational challenge for Palin. His and Terry Jones's insistence on using proper locations in Perthshire for *Holy Grail* – an insistence which paid off amply in the ensuing rather expensive, almost Hollywood, look of the film – exacerbated their own difficulties in pulling the project together.

'The Department of the Environment in Scotland refused to let us use any of their rotten crumbling old castles,' Palin recounts. 'They said Monty Python wouldn't be doing the kind of things that would be in keeping with the dignity of the buildings – so in the end we shot it where we could: we actually finished the film in our production manager's back garden at Gospel Oak.'

Keen as ever to be positive and optimistic, Palin rationalised the other Pythons' determination to maintain their independence. 'It's got a way of working itself out,' he said. 'It would be absolutely disastrous if we were all the same, and did the same amount of work and never grumbled. It would have been awful.'

Or, as Graham Chapman put it: 'Working in a group is great fun, but you need your own individual identity as well ... if you're stuck together for almost a year doing a television series, it becomes very difficult to have a separate existence other than within the group. You virtually have to ring up to ask if it's all right to have a bath. We must develop separately as individuals for the group to survive.'

In between arguing with stuffy Scottish bureaucrats and trying to round up stray Pythons, Palin still managed to satisfy himself creatively in his producing (as well as writing and acting) role. 'We were able to use the considerable talents of people in Python,' he said at the time *Holy Grail* was released. 'Terry Gilliam with his design and Terry Jones's direction and all of our feelings for historical period. We felt we were using an area of ourselves which we hadn't really explored in the television series.'

The characters the individual Pythons played in *Holy Grail* were very much built on the stereotypes Python fans were used to seeing them portray in the television series. Ordered to go on a quest for the *Holy Grail* by God (a Gilliam animation), Chapman played King Arthur, he who encounters the Knights who say 'Ni', with the old bufferish authority he perfected playing military types in the TV show. Cleese played a destructive, violent Sir Launcelot, Idle the cowardly Sir Robin, Palin the innocent, naive but none the less noble Sir Galahad. (Palin's best-received scene found him in a castle full of beautiful teenage damsels all with an urgent desire to be spanked and given oral sex. To his fury, he is rescued by Launcelot.) Jones's character, Sir Bedevere was marked out by wisdom and learnedness, a reflection, perhaps, of his hankering towards academia – post-Python Jones went on to write a scholarly work on Chaucer, among other serious books.

Holy Grail was premiered in Los Angeles, despite Palin's expressed preference for a British opening in the presence of a waxwork Princess Margaret. The premiere was not exactly the hottest event in Hollywood, but still had the desired effect of raising up a level

Python awareness, which had been restricted to campuses and PBS viewers.

'We didn't all go out for it,' says Palin of the *Holy Grail* launch, 'only those of us who like travelling in groups. John Cleese and Eric Idle stayed behind which was just as well really ... We'd never have got six into the hotel room they gave us. When we arrived we found that the public television service there was having its Pledge Week, so we had to keep going on TV and begging for money. We raised enough to pay all our fares home.'

As a result, perhaps, of having a traditional Hollywood premiere, *Monty Python and the Holy Grail* was far more successful in America than *And Now For Something Completely Different* had been. The film earned $50 million by 1983, and was even successful in the Soviet Union. It may have been that the Russians liked its mildly anti-religious subtext; they would have to wait four years until that theme was explored further by the Pythons in their next film collaboration, *The Life of Brian*.

The British launch party for *Holy Grail* was the cue for some uncharacteristically sharp comment from Palin about Cleese who, since he left Monty Python at the end of the third series, had been regarded as money-fixated by the rest of the group, and by the left-leaning Palin and Jones in particular. 'Now he has come back to us and said we should all get together to tour America and boost the series, which is about to be shown there,' Palin told one reporter. 'Presumably he wants to do the tour for money, but we have said "No".'

Cleese responded when prompted by saying, 'It is malicious to suggest that I am money-mad. I have no yearning to own a yacht or a Greek Island.' He went on to explain that, yes, money came into the picture, and was a reason he would like to do a tour, but that he happened to find that doing his own projects in places like New York and San Francisco more attractive. This level of virtual sibling rivalry was the closest Michael would come to clashing head-on with Cleese, but it was not unique.

Some years later, for example, long after the making of Cleese's film *A Fish Called Wanda*, in which Palin starred and was given a handsome slice of the profits by Cleese, Michael was still clearly, quite viscerally, unhappy with something about Cleese's commercial bent.

In an interview with the *Daily News* of Los Angeles, he announced rather surprisingly that it wouldn't bother him if he never saw Cleese's then ubiquitous ads hawking electronic products. 'It's just as well I don't. That's his affair. We've long gone past the sense where we felt jealous about going off and doing things. I've always felt that, when we did Monty Python, that was something that was self-contained. It was our own baby. It belonged to the six of us and I never wanted to use Monty Python characters to sell anything, really. They're so special because they haven't been bought up by some big company. They're just our own. But outside that, I think everyone's entitled to do whatever they want. If [Cleese] was just doing commercials and he wasn't doing movies, I would be very sad about that.'

What then, in the seventies and eighties was the state of relations between the Pythons, who were from 1973 onwards neither a team nor a group of individuals? And how did Michael operate as one of the six slightly spiky friends who, it seemed, couldn't live together and couldn't quite live apart?

'There was a time when we used to shout "Shan't", "Won't" at each other, like children,' Palin said at this time. 'We used to get together just to badmouth each other's projects. But we're family, you know – we see each other, we have a joint company together.' (One of the more eyebrow-raising examples of this tendency to badmouth one another's projects, for some admirers of John Cleese, was Palin expressing the view that Monty Python was funnier than *Fawlty Towers*. 'In a way, Python is funnier than anything any individual does,' he told the Python chronicler Kim Howard Johnson. 'For example, *Fawlty Towers* is unquestionably brilliant, but it isn't as unique and special as Python. I have a suspicion John knows that too.')

John Cleese has spoken of the way in which the close comradeship in adversity the team felt at the outset of the Monty Python gave way to constantly changing internecine alliances, 'like the history of the Balkans', as the programme grew more successful. 'We did hang on to the group security for a while – perhaps for too long,' agrees Palin. 'It took a long time after Python for people to get used to the fact that it wasn't a crime to want to go off and do something on your own.

'Now,' Palin said a few years later, in 1979, 'I think it did us a lot of good. We're all back together again, in great form, best of friends, just as it was when we started ten years ago.'

Keeping this happy status quo was far from easy or pleasant. He would scurry off when a furious Jones, provoked by Cleese's famous sarcasm, would sometimes physically attack Cleese in some relatively minor way. 'When there was squabbling going on,' Cleese says of Palin, 'he tended to dial out a bit and let people get on with it. He's not a man who will ever die on the barricades, but he will die with thousands of friends.'

Palin is often described as the peacemaker among the Pythons, as the one who spoke to all the others regardless of who was not speaking to whom at any given time. A rather more subtle description of Palin's role in the team is given by Robert Hewison, his old university friend, who remained close both to Michael and the entire group. He sees Palin more as a facilitator than a mere mediator. Speaking of his friend's ability at Oxford to channel the efforts of a diversity of talented egoists into a unified production, Hewison remarks: 'All this is exactly what went on in the Pythons in exactly the same way, with Michael always being the universal joint, the man who can transmit everybody's energies and keep everybody together.'

To those who worked with the team, it has to be said, the inter-Python clashes were neither obvious nor intrusive. According to Hazel Pethig, the costume lady, years later, the Pythons were all equally nice. 'John, Michael, Eric, the Terrys and the handsome one who died, they were all such lovely men,' she said. 'Especially Michael.' The thing that impressed her was that whenever somebody had to do something unpleasant, like fall in a pond, Michael would volunteer – and do it with apparent pleasure.

As she fussed over the costumes, Pethig would be half-listening to the team debating who was to end up in the canal, and she could not help noticing how much Michael didn't mind if it was him. 'It wasn't that the others were unwilling, exactly,' she recalled. 'It was just that Michael really didn't mind.'

He was sunny, cheerful, busy and fulfilled. 'I think writing a novel is the most creative thing you can do, or a play,' he said in 1979. 'I've just finished one of each. Just back from the typist today.

'I'm terribly happy with my wife, my children, my house, my work,' he went on to confess, at the very time when Cleese was descending into depression after the collapse of his first marriage to Connie Booth. 'I'm always optimistic about life,' Palin continued. 'My first reaction is always to say yes and try to enjoy myself, not looking for the nasty or cynical side.'

The idea for Monty Python's *Life of Brian* evolved among the team while they were travelling around the world in various combinations to attend premieres for *Holy Grail* and do publicity for the film. The original suggestion, acknowledged by all as having been made by Eric Idle, was for a story to be called *Jesus Christ – Lust for Glory*. This paradoxically, considering the furore which was to follow *Life of Brian*'s release, was thought to be too disrespectful to Jesus Christ.

So the thinking moved on to the idea of a film about a previously unknown thirteenth disciple, St Brian, who could never quite keep up with the more successful disciples. Then they moved away from the life of Christ altogether, and decided to make the film about Brian Cohen, who is mistakenly hailed as the Messiah by a crowd hungry for some, indeed any, religious leader.

Shot late in 1978 on location at Monastir, Tunisia, on Zeffirelli's sets for his *Jesus of Nazareth*, *Life of Brian*'s controversial concept scared off its original backers, EMI. In the end, the finance came from George Harrison. The combination was everything religious and political conservatives in Britain and the USA could have feared; money from the Beatles, whom John Lennon had speculated in 1965 were more popular than Jesus, was being used to pay for a popular entertainment which, the conservatives were convinced, mocked Christ. And in the middle of the maelstrom was Michael Palin, formerly one of the keenest members of the Crusaders at Birkdale School, Sheffield.

As EMI had guessed, *Life of Brian* offended people widely. When it opened in the States in autumn 1979, it upset both Christian and Jewish organisations and was banned in two states. 'We've been attacked by everybody,' said Michael on the publicity trail. 'The Catholics, the Lutherans and even a Rabbinical group. They've all leaped to the conclusion that it is a vicious and blasphemous attack on the life of Christ. But *Life of Brian* takes place in AD 33. Actually there is not a great deal of religious satire in it, although there is some comment on organised religion. Jesus is treated very respect-fully. But the religious critics in America have told people not to go and see it, which is wonderful for the box office.'

In England, where the film opened in November, reaction was less extreme, the censor passing it uncut, and reviewers feeling it was in bad taste – gloriously so, in the view of some – but not blasphemous. The day after the premiere, Cleese and Palin appeared on *Saturday Night, Sunday Morning*, a late-night BBC 2 programme with Mervyn Stockwood, the Bishop of Southwark and the Christian moralist writer, Malcolm Muggeridge. The confrontation, with Tim Rice as moderator, was described later by Cleese as the occasion on which he saw Palin angrier than he had ever witnessed him before or since.

While Cleese, progenitor of the 'Argument Shop' sketch, did law at Cambridge and was selected for a job he never took up with a leading firm of solicitors, and hence was well used to keeping his end up in debate, Palin is a far less combative soul who avoids confrontation wherever possible. Palin was nevertheless far from naive enough to imagine that Muggeridge and the bishop would be easy on Cleese and him. He admired both men, and prepared himself days before the programme, to the extent of making copious notes.

But Palin – ironically for one who had mocked it to such brilliant effect in Monty Python – was greatly overestimating the intellectual possibilities of the television studio debate format. For a former Crusader, he also badly underestimated the determination and closed-mindedness that establishment churchmen would bring to a debate which for them was do or die, not an occasion for the discussion of ideas.

The debate consequently contained no intellectual direction, no dialectic, no theology, analysis or historical theory. Stockwood and Muggeridge turned out merely to be two old tub-thumping hacks, manipulative and simplistic and populist. They started by declaring the film not only blasphemous but 'tenth-rate', and went on to refer to it as 'a miserable little film'.

Insisting that the film was a parody of Christ's life – despite Cleese's and Palin's adamant denials – Muggeridge suggested cleverly that if *Life of Brian* had parodied Islam instead of Christianity there would have been an outcry from the same people who were currently praising it. It was, in fact, a prescient point for Muggeridge to have made a decade or more before the age of Islamic fundamentalism and the Salman Rushdie fatwa. Cleese batted it down firmly, nonetheless, retorting: 'You're right. Four hundred years ago we would have been burnt for this film. Now, I'm suggesting that we've made an advance.' Muggeridge did not see it that way at all.

Palin in particular was treated dismissively in such discussion as there was. 'The bishop spent the entire time castigating us as if we were the most loathsome dogs in London,' Palin recalls. 'He practically demanded we be deported.' Palin also remembers Stockwood's professionally timed last word; fingering his crucifix, the bishop wished the two Pythons well of their thirty pieces of silver.

'After the programme was finished he came up to us, gave us a broad smile, extended his hand and said, "Jolly good,"' Palin reported in an American interview. 'That's exactly what we were getting at in that movie. The hypocrisy of some people. I don't object to people believing in religion, but I do have contempt for the clergy and trouble accepting organised religion. I'm wary of anyone imposing their morals on me and have very little time for the hypocrisy of a lot of churchmen.'

In reality, *Life of Brian* dealt harshly with many groups of people – leaders of left-wing guerrilla organisations, trade unionists, impressionable followers of *false* religious cults – but not with Christians at all. What the film was based on, of course, was the old Palin–Jones obsession with transplanting modern stereotypes into a historical setting – a characteristic they now dismissed as a desire to dress up.

What made *Life of Brian* unusual for a Python production (apart from its conventional narrative structure) was its positive message, that people shouldn't follow anybody, but think for themselves as individuals. It was very likely the fact that the usual Python surrealism was conspicuously missing which made Christians suspicious that the Pythons were suddenly getting serious, and were directing their fire at the faith.

Defending what was a serious (although also extremely funny) film was a new position for Palin to find himself in. Having to point out again and again that, yes, there is a crucifixion scene at the end, but that crucifixion was the normal method of execution by the Romans at the time, so it does not mean that the crucifixion of Christ is automatically being belittled, was far from his happiest moment; he found, as he put it at the time, that 'the whole theology thing has become a bit of a bore'.

He was, after all, a respectable husband, father, and householder of nearly forty. He had never wanted to make anyone angry, let alone blaspheme. So harmless did he regard the film that he had even had his family out in Tunisia on set with him. (Tom, Michael's elder son, remembers being frightened by seeing his dad in costume because he didn't recognise him, and enjoying watching him filming while he tucked in to the on-set catering.) Palin regarded *Life of Brian*, as he did intelligent critics, as a film which was perfectly compatible with Christianity, and might well have thoroughly entertained and amused Jesus himself. Cleese insisted it actually was a religious film. It was with feeling, therefore, that Palin declared the furore, and especially the ill-fated television debate, as the most disillusioning experience of his life.

There were plenty of advantages to having become virtually a film star, however. 'I've achieved two lifetimes' ambitions in the last couple of weeks,' he said at the height of the *Life of Brian* storm. 'To be on *Desert Island Discs* and to have my work discussed in *The Times* correspondence column. The latter was a terrible disappointment. The letters were hysterical. Someone called Allatt wrote to say he hadn't seen the film but he was against everything it stood for. We should have written and said we've never seen Mr Allatt, but we don't like him. The only sane letter was from Penelope Mortimer.'

Palin's *Desert Island Discs* choices were: Duke Ellington playing 'Things Ain't What They Used To Be', the Black Dyke Mills Brass Band's 'Londonderry Air', Elvis Presley with 'You're a Heartbreaker', the Finale from the film of *Oh, What a Lovely War*, the 'Lullaby of Broadway', the Beatles' 'Things We Said Today', 'Nimrod' from Elgar's Enigma Variations, and an excerpt from *The Goon Show* entitled 'A Tale of Men's Shirts' from their New Year's Eve 1959 show. His book was Thackeray's *Vanity Fair* (having considered something by the journalist James Cameron), his luxury was 'the most luxurious feather pillow that I could possibly have', and his one-disc-above-all choice, the Elgar. This, he explained, he always listened to on one of the then newfangled Walkman players when he was abroad.

There was a further four-year gap before the Pythons got together again for their third and final film, *The Meaning of Life*. The film was the result, he says, of a concentrated group writing effort when the team installed themselves in a villa in Jamaica to write a new screenplay. 'There had been serious doubts about whether we could make the material as good any more. The new film had to be different. We felt we had to break new ground,' said Palin.

'We haven't got a plot yet for the new film,' he admitted at the time. 'It might be about a war, or science fiction. But it won't be aimed at showing people how important we think we are, how serious we can be, how we're going to upset someone. As John says, let's show them how to make a *really* silly film.'

George Harrison was again the source of the finance, which for *The Meaning of Life* was £2 million. 'George is a wonderful patron,' Palin said. 'He will actually give you money because he likes what you do. But you never actually ask about what you presume to be the Beatles' fortune.

'I didn't think the Pythons would do another film but we got ourselves together and with Cleese as a sort of chairman and Terry Jones as the terrier of the group we got moving,' Palin continued. 'When we got to the villa, we found there were only four decent rooms. It was interesting to see who got which. I, of course, ended up sleeping in Cleese's shoe cupboard. We didn't have any ladies with us and the Jamaicans were curious about what these six Englishmen were up to. It wasn't the cricket, so they decided we were after a certain local herb and dying to blow our minds on the grass they insisted on offering us.'

In spite of Jones's efforts – he actually forced his indolent colleagues to sit down one Wednesday morning and start work when they were showing little inclination to do so and hadn't even the faintest idea of a title – it might have been better for *The Meaning of Life* if the Pythons had taken advantage of the local weed, or if the team had followed Palin's suggestion and gone home to make a new TV series.

The Meaning of Life was the last and the least critically successful of the team's movie projects, although it made a healthy $80 million at the box office. It went into production immediately after Palin's film *The Missionary* completed shooting, but *The Meaning of Life* had already been in development, albeit at the sluggish tempo of six men who had little financial need to work, for the four years since 1979.

In terms of creating a film with a theme, where previously there was nothing but a ragbag of disparate material, the Jamaica trip worked, as had a Barbados 'holiday' on which the team had hatched *Life of Brian*. 'Those trips work because they get us away from

London and our individual home backgrounds,' Palin has explained. 'If something isn't working we can't say, "Let's go home and try again tomorrow." We're forced to confront the problem. Still, there was a moment when we came close to giving up and just having a holiday.'

After the success of *Life of Brian*, the group set out to re-create another story. As Michael suggested, at one time the new film was to have been a Second World War epic, provisionally entitled *Monty Python's World War III*. They found, however, that the constraints of a conventional structure worked to the detriment of spontaneity; they may have been in their forties but, to a man, the Pythons were keen to get back to the unstructured anarchy of their pre-*Brian* days. In Palin's case, his career by the early eighties had encompassed plenty of extremely conventional filmmaking, and, ever the nostalgia addict, the idea of doing a Pythons revisited appealed enormously. Indeed, during the lengthy planning for *The Meaning of Life*, the Pythons did their famous, revivalist-style Hollywood Bowl shows, which were truly Greatest Hits compilations put on partly to make a great deal of money in America, and partly for the boys to have fun together again.

A broadly narrative patchwork about man's quest for the meaning of life was agreed on at the crucial breakfast in Jamaica. 'It's a modest little tale,' Palin commented, 'more like the old television shows. We've kept in material which over the past three or four years of writing has always come out on top of the pile. But it will be a very, very different film from *Brian*. About twenty per cent of the material is debatable – that's the area we fight over – but I'd say eighty per cent of the film is stuff we've all fallen about at, at one time or another.' Asked what was holding the project together, he replied, 'Money, and not even enough of that,' but quickly went on to show that he still wasn't prepared to be as upfront and American as Cleese.

'Actually,' he elaborated in a more typically English way, 'It's quite difficult to put into words what it is about, outside of saying it's about the meaning of life. We deal in eternal truths such as why we're here, what is knowledge, how much mud a man can smear himself with during a day's filming ... I think the danger is that we try to seek logic in Python when there is no logic.'

Palin's outstanding contribution to *The Meaning of Life* was acknowledged as the 'Sperm Song', an attack on the Vatican's opposition to birth control, which he had written in Southwold, of all places, with Terry Jones. 'Ev'ry sperm is sacred,' he intoned, surrounded by dozens of children, looking like a scene from *Oliver!* For Jones, who regarded *The Meaning of Life* as the Pythons' best film (well, he did make it almost on his own at times) the funniest moment in the 103 minutes was Michael's. 'It was something Mike threw in when we were shooting,' Jones recounted admiringly. The sketch involved the Grim Reaper paying a visit to a dinner party where the salmon was dangerously off. 'Just as the ghosts were suddenly going out of the door, Mike's character suddenly says, "Hey, I didn't even eat the salmon!" He just threw it in on that take.' (Palin's character, it is worthy of recording, was as Terry Gilliam's wife, in one of his most elaborate female impersonations yet, with big blonde hair, eyelashes, heavy earrings and a long cocktail dress in crimson.)

The first public showing of *The Meaning of Life* in the States, at a preview, broke a record of sorts: eighty people out of an audience of 300 walked out, revolted, it seemed, by Terry Jones's portrayal of Mr Creosote, the man who eats until he vomits, then eats again until he explodes. Universal, encouraged by the reaction, based their American poster campaign for the film on this incident. 'Have you been grossed out yet?' the slogan asked, and takings rocketed.

The Meaning of Life was, however, a film strictly for Monty Python fans, and failed to gain the admiration of some people who saw in *Life of Brian* a film of real weight and substance. Michael Palin, as ever, was optimistic about the Pythons' future after the film. 'The nice thing now is that I do not feel I depend on Python as a primary source of work,' he enthused. 'We all go off and do our separate things, then come back together again. There was a time when I thought we would never work together again but, after

The Meaning of Life, I feel confident we will do films together again.'

And indeed they did – but never as a group of six.

8

Kyle of Lochalsh

At some point in the eighties, it became evident that the pleasant, understated, relaxed facilitator of the Pythons, the apparently directionless, ego-free go-between, the nostalgia freak who assiduously kept up with all his prep school chums back in Sheffield and was probably only a breath away from taking up train spotting again, was also the most energetic and ambitious of all six. Palin is a workaholic, conditioned, he believes, by his upbringing to drive himself hard, even when he doesn't particularly need the money. 'Don't make a pact with the Great Employer in the Sky,' he often says.

And he never has. While Cleese would take months off at a time to catch up on his reading philosophy, and would regard laziness as an art form, while Gilliam and Jones would direct only when the fancy took them, and Chapman and Idle felt the need to do very little at all, Palin was ceaselessly prolific, as a writer, director, performer, travel journalist and even novelist. His interests have also encompassed a small publishing company, an eight-track recording studio in Neal's Yard, Covent Garden, and a children's book, *Small Harry and the Toothache Pills*.

It was also clear that he was far and away the best actor in the Python group, able to take on a wide variety of roles and immerse himself in them. Unlike the others, who are always principally playing themselves, and cannot manage a straight role without the shadow of Python interfering, Palin can become unrecognisable when in character. 'He's the only actor among us,' says Terry Gilliam, 'the rest of us are just caricaturists.'

His acting skill is not an area Palin is keen to dwell on, preferring to explain his prolificness and breadth of ability. 'With our pattern of working, there's always another thing in the offing; so if you get a bit of clear time off from Python, you've got to work fast,' he explained in the eighties. 'I wrote my children's book when I was supposed to be on holiday in Ireland. And I started *The Missionary* out of sheer frustration that the Python film [*The Meaning of Life*] wasn't happening. Of course, it suddenly came together and I ended up going straight from filming *The Missionary* to filming *The Meaning of Life*.'

As well as a great deal of money, Monty Python brought Palin widespread public recognition, even in America, where fame is harder to achieve than anywhere in the world. People, he said, now grabbed him in the street and asked, 'You're Eric Idle, aren't you?' More importantly, fame, money and not a little power brought him professional status, and the wherewithal to develop his own projects outside the familiar Python stereotypes. As a result, from the end of Python onwards, he was involved with a plethora of films, plays and books.

If there was a progression in his work, it was away from surrealism and towards more conservative, and slightly more serious, material. There is little doubt that he was, and continues to be, hampered in his acting career by his normalness, a lightweight quality which meant that he is often considered too unexciting and undramatic to play leading men. This is thankfully not always the case, however. Terry Gilliam has dared to use him unconventionally, in *Brazil*, when he cast Palin as a baby-faced state torturer with a penchant for pulling out finger nails. And the Liverpudlian playwright Alan Bleasdale gave Palin's acting talent its full head in the TV series, *GBH*, in which Palin played a mild-mannered schoolmaster forced to fight back against an insane left-wing local politician. In Palin's writing, his first solo film script, *The Missionary*, was influenced not by Python but by the Ealing comedies. *American Friends*, which he co-wrote and starred in as his own great grandfather, was even less Pythonic – a straight and engaging romantic comedy.

But in 1973, at the tail end of Monty Python, these mature projects were still a long way ahead. It was in that year that Palin and Jones wrote a TV play called *Secrets*, which was run in a BBC drama series under the heading 'Black and Blue', the premise being that the humour would be either black or blue, or both. Warren Mitchell played the lead in this story, an antidote to Roald Dahl's *Charlie and the Chocolate Factory*. *Secrets* was about a chocolate factory where some workers who have fallen in a mixing vat of molten chocolate end up as fillings for confectionery. After favourable consumer reports from areas where the chocolates have been accidentally despatched, the company attempts to reproduce the effect with more conventional meat, but the taste simply isn't the same, and there are complaints; so the factory advertises for people willing to be cannibalised – for a price. There are plenty of volunteers, and the chocolates – tactfully promoted under the name Secrets as containing 'non-animal meat' – are best-sellers. The play ends with an advertisement which boasts: 'We let people into our Secrets'.

Secrets was well received by the critics, and the BBC took a satisfying number of angry telephone calls on the evening of transmission. The first step towards freedom from being a Python had been struck. At the same time as writing *Secrets*, Palin and Jones were working on a book aimed at teenage Python fans, *Bert Fegg's Nasty Book for Boys and Girls*, which was reissued over the years in updated versions under various names. The book was a jolly rehearsal for parodic, rather relentless, Python-meets-boys'-comic themes which would recur later in Palin's and Jones's work; 'The Famous Five Go Pillaging', 'Across the Andes by Frog' and a soccer tactics cartoon strip featuring The Supremes give some idea of the kind of humour they were now mining.

The highly acclaimed series *Ripping Yarns* followed soon after the *Bert Fegg* book, and effectively took the book's Edwardian schoolboyish ethos on to television. A BBC director, Terry Hughes, wanted the Jones–Palin team to make a series, and they came up with a script for a pilot, called *Tomkinson's Schooldays*. The programme was made entirely on film, which meant that it could be given a distinctive Palin–Jones 'look'. An enthusiastic reception for the one-off programme led to the commissioning of the *Ripping Yarns* series.

Each of the nine *Ripping Yarns* was different in mood and subject, the only unifying feature being the suggestion that their provenance was juvenile fiction of yesteryear. They had titles like 'Escape from Stalag IIB', 'Murder at Moorstones Manor', 'Across the Andes by Frog' (again), and, in the second series, 'Roger of the Raj' and 'Whinfrey's Last Stand'. Even though they were obviously send-ups, the respect for the past which Palin and Jones have was sufficient to ensure that the backgrounds and atmosphere were authentic, a verisimilitude which heightened the comedy.

For Palin in particular, this was the stuff of which his still vivid childhood was made. As he told Mick Brown in his *Penthouse* interview, he grew up reading stories with titles such as 'The Ducker of Denbigh', where life was a school called Rookwood and its greatest problem was whether the rotters of Belltowers could be bowled out before tea.

'The key to a lot of the stories,' Palin explained, 'is that people don't grow up in that sort of society. The public school bully simply became an officer in the regiment, where he could bully his men, and then an MP or a high sheriff where he could bully the world at large. So you actually got a sort of institutionalised bullying which was inculcated in people from school.

'Similarly, manners and discipline and restraint were also inculcated from a very early age. Now we may think they are wonderful things, but the point is that they have to be looked at and questioned in every time and period. When I go to restaurants, I have to put on a tie; I always feel so helpless when they make you wear a silly jacket just for the sake of it. I always wish I could encapsulate somehow just how I feel about the sort of idiocy, this total lack of communication between me and them. Of course, at the time you can never think of the really witty line. But with *Ripping Yarns* I can do that, and if people laugh so much the better.'

'Tomkinson's Schooldays', the first and one of the best received *Ripping Yarns*, was a lengthy classic reversal sketch, concerning a school bully who is on a salary to oblige parents who send their boys to the school for the specific purpose of being properly bullied. In 'Whinfrey's Last Stand', Palin starred as Gerald Whinfrey, a upper-class twit who blunders into adventures, and regularly saves the Empire twice before lunch and once after tea.

Probably the best *Ripping Yarn* was 'The Testing of Eric Olthwaite', the story of Eric (played, possibly with a smidgen of autobiographical passion, by Palin), a Yorkshire boy regarded by his sister as 'a boring little tit'. Eric's only interests are in rainfall figures and shovels ('Howard Molson's got a new shovel ... he's hung it next to his other one'), and he is so tedious that his family abandon him, even taking the outside toilet with them. Eventually, the rejected Eric becomes mayor of his own town.

The story, which was actually filmed in Durham because a suitably grim 1930s-looking town could not be found in Yorkshire, was told with an attention to detail by this time typical of Palin – as was the hero, a classic Palin creation in the downtrodden, Mr Pither/Mr Putey mould; it seems Michael had a thing about beleaguered men with two syllable surnames beginning in a P.

Ripping Yarns was shown on BBC 2 and, not being terribly splashy or glamorous, did not gain a particularly large audience, but did run to two brief series, which Palin was quite happy with. 'We were constantly up against a tight budget. What we were doing could have been done by the drama department at the BBC without batting an eyelid. But because it was done by the light entertainment department, we were always having to cut corners. I felt the *Ripping Yarns* always just missed what I wanted them to be.'

He was not, therefore, terribly bothered about the series ending after nine episodes. 'I'm not sorry, because I think we are in danger of running out of ideas – much as Monty Python ran out of ideas on television,' he told the *New York Daily News*. Despite the vaguely Pythonesque flavour, he elaborated, the weaving of the *Yarns* was an entirely different discipline. 'In Python everything is done by committee, but in *Yarns* you have to make all the decisions about scripts and casting yourself. I think some of the actors consider me to be a bit of a martinet, but it can't be helped.'

In 1977, Terry Gilliam asked Palin to play his innocent hero in the film *Jabberwocky*, in which, as a naive and dim-witted cooper's apprentice, he finds himself mistaken for a prince and called upon to rid the kingdom of a monster. Gilliam's typically dark and messy view of the period required the cast to smear themselves with mud and pick their way through slime and rubbish, the kind of ordeal which, as Hazel Pethig, the Pythons' costume manager, had previously noted of Palin, never succeeded in diminishing his cheerfulness.

The following year, Palin was sequestered by another Python, Eric Idle, for a sixty-five-minute TV parody of Beatlemania, *The Rutles*. The cast included, as further evidence of the Pythons' pulling power even five years after the end of Monty Python, Mick and Bianca Jagger, Paul Simon and George Harrison, who, disguised as a journalist, interviews a fictitious character – played by Michael Palin.

In 1980, the BBC gave Palin an opportunity to indulge his earliest and greatest delight – trains. His one-off contribution to their series *Great Railway Journeys of the World* seemed at the time more like a pleasurable diversion than the vocational move which it would eventually herald, however. At this stage in his travelogue career, Michael was only one among a number of loco-loving notables such as Michael Frayn and Ludovic Kennedy. From the BBC's point of view, he was also cheap; other nominated *Great Railway Journeys* involved travelling thousands of miles across the United States or Australia, but Palin was happy to make a simple journey from his Gospel Oak home in north London to Kyle of Lochalsh on the west coast of Scotland, from where he picked up an old station sign he had bought for the railway memorabilia collection he keeps at home.

The journey was highly significant in Palin's development, as it meant being almost entirely serious – as well as being himself – for the first time ever on TV. 'I'm having to play Michael Palin and it's a difficult role,' he commented. 'I keep getting my walk wrong, and I don't know what to do with my eyebrows.' But the programme was as revealing of the gentle, wistful nature of Palin's personality and his reverence for landscape as any interview. At times, the film had something of the languorous, rhythmic fluency of the acknowledged finest TV train journey, the BBC's *Metroland* with Sir John Betjeman.

'I spent hours train spotting when I was a boy in Sheffield,' he revealed to a world that, nearly twenty years ago, was not aware of this devastating biographical detail for one so revered and trendy. 'So making this was like a dream come true. I must have been the railways' ideal passenger when I was a kid. I could spend hours in the cold, happily munching sausage rolls, waiting for a train. The later it was, the more it added to the tension.

'I gave up my love for trains when I started to go out with girls,' he added, 'but now I would settle down happily with a nice steamer and raise three small shunters for the rest of my life.'

The projects piled up, one after the other, and none ever quite predictable. In November 1981, Palin and Jones indulged themselves a little by writing a thirty-minute lunchtime play, *Underwood's Finest Hour*, for the Lyric Studio, in Hammersmith, west London. The play was about a woman having a baby while England needs sixty-five runs in thirty-four minutes to beat the West Indies. The play featured six actors and the voice of John Arlott calmly announcing the unexpected triumph of Underwood holding his ground where Boycott had just failed. Critic Ned Chaillet in the *Daily Telegraph* found it 'not unamusing' but called it 'more a tribute to cricket – in the shape of Derek Underwood – than a try at theatre'.

In the same year, Michael collaborated again with Gilliam on the screenplay of *Time Bandits*, a 'sci-fi-horror-comic-children's' film, although Palin's appearance in this film was in a minor role as one of a pair of lovers who seem to have been conducting an affair through many historical eras. The filming was beset by disaster; some scenes shot in Morocco had to be reshot because someone had his thumb over part of the lens, and Ruth Gordon, who was to have played Mrs Ogre, broke her leg two weeks before shooting. Palin came up with the directorial brainwave of the film, by instructing John Cleese, in his role as Robin Hood, 'to behave like the Duke of Kent'. Cleese was royalty itself, going around with his hands behind his back, wearing a silly wig and saying: 'I see', 'How interesting', and his famous, 'So you're a robber? Jolly good. Have you met The Poor?'

At the same time, during the endlessly protracted run-up to the 1982 Python film *The Meaning of Life*, Palin wrote *Small Harry and the Toothache Pills*, a public reading from which in the lobby of the Lyttelton Theatre technically constituted his National Theatre debut. The book's dental theme was inspired by stories he told his three children in the car while speeding across France from Helen's sister's house there, to catch the cross-Channel ferry. 'I was interested in a children's book as I've never really grown up myself,' Palin said on publication day. 'I almost got round to it when I was twenty or twenty-two but it never really happened. Since then I've been regressing gently back to childhood.'

As a result of *Small Harry*, Palin fans learned that he has 'a love–hate affair with my dentist. I'd had a lot of treatment from him as I suffered from a condition of the gums usually prevalent among teenage girls. As far as I know it is the only symptom I have of becoming a teenage girl. Now I'm rather hooked on going to the dentist. He even advertised the *Life of Brian* film for me, saying, "Help Michael Palin pay his dental bills – see this film." '

Charming and possibly challenging as the children's book was, Palin made another more important breakthrough in the frustrating, inspiration-seeking time leading up to *The Meaning of Life*. His film-making ambitions were steadily increasing, and in 1982 he wrote, co-produced and starred in a film backed by George Harrison and Denis O'Brien, which he called *The Missionary*. It was the first truly Michael Palin film, and had a direct link to Ranmoor and his childhood, when he used to be fascinated by the macho missionaries who would give lectures at St John's Church about their adventures. The film also benefited from another of his childhood observations at St John's – that ministers of the church afforded great comic potential. 'They are a very fertile area,' he says. 'Everything they do is regulated by ceremony, strict rules and po faces which cry out for a joke or two.'

The film was the story of the Reverend Charles Fortescue – 'crack missionary and popular hero' – who went to Africa from Southampton in 1896 and, as the film opens, returns from a long stint proselytising in the African bush to find himself in an Edwardian England steeped in hypocrisy and social prejudice with a fiancée, a rich, beautiful, nymphomaniac lover – and responsibility for a refuge for twenty-eight fallen women. No wonder Palin toyed long and lovingly with the idea of calling the film *The Missionary Position*.

'I liked the idea of bringing an outsider, a missionary who had been in Africa for ten years, into this very settled, very stratified society in order to disrupt the spectacle slightly and turn it on its head,' Palin said. 'But I wouldn't want to judge the people of those times too harshly. I know the class system was so much stronger and there was much injustice ... but somehow we haven't much improved. We just exchange one sort of moral tyranny for another.'

In the meticulous research phase of *The Missionary*, Palin spent time in the British Library to research the history of prostitution. 'I didn't want to write the script from what may have been my own misconceived prejudices. I wanted to find out if there were any serious attempts at reform. But the research bore out my suspicions. The Edwardians treated prostitutes as wicked women. They considered it their job to clean them up with carbolic soap and prayers. Researching sexual habits is very fascinating. In fact,' he added, 'I don't think you ever really complete your researches on a subject like that ...'

Palin loved the challenge of writing a full-length feature film which already had the enthusiasm and backing – to the tune of £2 million – of George Harrison.

'George has a marvellous attitude to film-making,' says Palin. 'As soon as he gives his approval it's just a case of steaming ahead and doing it. You don't get the feeling he's constantly looking at script changes or the balance sheet.' Harrison was a founder Pythonophile, who sent a congratulatory telegram after the debut broadcast in 1969. He was later a devout *Ripping Yarns* fan. 'He and Denis said, "If you can come up with a screenplay which we think works, we'll finance it." I couldn't ignore an offer like that. We'd been working on the Python film, and that didn't seem to be getting anywhere, so I took some time off to think about ideas of my own. That was a deliberate decision. There are certain things I would write only in the Python group and there are certain things that Terry and I can do together really well. But what I wanted to find out was what I could do on my own, whether I could write more than just a five-or ten-minute sketch – and could sustain a story and characters.'

Before he could sustain them, however, it was necessary to come up with them. Inspiration came, not out of the blue, but out of a fiendish gale, whose teeth he ran into on one of his regular jogs over Hampstead Heath. With the characters and story sorted in his mind, the combination of acting and writing was both extremely important to Palin and excessively draining, especially as he admits to finding writing 'jolly hard work'.

'I don't think I'm a very good writer,' he insists. 'I'm quite good at writing funny lines and coming up with funny ideas, but I'd love to be as good at a film script as someone like Harold Pinter.' The script work for a grown-up film involved extreme discipline. 'With Python anything went – chickens, Zulu gynaecologists, you name it,' he says. 'But, although when I was writing the script for *The Missionary* several outlandish creations tried to force their way in, I firmly but kindly told them they could go.'

The spirit of Pythonic insanity seemed to be as alive in the hands of Palin alone as it had ever been. Even the prologue to the published version of *The Missionary*'s script – hardly a passage destined for mass consumption – crackled with polished gags. 'There had been many legendary white men in nineteenth-century Africa,' Palin wrote. 'There was "Mad Arnold" Frobisher who used to attack crocodiles for no reason at all. There was the Reverend Cyril Toogood who walked forty miles before breakfast every day, and died of starvation after three weeks. There was "Chief" Arthur Wallington, a solicitor from Weymouth who turned native and took the name Odaka Ohuru Na ("the solicitor from Weymouth")...'

The cast of *The Missionary* was impressive. It included Denholm Elliott, Trevor Howard, David Suchet, Phoebe Nicholls, Michael Hordern and Maggie Smith, with whom Palin formed a particular bond of admiration. It was a sufficiently prestigious cast list to attract interest for the film in America. Palin was a bit English and reticent about Columbia's desire to bill *The Missionary* as a sex comedy, preferring to see it as 'an elegant look at Edwardian morals and manners'. But he was soon persuaded, and realised that it needed to be packaged in a certain way for America. 'I could just see this couple in the Mid West reacting to that. "Gee, honey, what are we gonna do tonight?" "Well, we can either go to a rodeo, or go see 'an elegant look at Edwardian morals and manner." It just wasn't on,' he joked.

To a considerable extent, Palin was, at nearly forty, becoming rather more assertive than he had previously been. He believed some of the actors on *Ripping Yarns* regarded him as a tyrant, and was not greatly apologetic about it. Now, fairly satisfied by *The Missionary*, he was positively confident. 'I'm arrogant enough to feel there's the right balance in *The Missionary*, and I'm in control,' he said. 'Control is what writing it was all about, while still being able to work with a director and crew, giving them full rein. Artistic control is important, but beyond that I'm not interested in being a Führer.'

The Missionary, perhaps as a consequence of the more dominant mode Palin was switching into, was the cause of his famous – celebrated, indeed – loss of temper when he was interviewed on hot April afternoon by two wonderfully bumptious young Oxford undergraduates, Edward Whitley and John Alachouzos, who came to his house as part of a book they were researching on Oxford graduates. They had already seen people like John Mortimer and Indira Gandhi, and had just seen the newly released *The Missionary* at the Marble Arch Odeon.

Palin's fury, which culminated in him walking out of his own house practically sobbing, has intrigued journalists for years, and is frequently referred to by writers like Craig Brown and Richard Ingrams as a compelling reason for admiring Palin on the grounds that, far from being nice but dull, he actually has a healthy dose of ego and could even be, in the nicest possible way, slightly loopy. It was certainly an impassioned performance by Palin, who came out of the encounter for most people (including Whitley and Alachouzos) as the winner.

The book which came out in 1986 under the name of Whitley alone (he is now a highly successful author and biographer), was an amazingly sparky collection of interviews. The notorious Michael Palin chapter continues for several pages very interestingly and without a hitch – some of Palin's views from it on Oxford are reproduced in Chapter Four. Then things started spinning out of control.

'*The Missionary* was Michael Palin's first solo film made outside the umbrella of Monty Python,' Whitley wrote in his account in the book. 'I hadn't enjoyed it, and these are the last few minutes of the interview ...'

'Did you feel that *The Missionary* had the same quality of humour as *The Life of Brian*?' Alachouzos, a Balliol history student, asked.

'*The Life of Brian* was a bit harder than *The Missionary*,' Palin, still unaware what would soon happen, but sounding a little wary on the tape, responded. He explained that *The Missionary* 'had a rather more gentle quality to it, which was just telling a story. Brian was a series of sketches and observations abut life now as well as life then; I don't think *The Missionary* had quite that aim.'

Alachouzos ploughed on regardless. 'Because it had struck me,' he drawled, 'that the style of humour was out-of-date and rather slapstick.'

'I'm sorry you found it thus,' Palin replied, politely, but with an obvious edge creeping into his voice.

'That scene, for example,' Alachouzos continued, 'when you explain to your wife what a "fallen woman" is, and she asks if it's somebody who's broken their ankle. "No, my dear." Somebody who's broken their leg? How could you put that into the film?'

It was this question at which Palin finally flipped. 'Oh dear! I'm sorry. It's just that I've got to go,' he said. Whitley writes that he stood up and turned away. 'He suddenly wheeled back to me, shouting, "I mean, how can you ask a thing like that? What do you mean: how can I put it into the film? Because I happened to think it was funny, I thought it worked. You didn't, fair enough, but don't come here and ask me, how can I dare put something like that in a film? Honestly, that's the most pissing awful thing I've ever heard ... If you didn't like the film, you didn't like the film, but don't say, "How can you put it in there?" '

'He stuck his face right up to mine,' Whitley continued, 'so I could clearly see the veins jumping in his forehead. "Because I'm an imbecile, *because I'm no good at writing fucking comedy* – that's why I put it in there." Palin then walked out; "Right, I'm off. Cheerio," he said, adding as he clattered down the stairs, "I hope your thing comes out really well." '

As he ran down the stairs, the muffled sound is heard of Palin saying, 'You've got lots of interesting ideas there,' as if it were the rushed end of any everyday university tutorial. 'I realised that this was not one of his skits,' comments Whitley.

The next sound was of Palin's footsteps bounding back up again, and of Whitley lamely asking, 'Mr Palin ...' Palin by now is shaking with outrage as he clears up the coffee cups all three had been happily drinking from minutes before. The cups audibly rattle in his hands. 'Don't "Mister Palin" me,' he continues. 'I'm not a man who gets angry very often, but I find that you have been amongst the rudest of people I've ever had to talk to. You've just got your own boorish ideas ... I'm prepared to discuss things in a reasonable attitude, and I think there are lots of criticisms I would make, but to say to me, *"How can you put something like that in?"* What do you mean, how can I put it in? I don't know what you mean. I've got to go, so I'll just have to say goodbye.'

Again, Palin clatters down the stairs, muttering to the two students – rather sweetly under the circumstances – 'You can write me a nice letter or something.'

'I was left sitting in his house amongst the satirist's memorabilia,' Whitley concluded. 'Mr Palin, it seemed, was exempt from his own dictum: "I feel that there is very, very little that we shouldn't say or couldn't say about anybody at any time."'

Whitley, then an English Literature student, is now a very respectable, good-natured – and still slightly chastened – family man, the author of Nick Leeson's biography and collaborator on Richard Branson's autobiography. 'All the other people I interviewed kept their distance, really,' Whitley says today, 'because I was very young and when you are seeing John Mortimer etc., they have this great gravity about them. But Michael Palin was determined to undercut any sense of formality. He was very hip and groovy and friendly.'

He explains that he and Alachouzos wondered on the way back to Oxford whether the most ethical thing would be to erase the tape and pretend the curtailed interview had never happened. It did not occur to them that the cassette contained sufficient material to make Whitley famous – and to re-align Palin in the public mind in a rather better, even more human, light.

'I think we rather sheepishly put our things together and left,' Whitley recalls. 'We were so embarrassed because several of us were going off left, right and centre, and we thought we had just completely messed this one up. But then we decided that we wouldn't erase it. We got back to a dinner party. There were about twenty people in the room and we said, 'Look we've got this thing we think is rather extraordinary.' We put it on and people just couldn't believe it. They were stunned. There were a couple of interviews in the book, which finally came out about four years later, which caught people's attention, but that was one which amused Richard Ingrams, and he wrote some really funny things when he reviewed it for the *Spectator*. He chose it as his book of the year for '86.

'We thought we were being just very frank,' Whitley explains. 'Because he seemed such an approachable man, I thought we could tell him straight what we thought about it. I hadn't realised that, like all actors, you could criticise so far, but only so far. He was trembling. We felt utterly astonished. I can't remember if I did write to him. I think I might have. I hope I wrote to him anyway. I think I sent him a book in a rather tongue-in-cheek way, saying, here it is for better or worse. I didn't hear anything back, but I know a number of people have spoken to him about it since.

'I went into banking after Oxford, but when I started off being a journalist, I used to write a bit for the *Standard* and the *Telegraph* and go to those *Private Eye* lunches and things like that, and it came out there. Apparently, he was embarrassed. It was the one time that he has let himself go in public. He is obviously a nice guy, and I don't blame him for losing his rag, because I think we were obnoxious. We did have our own opinions, we weren't listening to him. We would have driven anyone mad. No, he probably shouldn't have reacted like that, but we were horribly cocky and arrogant and vile as well, so I have a lot of sympathy for him.'

Alachouzos, who is half Greek, now works abroad, and is even more embarrassed than Whitley about the interlude. 'We were just a couple of pretentious boys,' he says. 'We saw a film, we didn't like it, we were rude about it and he was very pleasant. It reflects worse on us than it did on him. Edward wrote it up in a particularly funny way, and that's fair enough, but I wouldn't make anything more of it. All these actors and comedians are quite sensitive people, and I don't think there is anything novel about that. If you basically go along to somebody's house and you tell them you think they've made a crap film, they have got every right to kick you out of their house. I am not very proud of the incident and I write it down to experience.'

Although Whitley's writing of the book, and the Palin interview in particular, were the beginning of his own success, he has never met Palin since. This is a good reason why, even fifteen years on, neither man was aware of a remarkable coincidence, which would amuse them equally: not only did both Whitley and Palin go to the same school, Shrewsbury; they were in the same famously humorous house there, Riggs. Only a decade and a half or so separated them.

9

Hollywood

Two years after *The Missionary*, in 1984, Michael was asked by Alan Bennett to play a very typical Palin role in the film *A Private Function*, as Gilbert Chilvers, a nice, meek chap – a chiropodist – driven to anti-social acts by an overbearing wife.

'I find that I am drawn to characters who are losers or failures, or at least appear to be,' he explained, not for the first time in his career. 'I find people like that more interesting than heroes, or the accepted archetype of what the successful person is supposed to be. I mistrust all that. I think it's far more important to know and understand people ... What appealed to me immediately about playing Gilbert is that they wanted me to do it straight and I did. Malcolm Mowbray [the director] kept on at me to be dull. Whenever I got out of line, he would say, "This man is not having a nice time – remember that."'

Palin's co-stars in *A Private Function* were Maggie Smith, again, as Joyce, Gilbert's horrific wife, and a pig, Betty. The film was set in Yorkshire in the middle of the black market boom of 1947, which was spawned by severe post-war rationing. A pig is being illegally reared by the respectable citizens of a small town for an important function which is private, but which civic dignitaries will be attending.

Palin was well aware of the dangers of being upstaged when acting with children or animals, but nobody had warned him about the special problems of acting with a pig. 'Alan Bennett said, "I want you to play the part of a chiropodist,"' Palin explains. '"The job might possibly entail some unpleasant work with a pig ..." but none of this put me off because I think Alan Bennett is one of the funniest writers of English comedy around. And to work opposite Maggie Smith – it's not the sort of thing one turns down ... I was trying to work on a script, a sort of period piece about polar explorers like Scott. It was a comedy about being stuck on an ice floe, but it wasn't coming along.'

It wasn't easy, according to Michael's account. 'The pigs had been trained to a certain level by a company called Intellectual Animals, but even so they probably added a week to the shooting ... The trouble with all of them is that pigs keep falling asleep. I mean you can't stand over them and say, "Come on, love, just give us another hour."'

The pig was quite bright by all accounts. 'She didn't do any philosophising that I noticed,' says Palin. 'But by pig standards she was a bright pig ... a twelve O-level pig, I'd say. Still, at the end of the day, she was just a pig. We were told that without training there was no way you would have got her through the front door of a house, never mind trotting up and down stairs and stealing fruit from a bowl on the table – a fruit bowl that was liberally sprinkled with pig pellets by the way.

'The pig was very nervous, especially at the beginning. She'd come on the set and have a crap straight away. Everyone would laugh and that would make her do another one. It was as regular as clockwork. You know, a bit like a train. Every twenty minutes it would happen again. Which meant another job for Andrew, the boy who followed Betty around with a bucket ... She got a lot better as time went on. But it must have been pretty odd for her ... the clapperboards were going, I was running up and down stairs in my underpants and Maggie was running around screaming.'

While being interviewed by an American journalist about *A*

Private Function over a modish salad in New York's Russian Tea Rooms, Palin let slip a sensational revelation. 'There were not one, not two, but three pigs,' he told Desmond Ryan, movie critic of the *Philadelphia Inquirer*. (Palin's talk of pigs 'commanded the attention of the waiter, a passing busboy and nearby eaters', according to Ryan.) 'And the only way to get a pig to nuzzle your foot is to douse your shoes in sardine oil. When you see the pig following me around, it's not for my personality or my looks. It's the sardine oil. And the smell! You have to throw away your shoes afterwards.

'The three pigs we had – Betty One, Two and Three – were very different. Only one of them could act. That was Betty One, but she had black marks on her bum that we had to keep covering with make-up so you couldn't tell her from the other two,' he continued, Ryan noted, 'to a now-rapt audience in the restaurant that, as Hollywood's East Coast watering hole, has served more than its share of hams'.

'Getting Betty into a car was very hazardous. You should have seen us on this little B road in North Yorkshire late at night, everyone looking at their watches because the crew went on to double-time after midnight. She was pretty hard to shift, being so heavy, but I managed to get her into the front seat and then I got into the driver's side. It was all a bit of a tight squeeze and the pig panicked and dived straight across me, her right front trotter going straight into my crutch. She was pinned down there and I was trying to get this trotter off my privates, and everyone was yelling at me not to panic ... The pig, screeching like a 100cc motorbike with its clutch slipping, eventually calmed down.'

Although he found five weeks of concentrated pig smell pretty revolting, Palin still claims, for the publicity at least, to like pigs – but admitted that nothing would put him off eating pork. 'I'm a pork freak. It's my favourite food and I'm afraid it remained so throughout the film,' he said. 'I was a bit embarrassed eating bacon butties the first few days when the pig was walking by me. But then I thought about how much I love bacon, and bacon comes from pigs, and so I must love pigs too because I give them a very good home. There was one scene at the beginning, when I had to carry a carcass downstairs that had been hidden from the food inspector in this old chap's bed. By the end of the day the meat, which had been fresh in the morning, had really begun to go. I became a vegetarian for at least a day and a half after that. Then it was back to the bacon butties.'

A Private Function had a royal premiere in November 1984 in front of Princess Anne at the Odeon in London's Haymarket, but still Palin did not expect the film to become a blockbuster, because it required the audience to know something about the recent, but curiously forgotten, austerity years in Britain – a period which interested him because he lived in it, but was so un-sexy that it was rarely used as a background to a film.

One of the main careers Michael had considered at Shrewsbury, and later at Oxford, was journalism. He was perfectly suited for it, and wrote, with Robert Hewison, a little column in the university newspaper. It was a piece of limited, yet worthwhile, imagination, then, that found him in 1984 after *A Private Function*, as the subject of a Channel 4 documentary, *Palin's Column*, in which he undertook to write four weekly newspaper columns for the *Isle of Wight County Press*.

Palin's efforts were welcomed by most readers, according to the newspaper's editor, Peter Hurst. 'Michael Palin is so well known, so popular, and although he tried to play down the celebrity side he was instantly recognisable. The island is a hothouse of controversy so nothing pleases everyone, but generally there were eight-to-two in favour of the idea.'

Palin became convinced that Hurst wasn't among the eight; 'I got the feeling he was not too happy about television people coming and mucking about with his paper.' Even less happy was Palin himself. He was totally thrown that here, in Hurst, was a man seemingly impervious to his charm. It washed over and around him but Hurst was made of too stern a stuff to relax his guard. He was polite but distant. Every attempt to draw him out was rebuffed. Hurst was not going to play the game.

Palin threw himself nevertheless into the island's cream teas, Morris dancing, pet cemeteries and gossip about fossilised dinosaur droppings with every appearance of enthusiasm. He stayed at eighty-seven-year-old Dorothy Wright's B&B while filming and the two were impressed by each other. She called him 'Fairy toes' because he was so light on his feet. 'She ran her guesthouse and her life the way she wanted,' Palin says. 'She was very much like my mother in that way. She liked washing my socks and preparing the breakfast. All I could do for her was to place her bets at the betting shop – and she usually won.'

'I have always thought that the detail in people's lives is more interesting than the broad picture,' he explained. 'I suppose that what I'm trying to do in all sorts of vaguely artistic ways is to celebrate the differences in people. And when you look at any community under the microscope, people are a lot more different than you think.'

During work on the series, Palin was accused of cheating in the Isle of Wight Conker Championships. Charged with having doctored his conker, Palin said: 'Yes, it was pickled for me by a firm of conker consultants. I'd rather not say exactly what they did. But there were no illegal substances, no steroids, although I believe vinegar might have been applied. It might even have been lightly baked.'

The following year, he was anxious to clear his name. 'The great conker debacle,' he revealed, 'was a set-up', invented by the production team to pep up the occasionally flagging narrative of the series. It also provided many column inches of free publicity.

In 1985, Palin's film biography took another of its periodical quirkier turns when he played an inept adulterer in a thirty-minute short directed as a first-time effort by a photographer, Eva Sereny, and called *The Dress*. The film was shown in the UK with *Beverly Hills Cop*, so at least had the rare benefit for a whimsical little British film of a captive audience. In it, Palin co-starred with Phyllis

Logan as a conspiratorial family chap caught by his wife while buying a dress for his mistress.

'I don't think it is an antidote to adultery. I certainly didn't undertake it as a morally improving text,' Palin said of *The Dress*. 'I think it just makes the point that sex is important in marriage.' Palin made *The Dress* as the result of a conversation with Sir David Puttnam: 'We have lunch on the odd occasion,' Michael says. 'Just to catch up on the gossip. He said I'd always been interested in doing a serious role and suggested I do this. I liked the idea of doing a short story on film. It was made in just seven days. It was a bit of a rush and very tiring. When it was over I knew how God felt on the seventh day.'

He enjoyed the experience of being serious on film, but not whole-heartedly. 'I like the idea of acting without trying to be funny, but even at forty-one you still sometimes feel the urge for foolishness and silliness.' *The Dress* did supply Palin with one of his more embarrassing moments a couple of years after it was made and, for the most part, forgotten. 'Apart from *A Fish Called Wanda*, most of the films I've made aren't suitable to be shown on airlines,' he says. 'But I was coming back from New York once and tucking into my meal, when I looked up at the screen and there I was. It was a short film that I made called *The Dress*, in which I play a randy husband with a mistress. It gets quite steamy and ends up with a bed scene. I felt this awful embarrassment and looked around but hardly anybody was watching it, so no one connected me with the film. It was a very strange moment.'

In *East of Ipswich*, which Palin made the following year, he was back firmly in nostalgia mode, an area of film making he is aware can be a bit of a ghetto, 'a little, irrelevant nostalgic niche' as he puts it, but could not during his thirties and forties seemingly avoid. He complained at the time of *East of Ipswich* that when he did something contemporary, he found himself forced into judgements, and he didn't want to use his work to make moral points.

East of Ipswich was one of the few films Palin has written and not appeared in, although in one sense of course he is very much in it. The film is heavily autobiographical most of the time, but diverges in quite important ways from his own boyhood holidays in Southwold. Palin was especially anxious at the time to emphasise that not everything that happens to his gawky seventeen-year-old hero is drawn from life – particularly the part near the end where he has sex in a field at night with a fearsomely rampant Dutch exchange student.

The father in the film has close similarities to Ted Palin, being brittle-tempered and dragging him round local churches when the boy would rather be sizing up the local girls. And the boarding house, with its dragon landlady, is very like the guesthouses where the teenage Palin and his parents spent summer holidays in the 1950s.

Even the weather was nostalgic for the filming. *East of Ipswich* was shot in Southwold during a cold, wet June spell in 1986. 'A pretty mad thing to do, trying to capture the English summer,' says Palin. 'Even the dogs were wearing overcoats.' The filming also gave Palin an excuse to spend time with his mother, who still lived in Southwold. His father had died of Parkinson's Disease in 1977, but Mary Palin lived on until 1991.

Although it was delightfully light and easy on the mind, *East of Ipswich* did have a serious theme, which Palin describes as 'the terrible anxieties of a boy growing up who is not allowed to grow up' – through parental disapproval as well as his own ignorance.

As if to demonstrate his inability to write anything contemporary without having a burdensome judgement to deliver, Palin wrote his next film, *Number 27*, for BBC 1 when he realised he profoundly hated the scourge of those late eighties days, yuppies. *Number 27* starred Nigel Planer, Helena Michell and ninety-year-old Joyce Carey – who (in a delightfully Palinesque mixture of showbusiness, train spotting and nostalgic detail) was the lady behind the railway bar in David Lean and Noël Coward's 1945 film, *Brief Encounter*. *Number 27* was a story, Palin said, about 'bulldozers – mechanical and human – greed, incompetence and car telephones.' The film starts comically but the humour gets blacker and blacker as a team of property developers try every trick they know to force a lovely old lady out of her home. The house – number 27 – is inconveniently sited in the middle of an area of East London which the developers want to yuppify.

A Fish Called Wanda, which nearly coincided with *Number 27*, was almost at the opposite end of the film scale from *The Dress*; this was a film which no airliner in the world seemed capable of taking off without. Although it was, of course, entirely John Cleese's project, and made Cleese an undisputed international film star, it also made Michael Palin an even bigger name than he had previously been, and earned him an Oscar for Best Supporting Actor, despite his having had only a handful of lines. Additionally, thanks to Cleese's generosity, *Wanda* provided Palin with a huge amount of money.

Such was Cleese's desire to make the *Wanda* team as much like a family as he could, the stars – Palin, Jamie Lee Curtis and Kevin Kline – were all put on a proportion of the film's profits. In Hollywood, such a deal is regarded as a thoroughly bad bet for an actor, and the Americans in particular joined the cast largely to be in what looked like being a wacky English comedy rather than to make money. However, *A Fish Called Wanda* turned out to be the most successful British film of all time, surpassed only years later by *Four Weddings and a Funeral*, so Palin and the other principals all earned handsomely from it.

From a purely emotional point of view, the most striking feature for Palin of *A Fish Called Wanda* was that his part was as a chronic stammerer. This was not a mere co-incidence, of course. Palin and Cleese had been friends for nearly twenty-five years when Cleese was writing the film, and he knew all about Michael's father's appalling stammer. He consulted Palin in detail about the mechanics of stammering and finally asked him to play it. 'I wouldn't have dreamed of doing it while my father was alive,' Palin admits.

The film was strongly criticised in the United States as insensitive to stutterers, a charge that Palin, in another of his rare fits of pique, calls 'very stupid'. He has no remorse about the role, nor, he has said, will he ever forgive Michael Shamberg, the producer of *Wanda*, for apologising to an organisation for his part in the film.

Pythonesque as it may seem, Palin's performance as Ken in *Wanda* actually promoted a demonstration by militant stammerers in Los Angeles. Ted Palin was, at long last, and by the most indirect route imaginable, making his mark on the world. The *Los Angeles Times* reported on the demo: 'Outraged by the "cruel and demeaning" treatment of a character who stutters in the Academy Award-nominated comedy *A Fish Called Wanda*, members of the Orange County chapter of the National Stuttering Project picketed Tuesday outside the offices of MGM in Culver City. During the peaceful two-hour demonstration, ten members of the non-profit self-help organisation carried signs that said, "Wanda Insults People Who Stutter" and "Educate, Not Humiliate".'

Kevin Kline's character, Otto, was 'very cruel and demeaning', to Palin's Ken, according to the leader of the protesters, Ira Zimmerman, a redundant aerospace worker. 'I've been stuttering most of my life – almost forty-four years – and I have never heard more people laugh when I stutter than since the movie came out,' Mr Zimmerman was quoted as saying. 'If this is happening to me, it's certainly happening to other people who stutter, and it's certainly happening to youngsters who stutter.'

Another demonstrator, Annie Bradberry, told the *LA Times* reporter that whenever she brought up the movie people began to mimic Palin's stuttering. She had waited until *Wanda* was out on video before seeing it – 'I could not sit in a theater with people laughing at it,' she said. 'It makes me angry because I think of the children out there. Now that the movie is on video, it's into the hands of children, and children are basically cruel to other children with handicaps.'

'The worst thing about the film,' added another member of the stutterers' group, 'is the ending, where all of a sudden Ken's stuttering goes away after he runs over Otto with a steamroller. In other words, what was behind his stuttering, one could assume from that, was a lot of repressed feelings and lack of self-confidence and so on. The point we want to make more than anything else is that people who stutter are no more repressed, nervous or shy than anyone else.'

Mr Zimmerman delivered a list of three slightly optimistic demands to MGM. His group wanted the company to: 1) 'Prominently display with future showings of the movie a disclaimer, written last fall by *Wanda* producer Michael Shamberg, saying he does not want audiences to draw any negative inferences about people who stutter.' 2) 'Begin working on a movie that accurately portrays the problem of stuttering, portrays the appropriate listener response and emphasises the achievements of people who stutter,' and 3) 'Assure that the portrayal of handicapped people is accurate and preserves their self-esteem by obtaining medical and professional consultation on all future MGM movies.'

The *LA Times* also spoke to Shamberg, who said he was sympathetic to the demonstrators' concerns. He added, however, that 'for me, anything is fair game for comedy. I think *Wanda* was portraying one stutterer humorously, and it wasn't about stutterers per se.'

Proving that clouds really do have silver linings, Ira Zimmerman went on, emboldened by the *Wanda* demo, which he acknowledges as his 'coming out', to carve out a niche for himself as Hollywood's leading authority on stammering. Working from an office which on its wall has a framed letter of apology from Kevin Kline, he is the joint author of a brochure sent to all studios, 'Guidelines for the Portrayal of Stuttering in Movies and TV', and was hired in 1992 as a technical consultant for TV's *Quantum Leap*, working with the star Scott Bakula, who was playing a character who stuttered in one episode. The episode later received an award from the National Council on Communicative Disorders. And thanks to Ted Palin's original stammer, as portrayed by Michael and protested about by Mr Zimmerman, the speech defect has received its ultimate accolade; the *LA Times* now refers routinely to 'the stuttering community'.

Outside the stuttering community, meanwhile, *A Fish Called Wanda* did Michael no end of good. The only downside to the film was that, for a while, he grew to hate eating in restaurants because fans would so often try to imitate the scene where chips are stuck up his nose. It irritated him, he said, 'because it is so unoriginal'.

Although the stammering argument also annoyed Palin, he was by no means unaware of the issue and, in his own, more practical, way, ensured that *A Fish Called Wanda* did a great deal of good for people back in England with the affliction. In March 1993, he opened the Michael Palin Centre, Britain's first specialist unit for stammering children. The centre treats children as young as two and a half, while therapy does not normally start before the age of seven. Palin contributed money to the unit, which is off Farringdon Road in London, as well as his name, although the chief sponsor was the businessman Gerald Ronson, whose youngest daughter, Hayley, stammered.

Michael explained at the time that he was anxious to dispel the idea that he regards stammerers as figures of fun. 'The image of the stammerer is as solemn, taciturn and humourless. This is bull,' he said. 'My father had a lot of words to say but cruelly life frustrated him. We would pray that something would change and the words I know he wanted to say would flow without hindrance.' Palin and the actor Derek Nimmo, who stammered as a child, both became vice-presidents of the Association for Research into Stammering.

He told the press that he had been upset by criticism of his stammering role in *Wanda* four years earlier. 'It's probably better to show it than pretend it doesn't exist. Hundreds of thousands of children and adults suffer – but therapy works. It can be alleviated to the point where it's almost unnoticeable. Many people do not realise Winston Churchill had a stammer – one of the great orators of the twentieth century. If the association of my name with this centre helps to raise awareness and support, it will be one of the best things I have ever done with my life.'

Palin's next film, which he conceived and co-wrote in 1991, was even more deeply personal than *East of Ipswich*. In the new film, *American Friends*, Michael played his own great-grandfather, the Reverend Edward Palin, after being inspired by reading his 120-year-old diary. In this, the Palin ancient had chronicled his love affair with a seventeen-year-old American he met while on a Swiss walking holiday.

The diary had found its way into his attic several years previously, when Michael was contacted by a distant cousin in the west country, who felt the Revd Palin's effects should be in the care of the senior surviving Palin male heir.

'My sister and I drove down to Cirencester and collected a big, unwieldy package,' he recounted in an interview with *You Magazine*. 'Inside was a collection of photographs in peeling frames, chunky devotional books in leather with brass clasps, ledgers, account books, some First World War medals and assorted notebooks. After cursory examination they ended up in the attic cupboard as I raced through the country doing *Great Railway Journeys* and scribbling down ideas for a film called *Time Bandits*.

'When several years and projects later we had to clear the attic cupboard for plumbing reasons, I took down the dusty parcel and began to sift through in more detail. Much of the material seemed to have belonged to a prolific but undiscriminating Victorian bachelor, a man obsessed with lists, who wrote excruciating heroic poetry and could knock off a sonnet or two in Greek or Latin. The least conspicuous of the notebooks, unmarked and unlined, contained a diary which began, "Ragatz 1859. How I got there." I read for a while but couldn't sustain interest in the detailed weather observations, the dates and distances, and thumbnail portraits of large rocks.'

Another several years passed before Palin thumbed through the diary again. 'I persevered,' he explained, 'and almost at the end of the diary, stumbled on the moment when Edward Palin, my great-grandfather, first stumbled upon young Brita. Stumbled and rapidly fell.'

Edward Palin, further research discovered, was one of the most brilliant divinity dons of his generation, the vice-president of St John's College, Oxford, and a man with all the glittering prizes of academia ahead of him – until he met Brita, who was a New Jersey resident of Irish descent.

At the end of that holiday he went back to Oxford determined to become a married man. But when he announced to the college authorities that he hoped Brita would become his bridge, they refused to change the strict rules on dons being bachelors. He was left with no option. He had to leave his job. Edward Palin married Brita in Paris six years later, and ended up contentedly installed as the vicar of Linton, in Herefordshire. The couple lived happily ever after, and raised seven children, the eldest of whom, Edward, became a Norfolk doctor. His son was born in 1900 and, forty-three years later, he in turn produced Michael.

'It was absolutely marvellous discovering this little black book. Like opening a window in a very dark room,' Palin says. 'I thought then, it's a good story, and it seemed more interesting because it happened to my own ancestor. What I wanted to try and do was improvise what might have happened between him meeting the girl and marrying her six years later ... I remember mentioning it to Eric Idle in a St John's Wood restaurant in June 1986 and he instantly said, "You should make a film of that."'

Idle recognised the basis for a charming film, but what most enchanted Palin were the quite spooky parallels he spotted between himself and his ancestor. Michael also succumbed to his first love and married her. He also likes to take walking holidays alone, with a notebook as sole companion. 'I even keep a diary at home to keep tabs on what I see and do, otherwise I think the days will just disappear off the face of the earth,' he explained. 'What I couldn't put out of my mind was that I was a product of their relationship. Somewhere in my genes was Brita's Ireland and Edward's Oxford, and that was a good feeling, because theirs was almost certainly a happy and fulfilled partnership.'

The funding for the film, which was eventually released in 1990, was raised in Britain. Once the studios knew Palin was to play the lead, there would have been no problem getting backing from America. He held out, though, because he did not want to see his heritage turned into Hollywood schmaltz. 'I could have taken American money but I'm afraid that would have meant American interference,' he says.

Potential backers inevitably wanted more humour and Hollywood stars to attract finance for *American Friends*. Palin stuck by his original concept and his chosen actress, Connie Booth ex-wife of John Cleese, whom he wanted to play the older companion Brita was travelling with when Edward Palin met her. With the project becoming dangerously close to being an obsession, he finally, after many obstacles, worked out a deal with an independent British company, MCEG Virgin Vision.

A little-know, New York-born actress, Trini Alvarado, played Michael's great-grandmother-to-be after Palin searched long and hard, auditioning dozens of young American actresses. When asked by the *Washington Post* how he settled on Alvarado for his love interest, Palin laughed, and replied rather oddly, 'I can't tell you that, it's just so disgusting. It's appalling. I arrived in New York, had a few drinks, and I can't talk about it.' Palin immediately knew she was the one, he admitted, wined and dined her, and bombarded her agent with calls until she accepted.

'She is a very good actress but she also looks right – very period, with her dark hair and pale skin,' he said. Alvarado finally said yes, not least because, as she said, 'I have always been a Palin fan. I love Monty Python, and Michael bought me a very good lunch.'

Palin co-wrote the script of *American Friends* with the director Tristram Powell, the son of Anthony. It fictionalised the Revd Palin's story, turning Michael's great-grandfather into Francis Ashby, an ambitious, conscientious scholar at St John's College. Brita and her older companion, who she was in Switzerland with, became Miss Caroline Hartley (played by Booth) and Miss Elinor Hartley (Alvarado).

American Friends won the 1991 Writers' Guild award for Best

Screenplay, although the critical response to the project to which Palin had given his greatest film-making passion to date was warm rather than effusive. *The Times* described the film as 'this attractive if languorous romance . . . under the weight of Victoriana, the slender story sometimes slows to a halt and buckles; while Palin himself, bereft of his impish Monty Python twinkle, proves insufficiently robust an actor to cut through the blanket of refinement. Yet the film survives, just about, on good taste and charm.' The *Independent's* critic wrote: 'Michael Palin's film is something of a gentleman's water-colour, pleasant and quietly skilled rather than hilarious or highly charged . . . It is a real achievement to have made a film about Victorian England which trades neither in knowing smut nor fuzzy Imperial nostalgia, and admirers of Palin's *East of Ipswich* mode will not be let down.'

American reaction was more upbeat. The *Boston Globe* enthused: 'Michael Palin's *American Friends* is a film of endearing warmth, delicacy and grace, plucked from his family tree . . . The film's honesty hardly precludes wit and, while it never makes the mistake of filtering the nineteenth century through the twentieth, it's more than just scented, nostalgic time travel. Its gentle tone and wry humor never conceal the decorous but smug and ugly misogyny at work in Oxford in the nineteenth century, and while more concerned with affectionate celebration of Ashby's response to it than with being a message film, *American Friends*, in its restrained way, nails it.'

American Friends was not universally well-received, however. The critic Tom Hutchinson wrote in the *Mail on Sunday*, for example: 'It's the kind of plummy period-piece which the past satirists of Monty Python would have squeezed mercilessly . . . Although I disliked *A Fish Called Wanda*, I prefer him having chips stuffed up his nose. Better watchable vulgarity than well-mannered, well-meaning waxworks.'

Back-to-back with *American Friends*, Michael acted – mutton chop whiskers swiftly shaved off – in a vastly different TV film, Alan Bleasdale's *GBH*, a six-part drama series for Channel 4. Palin played Jim Nelson, the headmaster of a school for maladjusted children in Manchester. '*GBH* is a breakthrough because it is the first contemporary thing I've done,' Palin said. 'It's an honest appraisal of Alan's attitude to socialism. He believes in a world in which the rich look after the poor but he's very disillusioned after what he's seen in Liverpool.'

For a lengthy slice of 1996, John Cleese's *Fierce Creatures*, the follow-up to *A Fish Called Wanda*, reunited Palin with Cleese, Kevin Kline and Jamie Lee Curtis. It was a long and eagerly awaited movie, in which Palin played 'Bugsy' Malone, the garrulous (as a respite from stammering) insect house keeper at a fictional English zoo.

The original comedy notion of a zoo which permitted only dangerous animals was hatched and written as an extended sketch by Palin and Jones as far back as 1967, when it was turned down by the BBC as a *Comedy Playhouse*. Whether the BBC was being stuffy or prescient all those years ago is hard to tell, but in 1997 *Fierce Creatures* met with a sadly low-key response – indeed, was pretty much a flop.

Palin and Jones had all but forgotten their early idea, which centred on casting Cleese as a Mr Burster who, Palin explains, 'hated all small, furry animals, and wanted a zoo full only of killers'. Cleese, with his famously capacious memory, forgets nothing, and phoned Jones nearly twenty-five years later to ask if he and Michael would mind him using the Mr Burster sketch.

In the publicity for *Fierce Creatures*, Palin said he was delighted to contribute to the new film. According to Terry Jones, however, interviewed by journalist Sue Summers for a fine investigative article in the *Sunday Telegraph* on the troubled birth of *Fierce Creatures*, Palin's instant reaction was a little less benign. 'John rang me up about six years ago and said he had a way of extending the idea if we weren't doing anything with it,' said Jones. 'When I told Michael, he was furious and said, "Didn't you talk money?" But I was always sure John would see us right, as it were, and he has been fairly generous.'

Fierce Creatures was eventually made by two directors and had to wait a year – much, although not all, of the delay caused by Michael's travelling commitments – for a new final third or so to be shot. 'It was clear there was something wrong,' Palin admits. 'Possibly it was the fact that all the main characters had been killed off by carnivores halfway through the film. We thought it could be corrected by editing, then John decided we had to reshoot and do some serious restructuring.'

It is a measure of the kaleidoscopic range of Palin's work that nobody ever knows quite how to describe him. Is he an actor, a comedian, a novelist, a travel journalist? He has always chosen to describe himself as a writer, and always ensured that when passports still carried a job description, writer was what was entered in his. Comedian was the last thing he wanted to be labelled as, even though he is known above anything as a funny man, and John Cleese (who requested Michael Palin as his luxury on *Desert Island Discs* in 1997) has described him as one of the funniest ideas people he knows.

Although he admits occasionally to being prone to depression, Palin is one of those rare funny men who is amusing most of the time in private. He kept his children reliably in stitches for much of their youth, but his thoughtful, serious side is never far beneath the surface. His taste in books and films tends more towards the serious than the comic, and he is far from being a student of comedy, believing strongly that it does not need to be didactic or provocative, nor have any ulterior motive other than to make people laugh. This is not to suggest he does not love comedy. He idolises Spike Milligan, and loves Woody Allen, whom he cites as an example of a comedian who succeeds through intelligence and honesty.

'But the things that do most often make you laugh are telling observations that relate to real life,' he maintains. 'Take something like the Alan Ayckbourn plays, which are fairly neutral, but make me laugh a lot. They do not set out to provoke or disturb or make any significant point about human relationships and how they ought to be, but while you're laughing you realise that what is making you laugh are clever observations about real situations – you are seeing something in a different way.'

Lenny Bruce is another favourite. 'He was going into very danger-ous areas – race, drugs, fears about Jews and, when he pulled it off, it was great because the laughter was cathartic. It's a terrific thing if you can make someone laugh about something which is serious and sacred, because very often those taboo subjects are the ones that need to be discussed the most.

'I do take things quite seriously myself,' he has explained, 'but at the same time I find that, with people who take things too seriously, I tend to get slightly worried in their presence; people who have certain areas of their life that they cannot laugh about, be it their marriage or politics or whatever – that's where I tend to part company with them. You should be able to laugh at anything and everything if you want to, without being accused of being an insen-sitive maniac.'

Palin's post-Python workaholism has been nurtured since the early days by the Pythons' joint business organisation, a studio/office complex called Prominent Studios in Delancey Street, Camden Town. Here, the Pythons continue even today to hold board meetings to discuss the administration of the millions they still earn from their old work, and to allocate funds and backing to new projects. Prominent Features, one of the many companies under the same roof, has been the umbrella under which four of the Pythons' individual films have prospered – *American Friends*, *A Fish Called Wanda*, Terry Gilliam's *The Adventures of Baron Mun-chausen* and Terry Jones's *Eric the Viking*.

Palin finds the continuing existence of the Python organisation an enormous comfort and support. 'We went out on a limb but as part of Monty Python,' he says. That connection with his old life as a Python made him feel less isolated than he might otherwise have been. 'I wasn't responsible, I didn't have to make those mega-decisions. Nowadays people say, "Michael, what do you want to do?", "Michael, name your terms". Well, you can't have control and a quiet life.'

Sporadic ego clashes down the years have not soured the fun of the Pythons' decades of working more or less together. 'Whenever we have a meeting, we say, "We should have a snooker table, we should have fruit machines, videos," so we can all sit around like a rather luxurious British Legion Club for ageing comedians,' Palin joked to journalist Minty Clinch, 'but then the accountants say the space is worth X thousand pounds a minute so we can't afford it. Still, it's a nice place.'

The Pythons Palin sees most are Jones and Gilliam, though he has spent more time with Cleese in the past decade through working on *A Fish Called Wanda* and *Fierce Creatures*. Eric Idle spends most of his time abroad. Graham Chapman, of course, died in 1989. Still, the others are all good friends or, at any rate, Michael thinks they are, which may only be a tribute to his niceness.

'Graham's death made us realise that there was a friendship between us, not all-pervading but based on mutual respect,' Palin confided further in Clinch. 'I miss Graham an awful lot. I was with him when he died, which I've never done before. I don't know if he was conscious but I talked to him about the things he liked to hear – projects going wrong, things like not being able to raise the money for *American Friends*. I knew he'd love that. In a sense he was the oddest of all of us, a man of science and medicine and a wonderful defuser of sacred cows.'

Will there be more Michael Palin films, or has he finally wearied of the tiresome movie world after the struggle to get *American Friends* made, and the *Fierce Creatures* fiasco? Friends of Palin suggest that he has indeed become disillusioned with films, and we may wait a very long time before seeing another. With more than £4 million reportedly to his name, he insists he will make no more travel documentaries. And he has repeatedly said of late, by way of a clue to where his mind is dwelling, that he regards the novel as the highest art form of all. Palin loves writing: 'It is the nearest thing to whispering in someone's ear,' he has said.

Two of his latest projects have been a West End play and a novel. Palin's play, *The Weekend*, opened at London's Strand Theatre in May 1994 to disappointing critical response. The play was actually written in 1980, and now marked Palin's West End debut. But the late Jack Tinker of the *Daily Mail* was disappointed: 'Buried somewhere deep inside Michael Palin's first full-length stage drama there's a fascinating play struggling to get out,' Tinker wrote. 'It hammers loudly on its coffin lid just as Mr Palin prepares to lay it to rest with the final curtain.'

Palin has spoken a lot about how *The Weekend*, a living-room comedy that develops a dark side, relates to his father, his parents' marriage and his own character. The massively popular Richard Wilson starred in the play as the cantankerous Stephen, and Angela Thorne played his long-suffering wife, Virginia. It is fascinating, perhaps, that, back in Sheffield, schoolfriends of Palin had likened Ted Palin to Wilson's Victor Meldrew character long before *The Weekend* appeared.

'It's about my father, I suppose,' Palin said of the play and Wilson's portrayal of Stephen. 'He, like Stephen, was educated at Cambridge and was successful during the 1920s. Then, I think, something happened, with the Depression, another world war, the austerity years, bringing up two children. Things did not work out the way they were "supposed to" for someone from his background. There was a bitter edge to him. I don't know the answers. I've created a fictional situation to work through the questions I wanted to ask.'

Virginia shared qualities with Mary Palin. 'She just keeps going,' he explains, 'and has her own life in a sort of watertight compartment. I think that's probably how my mother coped with living with a man like that.' In writing *The Weekend*, Palin was reconsidering that relationship: 'How a love affair turned into a combative stand-off between two people; how understanding turned to lack of understanding; how a marriage that had become a kind of imposition, nevertheless survived . . . It's a very eloquent play about non-communication'.

Palin enjoyed the disciplines of a playwright as he followed his work through the rehearsal period, led by director Robin Lefevre, and a lengthy tour before its West End opening. 'After all the performing, it's been kind of odd being the writer, but I've quite liked being the figure sitting at the back of the room. I became fairly fussy about where the pauses go in a line and I'd get a bit possessive and fight for certain things including some which have gone. But it's been a very genteel battle, nothing like the writing sessions on Python. They made this seem like a week in a health farm.'

Jack Tinker did not dismiss the play completely: 'Far from supplying a neat ending, it leaves one going out into the night regretting what an interesting play he hadn't quite managed to write. However, I'm sure he will. This is, after all, a first. Had his name not been on the title page, it might well have surfaced to encouraging sounds in far less make-or-break circumstances.'

The play brought celebrities out in force to the opening. Support came from Terry Jones and Terry Gilliam. Playwrights Alan Bleasdale and David Hare were there, as were the novelist Douglas Adams, actors Geraldine McEwan and Jonathan Pryce, the BBC's Alan Yentob and Sir David Attenborough, whose recorded voice contributed some vital lines on the voracious sexual habits of the praying mantis.

'The reviews all contained the word dire,' Michael admitted bravely. 'Richard Wilson saving a sinking script was the only good thing they could find to say about it. I felt I'd been mugged. But it hasn't stopped me taking the risk of being mugged again ... I'm still confused about what happened to the play. We had a great tour, Robert Fox had the confidence to go into the West End with it, then we got totally savaged on the first night. It seemed like this little club of theatre critics was saying, "We don't want you chaps from TV in our world." But if I feel there is another piece I can do for the stage I won't be put off.'

One plus for a modestly beleaguered Palin – he had not put any of his own money into the play. 'I was always told never to invest in your own production,' he said. 'If no one will invest in it, it must be trash.'

Far more successful was Palin's next head-on-block exercise, his novel, *Hemingway's Chair*, which came out in 1995. 'I had always wanted to write a novel since my schooldays at Shrewsbury,' he said when *Hemingway's Chair* was launched. In fact, I did write a novel in 1977. It starts off jokey and ends up serious. I sent it to two publishers. One said the jokes were great but the second half was a bore. The other said I couldn't write comedy but that the serious stuff showed real talent. I locked it away in a drawer. It's still there.'

Hemingway's Chair was well received. It was despatched to reviewers complete with a jokey promo tape in which he said his book was 'on sale at all good bookshops, some shoe shops, and the odd butcher. *Very* odd butcher...'

'I shall never earn a tenth as much from a novel as I might make from going to Hollywood,' he said. 'But I don't want to do that. Creative success is what matters, not the money. For me, wealth buys the freedom to do what I want. I hate the life of tycoonery.'

Hemingway's Chair was a tough book which surprised those who have seen a strain of sentimentality in Palin's work in his championing of what he calls 'the ordinary person', the underdog. It is about an ordinary bloke called Martin Sproale who lives a quiet life working for the Post Office. He is obsessed with Hemingway, whom he begins to emulate when a female American Hemingway scholar arrives in town. Palin read *For Whom the Bell Tolls* at school: 'The nearest you get to doing a sexy book for A-level. The earth moved and all that. I saw Martin as someone who admired Hemingway in a trainspotter's, list-making way which suited someone who worked in a Post Office; he knew all the diseases Hemingway had, and how many times he banged his head when drunk.'

Hemingway's Chair was a *tour de force* against the evils of consumerism. Sproale, the postmaster, rises dramatically to the occasion when his local Post Office is faced with closure. 'There's a lot of Martin in me,' Palin admitted. 'Outwardly a rather conservative, steady sort of chap – but underneath a certain madness, the conformist who wants to break loose. I rather like people who cause trouble ... I find it very hard to write about people I don't like. I can write about people I like, without necessarily liking everything they do, but I can't fill a book with alienating or alienated characters.

'There is a real fear that the franchising of the Post Office will gradually reduce its role in the community to some fully automated system, in which you would have no human contact whatsoever. And it was this issue of human contact and communication in the face of increasingly sophisticated electronic gadgetry that really interested me,' said the man who remains proud to be low-tech, writes by hand and shuns all possible gadgetry.

Palin's vision of a centrally programmed society stops just this side of paranoia. He believes the growth of out-of-town shopping centres is the thin edge of the wedge. 'If people don't meet face to face and respond to each other as human beings in the Post Office, the local high street shops, whatever, they will have to rely an awful lot more on what they read, either in newspapers or on screens. My fear is that this will make us all much easier to govern.

'I feel reassured by the high street,' he explains, 'where you might go into several shops to find exactly what you want, and I have an antipathy to malls, where everything is made so easy for you that you buy lots of things you don't need. I resent those kinds of environments, because I feel they've taken the element of personal decision away from me. I can't even talk about the weather, because there is no weather. I suppose you could grumble about the choice of Muzak, but somehow it's just not the same.'

All of which anger and fulmination is not to say that Palin has lost his comic edge. One of the pleasures of *Hemingway's Chair*, wrote E. Jane Dickson in the *Daily Telegraph*, is the nicety of his social observations. Pamela Harvey-Wardrell, a crashing small-town snob, is described as 'a woman of such epic and ineffable unself-consciousness that, if born poor and unwelcome, she might well have been certified mad'.

The central thrust of *Hemingway's Chair* was, along with a great deal of what Palin said in publicising it, a cry against the modern world. 'I never feel quite in touch with the nineties,' he admitted recently in a way which suggests he may be a bit listless now, and may embark on a more relaxed, less workaholic life. 'For me, contemporary is the late sixties, when most of us were writing for David Frost.'

10

The World

The mutation of busy Michael Palin in his late forties from actor–writer–novelist–dramatist–comedian to actor–writer–novelist–dramatist–comedian–professional traveller was a perfectly predictable development. He had, after all, stated unequivocally at the age of eight that he wanted to grow up to be an explorer. And as a boy he was a train spotter, although not one transfixed by the wonder of lists of numbers crossed off in his train spotter's handbook. For Palin, the allure of the trains on Sheffield station was where they were going to. 'I'd gaze at trains going from Edinburgh to Devon and think, "If only",' he says.

His father had travelled extensively as an engineer – to India, Egypt and America – but, to Palin continuing puzzlement, he never once talked about his experiences, did not tell so much as a single story. Whether it was reticence, fear of being a bore, some lingering sadness about his adventures which he never told anyone, or merely that his stammer would have made it all such hard work to describe, Palin can only guess. 'There was a side to him which he kept very suppressed,' he says. 'I longed to hear stories of his foreign travels, but it wasn't to be.'

From the moment he was independent and could afford to travel, he did so. That said, his first journey out of Britain was not indicative of a famous traveller in the making. 'It is ironic that I hardly noticed my first trip abroad,' he wrote in the *Observer* in 1992. 'I was nineteen and went with a university ski party to the Tyrol. At that time, people interested me a lot more than places ... I could have been in Accrington rather than Austria for all I remember of the scenery. At twenty, he showed great steadfastness and self-reliance, fending for himself in Germany when he ran short of money and couldn't afford to join his Oxford friends at their villa in Greece; that was a fairly hefty clue that Palin was a traveller and, at heart, a lone traveller.

His early world travels were entirely a team thing with the rest of the Pythons, and sound much like the exploits of any group of young blokes on tour. 'We used to be rather disgraceful travellers,' he has admitted. 'Graham Chapman liked his booze and the weaker minded of us would follow him – although not at the same rate. I remember once when somebody got very ill on the plane and the crew actually asked if there was a doctor on board. Graham, who was a doctor, volunteered. This was the person they had just been trying to restrain five minutes before – 'I think you've had quite enough now, sir' – suddenly being shown down the aisle to administer to a sick passenger, which he did very well. He was a very good doctor.'

A Python's eye view of the world was not that of either a tourist or a traveller. He wrote in his *Observer* piece: 'As we toured Canada with our stage show during an airline go-slow, I learnt where to find a stuffed parrot in Winnipeg after five p.m. I saw Paris at the end of a large fish with which Graham Chapman knocked me into the lake in the Bois de Boulogne. I saw the remarkable landscape of southern Tunisia from the top of a cross – while singing 'Always Look on the Bright Side'. I saw Hollywood from inside the Bowl and Philadelphia from a helicopter flying us in to appear on a TV chat show. The host thought Monty Python was one person and seats had to be hastily found for us all, except Terry Jones who had by that time perched himself on David Soul's knee.'

As the Python era faded, however, he became an assiduous lone traveller, with no TV crew chronicling every moment; the re-invention of Palin as traveller, sometimes alone, sometimes meeting and befriending people as he went, was, then, in no sense a television stunt. He was already a travel addict when his television travels began in his forty-sixth year. 'I'd pick a European city I'd never been to and spend a week there losing my way and smiling a lot. Each time I became a little more courageous, straying farther off the beaten track and not being put off by closed doors. I was never bored or sated. Quite the opposite; I wanted to see more.'

Many people imagine themselves travelling solo, but are put off by the necessity most of the time to eat alone; not so Palin, who quite worries his friends by his predilection for eating large meals in smart restaurants on his own. Sometimes, however, he finds himself dying to tell someone what has happened to him – as good a reason as any for his later starting to share his enthusiasm for travel with millions.

In Barcelona once, he went for dinner in a grand restaurant, 'The sort of place where they give you six glasses and fourteen spoons and practically change the tablecloth between courses,' he explained to Lynn Barber in a 1988 *Sunday Express* interview. 'Because I went there early and the Spaniards dine very late, I was the only person there. I was terribly embarrassed. And the waiters kept bringing out these specialities of the house to show me – huge fishes and slabs of meat, and finally a lobster. I looked at this lobster and didn't know what to say about it. I knew I didn't want to eat it, that was for sure, and then the waiter said, "He not deada; he just very colda," and I was thinking, "Oh, I wish the other Pythons were here, this would be a great Python sketch." And then the waiter suddenly said, "And how is Brian's life?" and I realised he knew. All this treatment was because I was a Python. Which was funny, but it was a bit of a shock, being recognised in Spain.'

Such travels did not constitute quite the kind of exploration Palin used to read about, and be told about by lecturing missionaries, as a boy. But they were a great statement of freedom for a very conservative, regular family man from north London, whose growing wealth and occasional spare time gave him the chance to dare to follow his curiosity.

He tried to build travel into his work. He would, he says, set scripts quite arbitrarily in some far-off location for the purpose of going there. And he developed a habit, if he had some big writing project to finish, of choosing a quiet hotel in a part of Britain he did not know, and working from dawn to dusk with a lengthy 'exploring break' at lunchtime. 'In this way I discovered the Cheviots, the spectacular north Devon coast, south-west Scotland and the Borders, Dorset, Westmoreland and the Yorkshire Dales – out of season and between paragraphs.'

After *Life of Brian* catapulted him to superstardom in 1979, Palin said: 'My one serious ambition is still the same – to be an explorer. I do seriously want to find out what it's like to be eaten alive by a piranha fish.' The following year, he filmed his contribution to *Great Railway Journeys of the World*, which sowed the seed of TV travels to come, but it was nearly ten years before *Around the World in Eighty Days*, the 1988 BBC series which launched the career for which Palin has become almost as famous as he was as a Python.

It was all the idea of Clem Vallance, an ex-Cambridge Footlights contemporary of Eric Idle, who had been directing and producing light documentaries at the BBC almost since he left university. Vallance knew, as did many people who were acquainted with Michael, that he was a fanatical, but still somewhat unrequited, traveller. The idea of loosely recreating Phileas Fogg's fictional journey was so clear, uncomplicated and simple, that, in the world of television, which adores clear, uncomplicated and simple concepts, it was bound to be a winner. The journey was to be done by land only, and with the presenter carrying a minimum of luggage 'in a carpet bag' as Phileas Fogg did in Jules Verne's novel. Even the name of the proposed travel documentary, borrowed directly from Verne, had a simplicity about it which was actually rather brilliant. But had it not been for Vallance's persistence and mild deviousness, *Around the World in Eighty Days* might never have happened. Worse still, it might have been *Around the World in Eighty Days* with Noel Edmonds.

Vallance explains that he dreamed up the idea as a vehicle for Palin, but that it lay in a BBC drawer for five months. When it came up for consideration, the view at Kensington House, the then BBC documentaries centre in Shepherd's Bush, was that it was all very well, but needed a 'BBC 1 name' to front it; it is a measure of how perceptions of Palin have changed that, as late as 1987, he was still regarded as a bit fringe for a mainstream show. The idea gripped the BBC that Alan Whicker, in retirement in Jersey, was the man for *Around the World in Eighty Days*. Vallance was dubious, but kept quiet, confident that Whicker was unlikely to be attracted by a project which involved such discomfort. Whicker was, with respect to him, probably the last person in the world suitable for a programme which involved travelling virtually rough around the world, and talking to ordinary people as he went.

Whicker accepted the invitation to lunch, nevertheless. 'Alan was taken with a group executives,' Vallance recounts, 'to a pizzeria in Shepherd's Bush. There, he spent the time explaining how he'd just got back from the Melbourne Gold Cup. At every opportunity, I kept pointing out the downsides to the proposed series. How uncomfortable and dangerous it would be on the dhow crossing from Dubai to Bombay, how he wouldn't be able to take his girlfriend with him. On the way back to Kensington House, we were all walking along in a group and someone whispered to me, "We've got him, I think." I said, "Of course we haven't." And as you'd expect, Alan wrote back to say it was sweet of you to think of me, but no thanks. Noel Edmonds wasn't interested, there was an approach to Miles Kington, which came to nothing. And so it came to be Michael's series.'

Vallance and another director, Roger Mills, have shared the direction of all Palin's travel programmes, which by some estimates have – before the latest series, *Full Circle*, is taken into consideration – made £2 million for Palin so far, and the best part of £20 million for the BBC. *Around the World in Eighty Days* brought such unprecedented audiences to BBC 2 that the second journey, *From Pole to Pole*, was shown on BBC 1. The companion hardback to *Around the World in Eighty Days*, written by Michael from his notes and research on route, went to twenty-two reprintings, the paperback to thirteen in five years. Total sales were 710,000 books, and Michael's royalty cheques were so large, they had to be signed personally by the Director General. 'The BBC told me I was second only to Noddy in world sales,' Michael told the *Sheffield Star* some years after that first travel series. 'That helped to put it all in perspective.' (Ironically, Clem Vallance laughs, some of the BBC executives who opposed using Palin were later promoted as a result of its great success – which was still only possible because a New York TV company put up a major slice of the funding.)

The magic ingredient Palin has as a travel presenter is not so much humour as a complete lack of pretension. His attitude to travel is both wildly romantic and steadfastly practical. He is enthralled by astonishing landscapes, fascinating people and customs, and occasionally concerned by worrying issues he stumbles across, such as the massive dam scheme on the Yangtse River in China, over which he expressed his environmental misgivings in one of the early *Full Circle* episodes. But he presents all these matters from the perspective of what ordinary British people find interesting and entertaining.

This Englishman abroad theme does not mean Palin is clumsy or boorish as a means of populism; but equally, there is no intellectual showing off, or patronising use of superior knowledge. Palin is the ordinary British bloke in foreign parts. He is stung by critical accusations of blandness, and insists that his telegenic naivety about foreign countries is real and not affected. In a sense the programmes are about serious tourism rather than the snobbish geographical one-upmanship which conceited people refer to as 'travel' in an attempt to make anyone who enjoys the occasional night in a decent hotel feel like a tourist, and hence inferior. He particularly tries to avoid lapsing into 'boring traveller' mode. Palin is, in literary terms, Bill Bryson rather than Paul Theroux.

Some critics have, nevertheless, accused the programmes of being dull. 'My heart sank when Mark Lawson in the *Independent* gave

Eighty Days a poor review,' Palin has said. 'But at least he made some constructive points. It was the *Observer* that really upset me. Their reviewer said *Pole to Pole* made him want to sleep and never wake up. Well, fuck you, I thought. All the effort we've put in, yet you won't put the effort into a proper review.'

The Palin way of travelling is most certainly not to interview the famous, either to take the mickey out of them *à la* Whicker, or to be worthy. 'We have sat down and tried to talk to people about the state of the country and even talked to politicians, but it just isn't my bag,' he says. 'It's very dull, and it doesn't fit in with the idea of moving on, and also trying as much as possible to be the everyman kind of traveller. Most people wouldn't interview the Prime Minister if they went to a country so we got to places like markets where you will find people ready to talk.'

It may seem odd, bearing in mind their essential Englishness, that Palin's travelling exploits have found such a huge international audience. When he was filming part of *From Pole to Pole* in a remote part of northern Norway, he says, 'I can remember interviewing people on this ferry. I said, "Gosh what a terrible place to live, it's dark six months of the year. What do you do?" And they said, "We watch your series on the television."'

What Palin taps into, it seems, is the hunger that exists, especially in the USA, for that quirky, Pythonesque Englishness he exemplifies. A classic moment of this quite archaic, Goonish fifties approach is seen in the 1997 Palin journey, *Full Circle*. Palin is in Shanghai, speaking about the extraordinary office building boom there, when he is drowned out by a lengthy ship's foghorn blast. He stands, bemused, as the blast goes on and on; the viewer wonders why the sequence has not been cut and done again. Then, as the racket finally stops, Palin says, 'I knew I shouldn't have had the prunes,' and carries on. As a moment of ad libbing, it is exquisite; in British terms, it will have resonated with viewers, but one only wonders what they will make of it in Milwaukee. Then again, anyone watching a Michael Palin travel film there will probably already be an Anglophile, and know all about prunes and the marvellously English obsession with farting and constipation.

He rarely attempts in the programmes to speak foreign languages, for example, although he is not a bad linguist. He can get by in French and Spanish, and in Russia learned the rudiments of the language, to the extent that, on a train between Estonia and the then Leningrad in *From Pole to Pole*, he managed to have a conversation with a little girl travelling with her parents. On *Around the World*, he took the BBC's *Get By In Arabic*, while in China, for *Full Circle*, he also tried hard to learn some Mandarin for its own sake, rather than as something necessary for the filming.

Palin is only too aware that what he does in his travel series is dangerously close to what the Pythons used to skewer. 'That's the danger in everything we do,' he says. 'I think some of the Pythons look at me doing a travel documentary and, occasionally, I may do a piece to camera and they'll say: "That's the kind of stuff we used to send up. We used to make fun of these things." I'm always very conscious of that possibility.'

Palin set off from the Reform Club in Pall Mall with his carpet-style bag, containing six shirts, six changes of underwear, two pairs of trousers, a jacket and tie, a Sony Walkman, six cassettes, a short wave radio, and a Panama hat. Less obvious in the film was the crew of eight with their forty-five heavy pieces of luggage, although part of the principle of all Palin's travel films has been never to hide the fact that there is a full, cumbersome film unit with him at all times.

In setting off from Pall Mall, Palin pioneered a wave of amusingly glib entertainment world figures, such as Clive James, Clive Anderson and Ruby Wax, travelling to foreign parts with a crew in tow. 'When we did *Around the World in Eighty Days*, it freed up travel documentaries from serious travel writers – who probably look down on television travellers, with our camera crews and (they think) limousines,' he says. 'People still think television is awash with money. But we get more mileage from staying in a village police station than in a Hilton or Four Seasons, which are all the same and completely unfilmable.'

Although Palin is perfectly game about being filmed while not looking at his best – indeed, his bowels and their funny turns have become to some extent a matter of public discussion thanks to his travel series – he has still to allow showbusiness considerations their occasional head.

Clem Vallance, who produced *Full Circle* as well as directing half of it, points out that Palin has always been adamant about not being made to wear any form of hat. 'If you asked him to wear one just for a sequence, he might do it, but you would know he wasn't happy about it,' Vallance says. 'When you think about it from his point of view, he has got to look presentable and acceptable for the camera at every stage of the most mind-bogglingly difficult journey. You are going through mud or whatever, there's no make up, nothing. He has got to look after all of that himself, or we have to try and help him. It is not a question of being the big star and stamping your foot; you have got to have an awareness of how your public will see you, and he has got a very good sense of what is appropriate and what isn't.'

By July 1997, Michael's brand of 'easy listening' travel seemed to have insinuated itself into the BBC's corporate culture, and spawned something he would be unlikely to approve of at all. According to a 130-page BBC internal document called 'Reflecting the World', which found its way to the press, senior management now believed that the only way of putting across foreign news to the majority of the British public might be to have celebrities rather than foreign correspondents present it. Only a handful of stars could draw mass audiences to stories concerning matters beyond Calais, it was suggested; the names which would stop people switching off were cited as Clive James, Clive Anderson, Sir David Attenborough – and Michael Palin. Chris Evans, Gaby Roslin, Ulrika Jonsson, Vic Reeves and Bob Mortimer were suggested as stars who should be considered for programmes aimed at younger viewers.

Some of Palin's journeys have, almost as a consequence of Palin's and the BBC's quest to keep up interest, involved an element of risk. 'I underplay this now,' he says, 'but when we started the dhow journey [from Dubai to Bombay], none of us knew what was going to happen, whether we'd get there. We had no radio link with anybody, so we were very cut off from the world and totally dependent on these people. The year before, the captain's brother had died at sea with a whole crew because a storm blew up, so needless to say, we were a bit apprehensive.'

It was the dhow which provided him with his most frightening moment. 'We were drifting down the Straits of Hormuz with no engine and no radar, and with mines bobbing up and down in the water on either side of the boat. That was the only time in my life I have ever thought – oh my God, I'm going to die.'

From the start *Around the World* was more than just another travelogue. It was the idiosyncratic wanderings of a complex character. Palin's stamina was unfailing. In *Around the World in Eighty Days* (which actually lasted seventy-nine days) he plodded on for more than eleven weeks without a day off. He could relax on some of the longer sea passages, but every day he had to do some film work and write up his journals. While there was only one of him, there were two camera crews involved in the production. They leapfrogged each other as the journey progressed. One exhausted crew was sent home and replaced in Hong Kong.

Palin went through periods of depression and homesickness on this first trip, some of which the camera captured. Helen had the decorators in for most of his absence and, while she missed him, she didn't actually pine. He kept in touch with her by telephone – 'She wasn't all that sympathetic,' he says. 'Because her advice to me had been short, sweet and simple: don't go!' To his daughter, Rachel, he sent an endless string of postcards. He has since developed a theory about phoning home. 'I never call home more than once a week,' he says. 'The point is that you might be looking out over the Pacific, but at home, the only thing they're worried about is that the washing machine's leaking or one of the cats has gone missing.

'I learnt a lot from the *Eighty Days* programme,' Palin says, 'but it is never enough. I did realise that you have to be incredibly patient and that, whoever you talk to and however much you prepare, the unexpected will always take you by surprise. And even if you take the biggest medicine chest in the world there will still be some strange creature that will burrow itself into your body.

'However, the most essential things to take are medicinal and toiletry requisites. You need to carry a lot of drugs (legal ones, of course). The strongest were Imodium and Arret (for diarrhoea). It is important that if you get ill in an out-of-the-way place, you have something that will keep you going until you reach a hospital. I believe that the medicine bag had a sort of a deterrent effect. My bags got lost at one point and, as soon as they had gone, aches and pains and stomach problems set in. I lost half a stone during the trip and found that my cholesterol level had gone way down from being slightly high. Obviously goat and rice is good for cholesterol levels.'

On his return, Palin also advised other would-be world travellers to take Jeffrey Archer rather than to attempt to read Greek philosophy or deep Spanish novels – he hardly opened his heavy stuff the entire journey.

Not every frame of *Eighty Days* met with total public approval. One scene in Kwangchow, China, in which a live snake was beheaded and disembowelled before being prepared for Michael's meal, was later condemned by the Broadcasting Standards Council. Viewers saw the restaurateur extract the snake's gall bladder, skin the animal and delicately place its head, tongue still flicking, next to the saucer containing the gall bladder. A complaint by the Reptile Protection Trust was partly upheld because the BSC felt the scene was shown at inappropriate length and detail before the 'family-viewing watershed'. But the BSC rejected the Trust's argument 'that the participation of Mr Palin, who had selected the snake for his meal, was tasteless'. (The meal, Michael recounted in the book of *Around the World in Eighty Days*, was far from tasteless, and was indeed rather agreeable to a man who has no fear of eating unorthodox animals. It included snake bladder liqueur, cat and snake soup, shredded snake with broccoli, deep fried snake balls, whole plucked rice birds and fresh fox.)

If anything were to stretch Palin's sunny temperament, it would have been a gruelling and sometimes dangerous three-month trip during which he had to work practically every day. Yet, as Stephen Pile, writing in the *Telegraph Magazine* pointed out, Palin made it around the world in seventy-nine days "without once having a tantrum, insulting a foreigner or hitting anybody" – and this despite the fact that at times he felt close to breaking point.

On day seventy-nine, he nearly cracked. 'We were all tired and fragile,' Palin recalled. 'I'd walked off the boat for one of the directors, when the other said do it again. I refused. I might have stamped my feet. Even ranted and raved. Many years earlier, when we were doing *Holy Grail*, I did actually go mad, after I was asked to crawl through the mud for the seventh time. It was a wonderfully liberating moment. All the Pythons stood up and clapped. They'd never seen me bad tempered before.'

It was a bad day for Michael. 'We were all very tired and our resistance was low. We made it back to London, only to find ourselves on the Underground with a bomb warning going off. We were two miles from our goal and I thought, "This is the end." ' He ended his epic journey standing forlornly on the wet December pavement outside the Reform Club. He had just been refused entry to the place where Phileas Fogg ended his eighty-day journey. 'They wouldn't let us in to film,' Michael said, a little bitterly, later. 'I had a feeling of absolutely genuine frustration at their unhelpfulness. They were pretty surly.'

Anyone less nice, the point was made, would have been homicidal before the first week of *Eighty Days* was out. He was filmed relentlessly, even during the blackest hours of a stomach bug on a dhow in the middle of the Persian Gulf, where the facilities were limited to a barrel. 'I would challenge you to find anyone who would say anything nasty about Michael Palin,' said Roger Mills.

After *Full Circle*, in 1997, Mills was still amazed by Palin's temperateness. That is not to say, Mills points out, that Palin is not insistent on professionalism. 'Yes, he does lose his temper. He's a human being. Mike's not a saint and I think he is fed up with the word nice. He loses his temper when he thinks that something has been incompetently done: if he is left standing around on a cold wet rainy day and he doesn't know what he is supposed to be doing. Very often in documentaries, particularly when you first get to a place, there is a moment of confusion. You are not quite sure which door you have to go into, or if the person you are supposed to meet is there. Tiredness is a factor in all this; something which looks like incompetence can result in him just letting fly and saying this is bloody inefficient. It doesn't happen very often, I have to say, but it does happen. But if there is a flare up, it is over quickly. Mike doesn't like losing his temper, and he says I am awfully sorry I lost it, but at the time . . .'

Michael's second journey, *From Pole to Pole*, broadcast at the end of 1992, was shorter at 12,500 miles, but more arduous, and took longer – five-and-a-half months – with a break of about ten days in September. This eight-hour documentary took Michael through seventeen countries – from Denmark to Russia to Turkey and down through Africa to the Antarctic. There was a commitment again to using local ground transport as much as possible. By travelling north to south, rather than around the globe, the team encountered extremes they never met in *Eighty Days*.

The route, along with the timing of the trip, during the latter half of 1991, also meant that Palin witnessed incredible political upheavals in the former Soviet Union, the Sudan, Ethiopia and South Africa. 'That year was an extraordinary year,' he says. 'Within two days of leaving Odessa in the Soviet Union, the generals' coup happened and the whole thing fell apart. We talked to people from Ukraine and Estonia who said, "Well, maybe in thirty years or forty years we'll get our independence." And they were independent by Christmas.'

There was a five-year gap before Michael took off again on his travels. Such a long intermission did not prevent the departure for *Full Circle*, shown during the autumn of 1997, from being a rushed affair. 'We had almost finished *Fierce Creatures*, and it was supposed to finish at the beginning of August so I could go off on this trip,' he explains. 'But, as they do, the film overshot, so four days before we left, I was still in a cupboard with spiders scuttling around in Pinewood studios. So going to Alaska and having a couple of nights' sleep by the Bearing Sea was a great relief and a great rest.'

The journey for *Full Circle* had taken some contrivance. 'We looked at atlases and talked in a rather jokey way about this being the way to see the Pacific,' Michael says. 'Then it formed into a geometric possibility to make a complete circle of the Pacific. The idea of stretching the Pacific exploration to two separate journeys, one on one side of the ocean and one on the other, was dismissed as being merely two *Pole to Poles*. Eric Idle, hearing of his friend's proposed journey around the entire Pacific Rim, helpfully proposed the series be called *Palin's Rim*. The suggestion was not taken up.

The subject of Palin's bottom did come up in a roundabout way quite early in the series, however. In one of the beautifully observed sequences so typical of Palin, the viewers were shown the high-tech loo installed in an otherwise traditional *riokan*, a rural Japanese inn. A more lofty traveller would doubtless have ignored such trivia in favour of some fascinating observation of the wildlife of rural Japan or an examination of some obscure art treasure, but then a more lofty traveller would not have held nine million viewers' attention.

'*Riokan* are that side of Japan which is very ancient and formal and delicate and precise – except for the loos,' he explained on Michael Parkinson's Radio 2 programme a few months before *Full Circle* was broadcast. 'This twenty-first-century loo had about twenty-three different functions and flushing devices. There were eight different ways of drying yourself, not including paper, ranging from a hurricane blast to a gentle breeze. There was a wonderful moment where our soundman had to go and record all these noises, because we filmed me going in there, but obviously the door shut and that was that. We were just going to have me trying to find how things worked. But then the sound man had to go in there, and all we heard for the next hour was, "Recording Michael Palin on the loo, take one." '

Full Circle included several quite dangerous interludes, some self imposed, others accidental. 'There were moments when we were filming a demonstration in Seoul that got quite violent,' Palin says. 'There were police with tear gas and riot squads in their coaches ready if the march got a bit out of order. We just joined in with the march to see what would happen.' (Not too much did, as it turned out.)

'There is a general level of anxiety which you carry throughout the whole journey. We had to go in a Russian helicopter which was about forty years old, and there is a sequence in the opening programme where it barely takes off. It goes about eight feet in the air, shudders a bit and then sinks to the ground and the proceeds off on its wheels up the road, and I was thinking, oh God.'

In Columbia, currently regarded as the single most dangerous country in the world for travellers, there was a moment of more than just general anxiety. 'We were being driven by an English reporter who lives in Chile round the seamiest streets of Bogata. There were a lot of streets just filled with drug addicts and rubbish and debris, and we weren't allowed to get out of the car. I thought, this may be a bit over-reacting, come on, and then in one street they started throwing rocks at the car, and then I was very glad we had a driver who knew what to do. We moved out of the area pretty fast. Also while we were there at one point there was a roadblock, where police were stopping people and searching cars. Again, this was in the very sort of downtown area of Bogata, and they let us get out for a bit there. Nigel the cameraman was busy filming, and I was just aware of four guys. They looked at us, and I knew that this was where the trouble was going to come from, not from the people who had their needles out. These were guys who were the minor pushers. Curiously, there was no attempt to communicate with us. The band of them just started to move towards the car. I said, maybe we should go now, and we went and got out of that.'

There was danger of a more containable kind in Queenstown,

New Zealand, where Palin refused to bungee jump. 'New Zealanders are all driven by this desire to kill themselves as soon as possible,' he laughs. 'We talked to the guy who popularised bungee jumping. I said, "You understand that I am just not going to do this. I have done all sorts of things, but not this. I see no point at my age in hurtling head first down a raging torrent with rocks in it. I do have a fear of heights where I feel I could easily jump off. I can climb rocks and mountains – I did a lot of climbing in the Andes, and I don't mind that, but if I know I could fall then I get a bit of a cold sweat. And when you know not only could you fall, but people are going to push you because that's there job, that is utterly terrifying."

'Eventually,' Palin relates, 'he said, "You know, it would be very easy if I held on to you." I could see Roger the director's eye lighting up – Michael bungee jumping arm in arm plunging down into the river and then bouncing up again, what a great sequence. I was on the verge of cracking but then he said, "We've had six million billion jumps and nobody has even lost a front tooth," and I said, "Fine, that means I am going to the first to lose a front tooth." After that he had clearly marked me down as totally chicken, but one of his assistants let slip later that they didn't get many people jumping over thirty-five, although there was a lady of eighty-eight who bungee jumped out of a helicopter which is the longest jump you can do – it's about three hundred metres and back up again. What a way to go. Paid for by her children!'

Full Circle also included a sequence in Australia which Palin regards as the hardest day's filming he has ever done. 'In the centre of Australia,' he explains, 'there are herds of wild camels, which were imported to build the railways in the 1920s and then were turned loose. They have adapted very well, and apparently are a very healthy stock of camel, much in demand from the Middle East for camel racing.' Unfortunately, they are at all not easy to catch, so a new breed of latter day camel-boys making a living lassoing wild camels and sending them off to the land of their camel ancestors. For a day, Palin was invited to join them camel rustling.

'They enjoyed winding us poms up the night before about what it's like: "Michael, this is the greatest adrenalin rush you will find anywhere in the world," and they laughed a lot, and of course I thought it wasn't going to be too bad, and of course it turned out to be almost sheer hell.

'You are put on the back of a little pick-up truck with a rail on top, and you stand half hanging on to this rail and are given a stick with a piece of rope on the end like a lasso. When you are up against the camel, all you have to do is put the stick over its head, and then they get down and do all the rest and pull the camel in. But it isn't that easy, because the camels aren't stupid – they're not wild for nothing and when they see someone coming up with a stick, they just go off in the other direction. Hence, the vehicles are driven like complete lunatics towards these camels, off the dirt track on to boulders, dried up river beds, small hillocks. You bounce along, get alongside the camels and then they start shouting at you, "Go on Michael, go for it NOW! NOW!" the camels are great, because they don't really look panicked at all. They just sort of rolled their eyes, and turned away gently in the other direction.

'We were using two cameras, one in the helicopter which musters the camels and the other in a vehicle filming me. And so it was all of the morning and most of the afternoon before I actually caught a camel. We missed one after the other, so by the end I was just so angry. I've rarely been so angry. I was getting thrown around, I thought I had broken a rib and I was just banging the side of this truck and effing and blinding and using all the filthiest language I could muster up. But in the end, I did actually get alongside a camel, lassoed it, and, as they said, it was one of the great adrenalin rushes of all time. It took me about four days to recover, but by the end of that day it was the greatest satisfaction I have ever had, to lasso one of these stupid camels. It was real adventure, of the most raw kind. It makes bungee jumping look like a medium dry sherry. And the great thing I discovered was that Jeremy Clarkson had been there and he'd only spent five minutes. They said, "Jeremy Clarkson, he's just a big girl's blouse." I said I promised not to tell any journalists.'

In the Australian segment of *Full Circle*, Palin also played a cameo part in *Home and Away* as part of an item on Australian soap operas. 'They were filming near Sydney, where we were based, and we just went up to look around. Word went along the beach, and they wrote a part for me. It was fame at last, because it was the only programme that my daughter watches. She was in her final year at Oxford University, and they all watch it. I told the cast that in Oxford this is the one they all watch and they couldn't believe it. I can go from pole to pole, whatever, but my street cred has never been higher than when I appeared briefly on *Home and Away*.'

Michael had to wear a tight rubber surfer's suit and interrupt a romantic scene. 'I had a surf board to carry, and I modelled my performance partly on Hugh Grant and the walk on John Cleese. I did a rather strange double take by the side of the Pacific Ocean, and remembered all that John had taught me about the double take. I executed it rather well, I thought. I had to say, "Excuse me, just thinking about taking a dip and wondered if there were sharks in there?" to which they say, "Any sharks? No, no." To which I say, "Jolly good, fine," and off I go into the water. But then she shouts at the last minute, "But there are some pretty nasty jelly fish." I stop on the edge of the water and say, "Thank you, thank you," and then double back. I am just waiting for the BAFTA summons for Best Fifty-five-Year-old In a Rubber Suit. Jeremy Irons will probably get that first.'

All the fun Palin had in Australasia was overshadowed a little, however, by what had happened a couple of weeks earlier, when he and the team were in a remote part of Borneo.

'Ironically, it was one of the few times in the whole journey that we were totally out of contact,' he recounted to Michael Parkinson on Radio 2. 'Now, almost anywhere in the world apart from where we were, you can get someone on the mobile phone. People ring from the top of Everest, "Hello, I'm on Everest, dear". We were interviewing some old guys who had been head-hunting and knew about head-hunting. When we finally got back to the hotel, there was a message from Helen, and there was a message from the wife of our assistant cameraman, who was expecting a baby.

'Helen had had a series of quite serious headaches, went for a brain scan and was discovered to have a meningioma, which is a brain tumour which is not in the brain but on the top of it, underneath the skull. The doctor said it had probably been there for a very long time, as these things gradually grow, but the headaches had got so bad that she had gone to seek some advice and, within about four days, she was taken into hospital, operated on and is now absolutely fine. My assistant cameraman had heard that his daughter had fallen out of a first floor window and cracked her head, and so both were seriously ill.

'That night, it was kind of eerie. It was almost like something supernatural had happened, but of course it wasn't, it was just coincidence that we'd been with these head-hunters while all this was happening, but it was a difficult thing to deal with at that time. I felt utterly and completely helpless and Helen was absolutely brilliant and just calmed me down, told me that there was no need to panic, and that she'd rather I came back as soon as she had had the operation, than rush back just before she went into hospital and worry even more.

'The surgeon at the National Hospital for Neurology and Neurosurgery was terrific and he phoned me in strange parts of the world to tell me very patiently what was going to happen with the operation, exactly what he was going to do, exactly what the risk factor was, which was fairly minimal. I am so grateful to him for just spending that time, because I didn't know what to do. I was about to drop everything and go but, in the middle of Borneo, it's not that easy; well, you can drop everything, that's easy, but going isn't.'

It was Clem Vallance who encouraged Michael to go home mid-journey. 'I said, fuck the series, Michael, just get on a plane and go home,' Vallance says. 'I then made arrangements for him to leave the journey a week later, and we missed out a section, and prepared for him to come back to Australia. He was away for a week, so we went across to another Indonesian island and shot some cover just in case we could actually extend the journey to there. We shot the sequences so that he could do a voice-over for it but, when I came to look at it in the cutting room, I found I couldn't use it because it lacked his personal touch, so I junked it.'

Vallance then sent the crew forward to Australia early to wait for Michael to come back. Palin's Pacific marathon consequently included a four-day diversion to London, where he arrived with such a bad cold, he needed nursing himself. Helen made a full recovery from surgery, and was soon back at work, with her driving licence restored, which particularly delighted her. 'It's a nightmare really,' Vallance reflects. 'I have been at this twenty years now in odd parts of the world, and there always is a time when you disappear for two or three weeks, and during that time anything could happen to your family and you wouldn't know about it. That's always the most worrying bit. Most places you can pick up a phone, and these days you can get home or call home or get a fax. The world has shrunk in that sense, but with the kind of travelling that we do there's always those dark sides of the moon where you are beyond contact.'

(The team could easily have equipped themselves, as BBC crews do in remote spots, with a laptop-sized satellite phone perfectly capable of working from the jungles of Borneo and was suggested to Palin during the publicity tour for *Full Circle*. 'Oh, dear, no. I'm very low tech,' he said. Other members of the team aware of such gadgets argue that the integrity of travel documentaries like Palin's depends to some extent on the team being effectively cut off for long periods.)

Palin's view on everything being a fair target for laughter was tested by the incident of his wife's brain tumour. Hearing from Palin that he had been filming a tribe of head-hunters when Helen had the operation on her brain, John Cleese joked, 'You could have brought one back for Helen.' Even from a close friend, it could have gone down badly, but Palin, already aware of the irony, laughed – and recounts Cleese's joke himself.

What, one might wonder, does Michael Palin do by way of a break when these mammoth world trips are over? What holiday do you buy for the man who's been everywhere? 'I like family holidays,' he replies. 'We now tend to go to France every year in the summer for as many days as I can manage, which is usually only about ten days or so. My sister-in-law and her husband have a little farmhouse in the Lot Valley in France, east of Bordeaux. It's very simple and very basic and you don't have to really do anything there apart from sit around for ten days, which suits me absolutely fine. I give the impression of always wanting to be on the move, but actually I love hanging around in cafés, having a drink, a long lunch or a glass of wine. That's what is really so good about travel. Go somewhere, sit down and watch the world go by and enjoy yourself. You can't do that when someone's saying, "Right, off we go, Michael. You have got to hang by one leg on this kangaroo while we put a rocket underneath it..."'

One thing Michael likes to do quickly when he gets back from months away is to unpack. 'It's very much part of touching base,' he says. 'I inherited from father a real desire for order. Everything has to be in its place. I think I go travelling because it destroys that sense of routine. Yet, even when I travel, I'm quite well organised, because you have to be. The unpacking is part of winding down. You no longer have to think: "Where are my socks, the mosquito net and the penknife?"

'It's essential to have a home base,' he insists. 'I like to have all the things I've been deprived of in my travels – brown bread, hard English cheese, white wine, making my own coffee, cooking for myself. It's a tremendous reassurance to come back to familiar things – your own fridge or bed, a restaurant or a pub. They all seem better for your having been away.'

With the world his oyster, he is obviously often asked his favourite place. 'I tend to like cities best,' Palin says on reflection. 'But I think the west coast of Ireland or Scotland are the most beautiful places in the world. They are both beautiful but accessible.'

Aware – almost too aware at times – that he is getting no younger, Palin maintains that *Full Circle* really will be his last televised trip on the current scale, but then adds: 'Whether it is simply curiosity, or some deep-seated need to keep testing mind and body, the exploring tendency will keep nagging at me until I've seen everywhere in the world. Now, *that's* something nobody's done yet.'

11

Gospel Oak

Most friends of Palin are agreed that bumping into Helen Gibbons on the beach in Southwold in 1959 was, along with bumping into Robert Hewison at Brasenose College three years later, the best thing that could possibly have happened to him. 'The thing about Helen was that she wasn't ambitious, and was very happy for Michael to take the ball and run,' says Hewison, who has known the Palins as a couple longer than almost anyone else.

Michael's and Helen's is a low key relationship – the very kind of alliance that is bound to outlast practically all others in the marriage-destroying world of showbusiness. Such marital and family stability has provided the ideal background for the routine-loving Palin to thrive creatively; paradoxically, it has given him the freedom he craves to be something of a loner much of the time.

Helen Palin has barely ever said a word publicly about their relationship; as a teacher turned voluntary bereavement counsellor, she is more than happy keeping a low profile. 'If one more person tells me what a nice husband I have, I'll scream,' is one of her few comments to a journalist. Michael, on the other hand, has spoken occasionally about their marriage. 'We have a practical relationship,' he said in Oxford once, on location making *American Friends*, when the question of his great-grandfather's romantic infatuation with a seventeen-year-old was very much up for discussion. 'Helen and I are very close, very fond of each other,' Michael continued, 'although I don't send her flowers very often. Marriage and bringing up a family is hard work – but it has been worth it. We have had terrific rewards all the way through.'

Like his three-times-married friend John Cleese, Palin is more than a little sceptical about love: 'I've had a romance or two in my life, but romance and passion? I think that's something you get out of the way at the start of a relationship. Romance and passion have always fascinated me. The way people become interested in each other, how the chemistry develops.

'It makes,' he said, aged forty-six on the *American Friends* set, and almost bitterly, one senses, 'a nice change to have a little passion in my declining years'. He was playing his great-grandfather as he said this, in the throes of his love affair.

He and Helen have never sat down and analysed the durability of their marriage. Unlike Cleese, he shies way from all types of psychological introspection. 'I like emotion and all that but at the same time I'm sort of fairly realistic too and down to earth,' Michael says. 'It's a most extraordinary thing, how people can survive that sort of just being together, day in day out, years and years of that daily, daily, daily contact.'

Helen and her husband share a sense of humour. 'Luckily, she is an extremely good judge of me, my work and my moods,' Michael says. 'We also share a lot of humour, which is terribly important. I make her laugh and she makes me laugh – mostly at myself.'

'He can be irritable,' Helen Palin volunteered to one visiting writer, 'especially when machines or plans go wrong. But he doesn't confront people. I wish he would sometimes. In a way he is too nice. I think he should be cross more often.'

'It's the same when I get fed up with endless media attention,' Palin says. 'I'll say to Helen, "Oh, no, not another piece in the paper," and she just says, "Well, stop going round the world then. Stop making eight-hour television programmes in which you're the only bloody person anyone sees!" She has a point.'

Helen, a sporty, attractive woman who plays tennis or badminton most nights, is not the kind of woman to hang around waiting for the phone to ring while her husband is off on one of his extended 'working jaunts'. They have an agreement that he calls only occasionally from abroad. 'I think absence makes the heart grow fonder,' he insists, 'and it also brings new influences into the relationship. If you're sitting in the same room watching TV every night suddenly your lives are so parallel there's nothing to talk about.'

The Palins have lived in Gospel Oak in north London since before the children were born, in a cul de sac of gentrified Victorian workers' cottages surrounded by high-rise council blocks. The road is so small that it does not appear on all maps. Rather than move upmarket as Michael became richer, they have taken the mildly eccentric step of simply acquiring more houses in the same street to knock together. They bought the first, in 1960, for £12,000. In 1977, to give his kids more space, they bought another for £17,500. That meant there was a gap between his two houses, as next door was lived in by Clare Latimer, proprietress of John Major's favourite catering firm, Clare's Kitchen. Clare's actual kitchen is now the Palins' parlour, because he managed to buy her house in the late eighties for £180,000. The Palins plus a shifting population of cats now have three houses out of four in the street. (Helen lived with twenty-six cats on the family farm and the Palins remain devoted cat people.) 'I only need one more house and I can put a hotel on it,' Michael jokes. 'Altogether they would fit into one of John Cleese's houses. They're a lot taller, but then so is he.'

The incongruity of a multi-millionaire and international show-business star living in a north London backwater – not to mention the irony of living in a house far less grand than his strapped-for-cash parents rented – is not lost on Palin. 'Over the years, I have thought, hmm, now I've made all this money, I could buy a castle. But Helen, who is practical, has pointed out I wouldn't know what to do with it. London is not a real city, like Sheffield, but people are tolerant. I get very little aggravation. People have known me from pre-Python days. If I moved to the country, people would come round gaping at me. I have roots here. I know all the shopkeepers. I'm not considered a celebrity.'

He has converted the loft into a light study, generally locked when he is not there. He calls the study his 'room'. It is, visitors report, lined with books, files and photographs, and has a little terrace looking out over an urban scene of tower blocks. There is a lot of built-in office furniture, and various mementoes on display – the inflatable globe he took on his *Around the World in Eighty Days* trip hangs from a shelf. A spiral staircase leading nowhere is the roost for a stuffed parrot. On the TV set downstairs, there is a large, pink, Terry Gilliam foot, in the garden a few oddities, such as a submarine machine gun, and a pair of Laurel and Hardy garden gnomes.

The Palin children are Tom, twenty-eight, William, twenty-six and Rachel twenty-two. All were educated at the neighbourhood primary school and then the local comprehensives, because the Palins do not believe in private education. 'It wasn't a political statement,' insists Michael. 'I'm not against public schools. I just want the state schools to be better. It seemed so sensible when we had such good local schools just across the road. Why have all those convoluted car runs?'

Michael always attempted to be the kind of father he wished his father could have been. The children ignored his fame. 'People who don't know us think we had a really bizarre childhood growing up around the Monty Python team,' Tom Palin explained in the *Sunday Times* magazine in 1997. 'But it was all pretty normal. Dad's never put on airs and graces, been remotely "actorish" or been filled with insecurities like so many other people in his profession. If he has ever felt insecure, I've never known about it ... When John Cleese, Terry Jones and Terry Gilliam used to come to the house, they were just Dad's friends, the people he worked with. It was fun, but it wasn't extraordinary.'

Academically, there has been an odd discrepancy between the

three Palin children; Tom managed six O-levels, is very athletic, and has gone into the music business as a producer and writer; he runs a company producing black R&B music. William and Rachel both went to Brasenose like their father, and are working in the media. The family is still close, meeting for lunch most Sundays – at which their father still manages to make them laugh. 'Dad comes up with stupid jokes, which make us chuckle,' according to Tom.

'They're mildly indulgent towards me,' Michael said of the children when they were younger. 'I think they regard me as a bit of a liability. If I ever try being funny in front of them they just get embarrassed. I'm still pretty childlike. But I hope they feel it's more entertaining to have a father who's doing something different than one with the same job, day in day out. We get on well – it's more like the relationship I had with my mother than my father.'

It has been a blissfully undramatic life at the Palin home. In January 1995, they were the victims of crime, but even that was a comedically bungled farce. Two drunken burglars took so long trying to break into the house that he had time to write down their descriptions while Helen phoned the police. He had been woken by the clattering of his letterbox as the would-be burglars tried to lift the front door latch with a steel tape measure. As Palin watched from behind the curtains, they taped window panes to prevent the glass breaking during the attempted break-in and talked loudly.

Police arrived in the early hours in time to arrest Nicholas O'Connell, twenty, and Glen Hilliard, eighteen, both of Kentish Town, north London. The pair admitted attempted burglary at Southwark Crown Court, and one received an eight-month sentence, the other, 140 hours' community service.

Palin was truly concerned for the hapless pair. 'I wouldn't want to see someone go down for eight months just for a bungled attempt to get into my house,' he said. 'But I gather that in this case one of the men also had another offence hanging over him. But it's hard to think of it as a serious burglary attempt.' He was anxious to play down any attempt to portray him in heroic mould. 'I was a bit hazy because I had just woken up, but I saw two people outside and as I watched one of them came towards the window. One did seem a bit unsteady, but they were so blatant about it. They seemed to take about an hour to approach the house and there were no heroics about it on either side ... I don't think you could describe it as a major assault on Fort Palin.'

After Ted Palin died, Michael's mother lived for another thirteen years, the latter part in a wheelchair. For her eightieth birthday, Michael took her to New York on Concorde, where she appeared with him when he hosted NBC's *Saturday Night Live*. 'She kept interrupting as I recited a monologue,' Palin complained. 'The audience loved it, her timing was terrific. She was totally unfazed by the occasion. I think she will probably be asked back, but I won't.'

His mother recalled the New York trip a few months afterwards, when interviewed by Martin Dawes of the *Sheffield Star*. 'I never, ever thought I would go to New York,' she said. 'That was kind of him. He got me on the show without warning me – they all knew except me.

'They love Michael in America,' she continued. 'When we were out sightseeing, a policeman recognised him. He was guarding the Chinese prime minister or somebody, but he had his picture taken with us. You can't imagine that happening in England, can you?'

In 1989, a year before she died, Michael dedicated the book of *Around the World in Eighty Days*, 'To my mother, Mary Palin, who hates me travelling.' She was eighty-six when she died after a stroke; 'She died with a giggle, and among friends – the way she would have wanted it,' Palin said. 'I'll miss her. She was someone I could share anything with.' She was buried near her home in Southwold.

Michael says today he has nothing but warm memories of his mother, 'a lovely woman', and he has come to forgive his father, though it is difficult when someone is dead, he says. 'You want them there, so you can forgive them unilaterally.' But he has stopped blaming his father. 'I know I've given him a hard time. I've made him the villain in my past. But it's not as simple as that.'

And indeed, it does not seem to be a mere case of the son rejecting the father's ways. Were Michael Palin not his father's son in many ways, it is unlikely for one thing that he would be so organised. Palin sets himself a quite strict writing rota, different for each project. When working on the script of *American Friends*, he described his routine: 'The usual day starts at eight with the disgusting pong of cat food pervading the house. I try to be working by nine, then run on Hampstead Heath for about fifty minutes at midday. It clears the mind and helps me work out bits of script. Then I'll write again in the afternoon. The cats often come upstairs to my study. Alby just sits around with his great legs all over the place. Betty interferes. She's bossy, is Betty, and usually starts sorting through my papers, tearing up reviews and organising the place.

'When I've had enough of work,' he concluded, sounding now more like Cleese than himself, 'I spend the rest of the day on input rather than output – reading, talking, feeding the cats. I'm pretty lazy really.' (Tom Palin admits to having inherited the organisation gene from Michael in the way he runs his business, too.)

The Pythons asked, not altogether jokily, what the meaning of life was, and Palin thinks he may be some way towards finding the answer. 'The meaning of life is to keep looking for the meaning of life,' he says. 'It is a continual process of discovery. I am what I've always been, somebody curious, probably opening too many doors and looking around too many corners. But I don't always want to know what's coming. If you know what is going to happen in life, it takes ninety per cent of the fun away. So if I *finally* discovered the meaning of life, I would curl up my toes and pop off.

'I find that freedom to do whatever you want contains a certain frustration because then you have to ask: What do you want? I love doubt. If you aren't feeling doubt at least twenty times a day, what is life about? Life is a total mess and you mustn't look for the perfect formula because it probably doesn't exist, and it certainly doesn't exist for me.'

One area of Palin's personal psychology which is not subject to very much doubt is, of course, the legendary and irksome 'niceness' business. People who know him personally confirm one after the other how nice he is. A voice not so much of dissent as of explanation comes from one senior BBC executive involved many times with commissioning Palin projects. 'Michael *is* nice, delightfully, incredibly nice,' he says. 'I have dealt with hundreds of presenters and I could, if I wanted, point to the downside of almost every one of them. I could not think of a single unpleasant thing to say about Michael Palin, but to an extent being nice is made easy for him, because he has an *extremely* tough and effective agent in Ann James, so some of the necessary nastiness, if you like, in negotiation is left to her.'

Niceness remains a characterisation that irks Palin, however. 'I pretty much loathe it. It's sort of a benign millstone. "Nice" to me tends to have overtones of being agreeable, harmless. There are many other things I'd like to be called rather than nice. I hate to say it myself, but "decent", "honourable", all those things that other people get called, would be better. Or just being called a complete shit would be better than nice.'

'If you use the word nice again,' he once threatened Hunter Davies during an interview, 'I'll call character witnesses. I'll bring forward my kids to prove I am abusive under strain and that I have bad taste in music. My wife, Helen, will testify to my groundless grumpiness and my acquisition of objects of questionable usefulness, viz, my buying of yet more chairs.' Thus, in Davies's article, did Michael Palin appear, if it is possible, even nicer.

Funny people can be – indeed, normally are – extraordinarily cutting and nasty. Which is why Palin's unusual blend of being extremely funny *and* extremely equable seems so anomalous. It leads to two assumptions which dog him; that he must be merely lightweight, and that he must also be too dull and conservative to be interesting. Once, on a Python set, a frustrated director shouted at him for being 'too bloody normal'. And Palin has complained himself that, whenever he tries to be serious, 'It just comes out as comedy, unfortunately.'

Niceness has had its benefits, however. Even in trashing a Palin book, one reviewer felt the need to apologise in advance. Adam

Nicolson, reviewing Michael's book of *Pole to Pole* in the *Sunday Times*, was loathe to say anything unkind about Palin. 'That's his appeal: he's the best version of us we could think of. His Next shirts, M&S belt-and-trouser sets, okay liberal attitudes and wrinkly face make him the man we want to be. There is no question that Palin is a modern saint. But he has written a boring book . . .'

Palin has said that he is easy going as a direct reaction to his father's grumpiness. His friend Robert Hewison observes, 'I hardly ever see anger in Michael. I think if there is any, it has long, long ago been diverted into comedy. One response to anger is to let it out in terms of comedy.'

Palin has even comedified on occasion the universal perception of his niceness. Talking about *Pole to Pole* before he set off on that journey, he was describing difficulties the team had in getting access to the Antarctic. 'You're not allowed to cross the Antarctic from one side to the other in a land expedition if you're flippant,' he said. 'You must be very serious or scientific. So I'll just have to do tsetse fly research or something like that. Or just test niceness in an extremely cold climate. "When wrestled viciously to the ground by a polar bear, Michael eventually said, 'Oh, bother' – which recorded point one in the niceometer."'

One side of his character about which Palin is pleasingly proud and unrepentant is the way he has managed, as he puts it, to avoid the worst danger, the thing he always dreaded: growing up. 'I thought there was some sort of mental change that happened to you round about twenty or twenty-one, when you shed the frivolous things of youth and wore sober clothes and took an office job. But somehow it just never happened, and I still think of myself as a child in many ways – not childish but childlike – which is quite a useful thing to be.'

Maintaining that sense of innocence is one way Palin staves off the depression which so many figures in comedy suffer from. He alludes to occasional attacks of mild melancholia, but the closest Palin will come normally to admitting to any kind of dark side is to confess: 'I am a worrier. There is some neurosis under the surface.

Unless you have strong support outside your working life, you can easily crack up.'

He even says he has occasionally been close to the edge of a breakdown, but he stresses that depression does not last long for him. 'I've occasionally contemplated walking to the end of the plank. There's a bit of madness in me, I'm glad to say. Sometimes that feeling has hit me when I have been rushing and over-worked. There is that feeling that you have to be all things to all men. You just feel unhealthy, run down and have less time to spend with your family and your children ... I end up saying, "No, I can't go out tonight" and being short tempered – just feeling like I am not functioning as well as I would normally.'

The suicide in 1992 of his sister, Angela, who was a depressive, shocked and baffled him. When his mother died, he has explained, it seemed reasonable and natural. She was a good age, she hated her wheelchair, she didn't want to be dependent on other people. Angela's suicide at the age of fifty-two was very different. She left three young grown-up children, and he found the unnaturalness of it difficult to come to terms with; he could not understand how 'someone so popular, efficient, who could bake such wonderful cakes, serve a tennis ball so well, would deliberately attach a tube to the back of her car ... she was so beautiful, extremely capable, bubbly, dressed well. No outsider would have realised how she felt,' he said. 'It's ironic that my sister, who killed herself, looked sane and I appeared mad because I was one of the Python team.'

He remains sceptical about psychiatrists, in spite of John Cleese's famed enthusiasm for most forms of shrinks. 'They were unable to help my sister,' Palin says bleakly. However, he was very willing in 1995 to front the BBC's Mental Health Week and spoke on it again about Angela. It was clear, according to Suzie Mackenzie, who discussed it with Palin about it for the London *Evening Standard*, that Palin held his father in some measure to blame for his sister Angela's death. He didn't cry at the time, Mackenzie related. The tears came years later. 'Almost any time. Tears of frustration, really, because I still didn't understand.'

Michael's 1994 stage play, *The Weekend*, touched on suicide, although it was written in 1980. 'One thing I did learn from my sister was how very dark depression can be. She said: "You will never ever understand it." And I don't suppose you can.' Maybe the Palins were awash with unacknowledged depression, he speculated at the time of *The Weekend*. 'There was an aunt his mother used to speak of,' Sally Vincent wrote in the *Sunday Times*, 'who once allegedly threw an alleged sanitary towel across the room. That was as barking as a Palin got, historically.'

In his physical health, as opposed to his rude mental health, Palin is a lean, fit fifty-four-year old, to whom a permanent tan and well-chosen, good clothes lend an elegant, enviable air. He does not look like a man who increasingly these days says he regards himself as getting old. He is 5ft 10in tall, and dropped to ten stone from eleven stone during his 141 day *Pole to Pole* trip: 'My cholesterol level also went down dramatically, which is not surprising when you are surviving on goat and rice for weeks on end.'

He used to smoke twenty-five cigarettes a day – but now runs six miles almost every day around Hampstead Heath, often bumping into neighbour and fellow fitness fanatic, Melvyn Bragg. 'It's a release,' he says of the rigorous exercise regime. 'When I'm running I'm away from the phone. If I'm writing, it's a great way to unclog the mind. I'm not a team runner. I like to run by myself because I do a lot of thinking. I never stop unless a dog bares its teeth, which hasn't happened for a long time.'

Even if there were a certain predisposition in Palin towards depression, he has done everything a man could do consciously to remove the major outside stimuli for it. People become depressed about lack of love, lack of fulfilment in their career, ill health, bereavement and money. In Palin's family emotional support is a given, he adores his work and is internationally adored for it, he has been blessed with good health and (with the help of being married to a bereavement counsellor, perhaps) appears to have survived emotionally the death of his parents and sister.

The money side has also been to all outward appearances blissful.

'I'm not absolutely certain but I don't think I have to work for money,' he said in 1983. 'It's a silly stage you get to where you earn enough to have to employ people to take care of all your bill-paying and you lose touch ... It's not like it used to be when I'd write a joke for David Frost and get paid £7. Now you don't see anything. It's all drifting around somewhere. I'm a bit worried. For all I know, someone might say: "You know that £4 million you made last year, and you know that supertanker that split up..." '

Since *A Fish Called Wanda*, Palin has been a very rich man ('John was incredibly generous,' he says). His fortune is estimated at more than £4 million. As late as 1992, he was still raking in £100,000 a year from sales of Monty Python shows, videos and books; even now Python revenue is said to be worth £16,000 a year.

Yet he is not very interested in money, as he told Lynn Barber in 1988: 'It's nice to know it's there but I've never wanted to alter my life radically. I like corner shops and getting on the tube and running round the Heath. I don't want to move up into a sort of rich world, having servants and helicopters – that's my idea of absolute hell.' He is wealthy enough to be generous with his children – he bought Tom a recording studio and William a flat – but, be it his father's training or Yorkshire parsimony, he has never learned to be extravagant with himself. His relatively modest car (the smallest Mercedes without electric windows – 'I like opening them at my own speed'), home and clothes attest to someone plainly determined to be cool about money. 'I haven't really had time to spend it,' Palin has said. 'My family aren't particularly interested in living in one of three houses around the world, or a couple of yachts.'

He is, at the same time, by no means financially naive. Indeed, Palin is now a media mogul; he was a co-founder of the MAI consortium which won the southern ITV franchise for Meridian. When he joined MAI, the company headed by the Labour Lord Hollick, it was not to be a financial wheeler dealer, however, but to campaign for 'popular, quality television'. 'I don't want a seat on the board,' he said in 1990. 'I am more interested in making programmes. It is important for there to be a diversity which safeguards standards. I want programmes of general interest as well as quiz shows.'

Palin has also been generous to such causes as the Michael Palin Centre (for stammering children). He was approached by two young Sheffield film makers with a historical docu-drama project called *Benjamin Huntsman – Man of Steel*, and was so impressed that he injected £40,000 into their project. He frequently gives money to good causes in Sheffield. He even donated his school briefcase, in which he used to carry Monty Python scripts around the world, to a Doncaster auction to raise funds for a body scanner appeal.

Some of Palin's seriousness has been directed over the years towards broadly political ends, especially in the area of his pet subject, public transport policy. He has turned down Labour party approaches to back its election campaigns, saying that although he sympathised with the party on many issues, he 'didn't want to give anybody *carte blanche* to use my name'.

In 1995, he announced that had he been a member, he would have voted for his fellow Yorkshireman and public transport enthusiast John Prescott as leader of the Labour party. 'I'm a big fan,' he said. 'He's a real fighter and clear, lucid thinker.' Some of his political feeling has manifested itself as a dislike and distrust of anything too commercial. He has made it plain that he is glad not to have seen any of John Cleese's TV commercials in the States, and has consistently opposed any breath of an idea of using Monty Python characters to back commercial products.

He once turned down £1 million to star in a series of commercials, although, seemingly to avoid the charge of priggishness, he was anxious to deny that he did so out of Left-wing piety, readily admitting that he appeared in commercials when he was hard-up. He even wrote to the *Evening Standard* in 1986 to deny that he was as pure as they had made him out to be.

'Connoisseurs of the self-righteous may have noted that, in your Ad Lib column on Tuesday it was alleged that I have only ever done advertisements for the Central Office of Information,' he wrote. 'I cannot let this slur on my amorality pass without correction. Those in the advertising business with long memories may recall a television commercial made with my great friend and mentor John Cleese, in the heady days of the early seventies. The product was a dog food called Hunky Chunks and, as far as I can gather, it was taken off the market fairly soon after screenings of the commercial. I think I still have a couple of tins somewhere.'

However, he said in 1990, 'I haven't done any TV advertising for a while and I don't want to. There are some nice people in advertising, but for every one there are three or four complete prats who seem to look after just one word or something. Someone like John Cleese can successfully put down the whole process of advertising while doing the commercial, and the bastard can get away with it. Well that's nice for him, but I just come across as the average Mr Nice Guy selling some kind of crap for somebody else.'

On the subject of transport, Palin tries to jettison all attempts at levity, but still, even in a serious letter to a broadsheet newspaper, cannot help writing quite brilliantly sparky stuff. 'Sir,' he wrote to the editor of the *Guardian*, 'It greatly saddens me to see a newspaper like the *Guardian*, with a reasonable reputation for good sense, taking such a woolly and negative attitude over the proposed rail cuts. To say, as you do in your leading article, that, "It is not easy to defend the full panoply of British Rail's rural network on any grounds other than nostalgia or a wishful belief that the day of *Thomas the Tank Engine* will one day return" is misinformed, irresponsible and shows a stunningly patronising and supercilious disregard for all those who use the rural networks.'

He went on to describe how he frequently used a threatened rail line between Ipswich and Lowestoft. 'It means that I can easily visit my mother, who lives alone in northeast Suffolk, without adding another car to the already overcrowded London approaches to the A12. When I arrive at Ipswich off the mainline train I do not find a branch line carrying ruddy-faced peasants in smocks asking if George the Fifth's dead yet, or misty-eyed septuagenarian train spotters clutching the *Shell Guide to Overgrown Sidings*. I find a train full, and very often packed, with local people going about their business. Schoolchildren, families who've been shopping in Ipswich, and either have no car or would rather not go through the hassle of crowded city-centre parking, men with business at the towns along the line – Saxmundham, Halesworth, Lowestoft, all thriving places. (Palin's train spotter past reached its apogee in September 1997 when Anglia Railways announced that a local train running through East Anglia was to be named after him.)

'I think the *Guardian* could learn a lot from *Thomas the Tank Engine*,' Palin's lengthy letter to the newspaper had concluded. It was obvious that Palin's passion for public transport amounted to far more than the nostalgia-driven enthusiasm of an overgrown train spotter, even though his train spotter past continues to amuse. (Russell Davies, coming to interview Palin for the *New York Times*, wrote: 'Other famous people answer their own front doors and make the coffee themselves, but only Michael Palin would compliment you on the route you took to get there.')

One day in the mid-eighties, he was at Leeds railway station, complaining loudly about British Rail to the nearest person to hand. That person just happened to be a leading member of a lobby group fighting for better public transport. Before he knew where he was, Palin had talked himself into being the new chairman of Transport 2000.

'I panicked initially. I've never been a committee man, never chaired anything, not even at Oxford; but I knew their work, I'd read their books and I believed in what they are doing. What I like about this group is that it is not cranky. It has many experts among its members and everyone worried about our cities and their own quality of life ought to be reading its research. Everything I do in life is a great leap into the unknown so I thought, all right, I'll have a bash.' For two years he championed railways, stopped the building of motorways, opened cycleways.

Palin's first task as chairman was to spearhead the BusWatch campaign. This was aimed at making sure government moves to privatise regional bus companies did not worsen services to passengers. 'Kentish Town is a good example of an area badly off for public transport,' he fulminated. 'If I want to get to the West End I use our Mini to drive to Chalk Farm, the nearest tube, because there isn't an efficient bus service.'

He also wrote, in his new capacity as chairman of Transport 2000, an article for the local government journal *Town & Country Planning* on why he was hopeful of the future of public transport. 'In the few months since accepting the chair of Transport 2000 and beginning to learn a little more about transport in this country I have been affected in roughly equal measure by Indignation, Despair and Hope,' the article opened.

It continued in similar vein, very nearly (but not quite, since he was entirely serious) parodying the sort of speech a local councillor would make in the hope of being quoted in, well, a magazine like *Town & Country Planning*. He outlined his Indignation at how cars were favoured in Britain, unlike in Europe. 'Now I know that much of my Indignation is emotional and naive,' he continued, 'and that I shall eventually learn why and how these things just cannot be changed overnight. Which brings me quite neatly on to Despair.

'The lack of any national debate on transport,' Palin continued, 'is partly the fault of secretive government departments and politicians looking for a more glamorous field in which to make their names. It's also the result of media apathy. Though the letter columns of newspapers provide incontrovertible evidence that people do care about their transport, it is rare to find this reflected in terms of coverage and features.'

To illustrate his sense of optimism for public transport, Palin continued his piece: 'The tide is running in our favour, and some of the most heartening evidence of all comes from abroad. In Los Angeles, Sacramento and Chicago they're turning highway routes into light railways and, even in Dallas, they've just spent $4 billion on public transport. Now *there's* Hope.'

In 1990, after he relinquished the chairmanship of Transport 2000 to become its president, he launched another bitter attack on the car, claiming the future of transport had finally swung away from roads and towards the railways. 'In the environmentally conscious nineties the accusing finger now points at the motor car – seen as a polluter, a clogger of cities and towns, a formidable instrument of damage, destruction and death,' he wrote in the foreword to *Rail For the Future*, a book published by the Railway Development Society.

In 1994, he was still on the attack, arguing against the case for more cars and roads in *Open Space* on BBC 2. 'The trouble is we have got so used to cars we can't imagine using them less,' he said. 'And it is increasingly difficult to manage without them because, as more people have cars, public transport has been run down and walking and cycling have become more dangerous.

'I dream about driving my car very fast through London,' Palin concluded, in a passage which must have caused many environmentalists to choke on their tofu. 'I think it's because I've been writing a lot of anti-car things recently and my dream's saying, "Come on now Palin, be honest, we all know about your Mercedes."

'I'm not totally against cars. I believe we have to get the balance right,' he elaborated. 'As a family we try and use the cars as little as possible. I cycle if the weather is good and I don't have to be somewhere smart and not sweaty ... I still find it nightmarish to be in a traffic jam opposite a bus stop with people waiting for a bus that I'm holding up.' People who play car radios too loudly also infuriate him, Palin has often said.

Occasionally, the name Michael Palin will make an unexpected appearance in newspaper-letter columns to grumble mildly about subjects other than transport. In January 1995, he wrote to the *Independent* about the dismissal of the governor of Parkhurst Prison, following a break out there:

Sir: I met John Marriot, the ex-governor of Parkhurst, while filming at the prison in 1993. He seemed to me a most humane and honourable man, concerned to treat as decently as possible everyone under his care, both the prison officers and the prisoners themselves. I remember being enormously impressed by his ability, his humanity and his commitment and, as a taxpayer, I was greatly reassured that our prison system should recognise the worth of such a man. Whatever may have gone wrong since, one thing puzzles me. If John Marriot has been made to take the rap for what the Prison Service internal inquiry called serious failures by local managers and individual prison officers, who is going to take the rap for the recent spate of national failures? Two obvious candidates come to mind, but as of this morning, Howard and Lewis are still on the run. Yours faithfully, Michael Palin, London, NW5.

Palin's letter is especially interesting with hindsight, as Michael Howard, the then Home Secretary, and Derek Lewis, director of the Prison Service, were very soon at loggerheads themselves.

Palin admits, as a workaholic who finds complete fulfilment in what he does for a living, that leisure time is more tricky. 'I find no problem in writing these silly things and standing up in front of cameras. I love it,' he has said. 'It's harder when you're at home or it's your evening off or you're at a party and people come up and expect you to be funny – that's what's difficult. At the end of the day, I prefer to read serious novels or watch serious plays or serious things on the television. People tend to think that all the time you're just laughing and gagging and falling over.'

What does Michael Palin do for fun? He listed running, cycling and walking as his preferred activities when asked about his 'favourite things' by the *Sun* in 1994. Friends note with fascination and some alarm his enthusiasm for eating in very expensive restaurants alone with a book. Food is a great pleasure to him, and the running keeps him slim enough to enjoy plenty of it, as the Palins did as a family in Sheffield. (Asked his favourite food by the *Sun*, he listed black pudding: 'I came to it fairly late in life after filming in the north. I had a black pudding sandwich made locally – the most wonderful thing I've ever eaten,' he said. His favourite drinks were Cloudy Bay Chardonnay from New Zealand, and Guinness. Top films were *The Life of Brian*, *This is Spinal Tap*, *Picnic at Hanging Rock*, and *La*

Grande Bouffe, favourite people, John Cleese and Dame Maggie Smith.)

Another leisure pursuit Palin is becoming increasingly keen on is art. He made a programme on 1930s railway posters many years ago, and in mid-1997 was working on another art documentary, this time for BBC Scotland, about the Scottish artist Anne Redpath, who died in 1965, and two of whose paintings form the centrepiece of Palin's quirky personal art collection. When he lent the paintings, *The Old Port, Menton* and *The Blue Tablecloth* to the Scottish National Gallery of Modern Art for a Redpath retrospective, the BBC asked if he would present their film.

He went to the south of France, where Redpath did much of her work, for some of the filming, as well as to Edinburgh. 'I was fascinated to learn the background, to discover how much artistic licence she had used,' Palin told the *Glasgow Herald.* 'Commitment and energy shine through, not just in the way her work is structured, but in the powerful way the paint is put on.

'I don't want to get pretentious, but I can feel her working,' Palin said of *The Blue Tablecloth.* 'The objects have ceased to be objects. There's nothing casual or arbitrary about them, nothing vapid.'

Having found and filmed the locations of his own paintings, Palin told interviewer Aileen Little how he enjoys looking at those of other artists he admires, especially those of the Camden group of painters, such as Sickert and Pissarro. 'It amazes me that these men left the suburbs of Paris for the suburbs of London,' he said. 'It takes a painterly eye to see the charm and beauty of an urban landscape.'

He likes to collect paintings which make him feel good, he revealed. He couldn't put up a 'tortured' Bacon or a 'painful' Freud. 'It's got to be something that makes me want to look, something pleasurable.'

Another of his pastimes may one day succeed in making Michael Palin what he has never quite managed to be – angry letters to newspapers aside – controversial. Like his great-grandfather, Edward, Palin keeps a diary, and his fellow Pythons are fascinated to know what it contains. Could it reveal a man not as nice as his public persona? Is he secretly storing up jealousies and personal loathings to explode on an unsuspecting world one day when he is very old, or even, like the parrot he tried to sell John Cleese, 'resting'?

'I've been doing the diary since the beginning of Python in 1969,' he told an interviewer recently. 'Typically there is very little about the early days of Python in it. I hope it wouldn't be a complete shock, because I'd hate to think that what I did was so utterly inconsistent with what I really felt that it would be a terrible, awful revelation to people. But bearing that in mind, yeah, there'll probably be some things that'll shock.'

No wonder, perhaps, that Michael Edward Palin tends to keep his study at the top of his modest house locked.